The First Book of

Microsoft® Word for Windows™

David Angell and Brent Heslop

A Division of Macmillan Computer Publishing

11711 North College, Carmel, Indiana 46032 USA

International Standard Book Number: 0-672-27332-2
Library of Congress Catalog Card Number: 90-63192

Acquisitions Editor: *Marie Butler-Knight*
Manuscript Editor: *Diana Francoeur*
Cover Design: *Held & Diedrich Design*
Illustrator: *Tami Hughes*
Production Assistance: *Jeff Baker, Martin Coleman, Joelynn Gifford,
Sandy Grieshop, Denny Hager, Betty Kish, Bob LaRoche, Sarah
Leatherman, Kimberly Leslie, Lisa Ann Naddy, Howard Peirce, Cindy
Phipps, Tad Ringo, Johnna VanHoose*
Technical Reviewers: *Neil Hoopman and C. Herbert Feltner*
Indexer: *Hilary Adams*

Printed in the United States of America

Contents

iv

5 *Previewing and Printing Documents, 137*

6 *More Formatting Features, 167*

V

7 *Creating Tables and Outlines, 195*

vi

Introduction

Word processing software has revolutionized written communications. Analogous to a carpenter's workbench with its carpentry tools, word processing software provides tools for editing, formatting, and printing documents. Earlier word processors often consisted of complex and cryptic commands. The user faced a long learning curve before mastering the word processing tools. These earlier word processors were limited in their ability to display documents as they would look when printed. They also required that the user learn additional programs to integrate text, pictures, and page layout features into a document.

Microsoft Word for Windows represents the next generation of word processing tools. Word is based on an easy-to-use *graphical user interface*, which reduces complex word processing tasks to simple menu commands or *icons* (on-screen symbols). Word for Windows' *WYSIWYG* (What You See Is What You Get) environment allows you to easily view and work with text, pictures, and page layout in a single program. As a document processor, Word for Windows provides a state-of-the-art workbench for building any type of document from a simple memo to an entire book.

How to Use This Book

This book is designed to get you up and running with Word for Windows, beginning with the essential tools and then expanding your skills to work with more powerful tools. The following description provides a blueprint for working with this book and Word for Windows. If you need to install Word for Windows, first see *Appendix A*, which explains step-by-step how to install Word for Windows on your computer system.

Chapters 1 through 5 orient you to the Word for Windows environment and cover the essential tools for crafting documents. Chapter 1 explains the layout of the Word for Windows workbench and how to choose tools by using the mouse or the keyboard. In addition, Chapter 1 also covers using Word's on-line help feature. Chapter 2 explains the basic tools for entering and manipulating text, as well as saving and retrieving documents. Chapter 3 shows you how to apply finishing touches to your document's text, including how to sand rough spots by searching and replacing text, correcting spelling errors, and using the Thesaurus to add texture to your writing. Chapter 4 covers basic formatting techniques for constructing the layout of your documents, including character, paragraph, and document formats. Chapter 5 shows you how to preview and print your finished documents.

Chapters 6, 7, and 8 build on the essential skills covered in the first five chapters. Chapter 6 expands your skills for applying more sophisticated formats, such as creating bulleted lists, formatting different sections of a document, and inserting footnotes. Chapter 7 explains how to organize information in your documents by using tables and outlines. Chapter 8 discusses adding a visual dimension to your document with pictures, spreadsheets, and charts.

Chapters 9 through 12 teach you how to harness Word's power tools to automate tasks, manage and work with multiple document files, and create dynamic documents. Chapter 9 explains creating and using Word's time-saving features, including glossaries, macros, styles, and templates. Using these features allows you to construct and reuse modules of text, formats, and command keystrokes. Chapter 10 covers Word's sophisticated file management features, as well as multiple document windows. Chapter 11 explains using bookmarks and fields to create *dynamic* documents, which integrate and automatically update information from sources within or outside your documents. Chapter 12 builds on the techniques learned in Chapter 11 to construct form letters, mailing labels, tables of contents, and indexes.

Conventions Used in This Book

This book uses various typographical conventions to help you quickly learn Word. Important points are bulleted and highlighted with color. New terms are italicized. Names of directories and files appear in uppercase letters. For example, C:\WINWORD\DOCUMENT.DOC refers to the file named DOCUMENT.DOC in the WINWORD directory on the C: drive.

Commands

Commands that require you to press two or more keys in succession are written in two different ways. When the keys are separated by commas, you should press and release each key in succession. For example, Alt,F,P means to first press the *Alt* key and release it, then press the *F* key and release it, and lastly press the *P* key and release it. You don't press the comma key.

When the keys are separated by hyphens (-), you should hold down one or more keys while you press another key. For example, Ctrl-Shift-F12 means to hold down simultaneously the Ctrl and Shift keys while pressing the F12 key; then release all three keys. You don't press the Hyphen (-) key.

In Word for Windows, most commands appear on the screen with one of their letters underlined, such as File or Edit. You can use the underlined letter in conjunction with the Alt key to access the command. Pressing Alt,F, for example, displays the File menu, and pressing Alt,E displays the Edit menu.

Activating a command is usually a two-step process. First you specify the menu and then you specify the command within the menu. To avoid repeating the same instructions over and over, we use a shortcut to express these two steps. When we want you to choose a command located in a menu, say the Print command in the File menu, we use the convention: File/Print. You press Alt; then press *F* to access the File menu and *P* to activate the Print command.

User Input and Computer Output

Text that you type from the keyboard is set in a special computer font, for example, "To start Word for Windows, type `winword` and press Enter." You type the letters *w i n w o r d* and then press the Enter key.

Computer output, such as error messages, questions from Word, and other information appearing on the screen, is also set in computer font. For example, "When you exit Word for Windows, Word asks you: `Save changes to Document1?`"

Special Terms

When you are working with menus and dialog boxes, the terms *choose* and *select* have different meanings. Whenever the term *choose* is used, it indicates that you should use the mouse to activate a command. In most cases, the keyboard equivalent follows. For example, the instruction "Choose the File/Print command (Alt,F,P)" means that you should click on the File menu option in the menu bar and then click on the Print menu option to activate the Print command. The keyboard equivalents, shown in parentheses, indicate that you should press the Alt key to activate the command menu, press the *F* key to activate the File menu, and, lastly, press the *P* key to activate the Print command. Notice that the keyboard keys that activate the command appear underlined throughout the text—as they do in Word for Windows' menus.

The term *select* refers to highlighting an option in a command menu or list box by moving the mouse pointer on top of the option and clicking (not double-clicking) on the option so that it is highlighted. Selecting options and text is explained in Chapter 1, "Getting Started with Word for Windows."

Quick Steps

Throughout this book, you will find procedures labeled **Quick Steps**. Quick Steps are step-by-step instructions for specific tasks. They tell you exactly how to accomplish a task, and they explain what the effect of each step is. Look for a large *Q* icon identifying each set of Quick Steps.

Acknowledgments

We would like to extend our appreciation to the many people who helped and encouraged us during the writing of this book. First, a warm thanks to Kim; without her support this book would not have been a reality. A special thanks to our friends and families for their valued support and for putting up with our grueling schedule of writing.

Special thanks to Tanya van Dam at Microsoft who always came through, providing updated information and support during this project. Thanks also to Alan Anderson, creator of Tiffany Plus, who provided us with vital information on working with graphics in the Microsoft Windows and Word for Windows environment. As always, thanks to Jeff House for his long hours of proofreading. A special thanks to Diana Francoeur for her exceptional editing of this book. We also want to express our gratitude to Fred and Bob at GEMS Computers, who went the extra mile helping us troubleshoot a computer problem when we were under a punishing deadline.

Microsoft Windows and Word for Windows provided us with the perfect reason to upgrade our systems. We would like to thank the following companies for their support in providing the hardware and software needed to complete this book. Computer Support Corporation for Arts & Letters; T/Maker for its ClickArt; Corel Systems Corporation for CorelDRAW!, the state-of-the-art drawing package; Cybex for the Companion, which helped us share a computer without the complications of LAN software; Image Club for its superior clip art; Intel, who helped us solve a memory crunch with Above Board Plus 8; Metro ImageBase for its Electronic Art; and Microsoft for Windows, Word for Windows, Microsoft Excel, and the Microsoft Mouse.

We thank NANAO Corporation for its Flexscan 9070U monitor, which worked flawlessly; LaserTools Corporation for Print Cache, the ultimate print caching utility; Seiko Instruments for its crisp CM1440 multisynchronous monitor; Video 7 for its 1024i VGA graphics board, which speeded up working with Word for Windows; and Informix for the visually stunning spreadsheet Wingz. Last but not least, thanks to Xerox Imaging Systems Inc., for Gray F/X, the most versatile of TIFF editors that enabled us to edit the figures in this book.

xii

Trademarks

All terms mentioned in this book that are known to be trademarks or service marks are listed below. In addition, terms suspected of being trademarks or service marks have been appropriately capitalized. SAMS cannot attest to the accuracy of this information. Use of a term in this book should not be regarded as affecting the validity of any trademark or service mark.

Arts and Letters is a registered trademark of Computer Support Corporation.

AutoCAD is a registered trademark of Autodesk Inc.

ClickArt is a registered trademark of T/Maker Company.

Display Write is a registered trademark of International Business Machines Corporation.

Epson is a registered trademark of Epson America, Inc.

Gray F/X is a trademark of Xerox Imaging Systems.

Harvard Graphics is a registered trademark of Software Publishing Corporation.

HP, LaserJet Series II, LaserJet III, PCL, and Hewlett-Packard are registered trademarks of Hewlett-Packard Company.

IBM and IBM AT are registered trademarks of International Business Machines Corporation.

Intel and the Above Board Plus 8 are registered trademarks of Intel Corporation.

LaserWriter, LaserWriter Plus, and LaserWriter II are registered trademarks of Apple Computer, Inc.

Lotus and 1-2-3 are registered trademarks of Lotus Development Corporation.

Macintosh is a registered trademark of Macintosh Library, Inc., licensed by Apple Computer, Inc.

Metro ImageBase and The Art of Electronic Publishing are trademarks of Metro Creative Graphics, Inc.

Micrografx Draw and Micrografx Designer are registered trademarks of Micrografx, Inc.

Microsoft, Microsoft Excel, Microsoft Windows, Microsoft Word for Windows, Microsoft Works, MS, MS Word, MS-DOS, are registered trademarks of Microsoft Corporation.

Mirage is a registered trademark of Zenographics, Inc.

Multimate is a registered trademark of Multimate International Corporation, an Ashton-Tate company.

Norton Utilities and Unerase are registered trademarks of Peter Norton Computing, Inc.

PageMaker is a registered trademark of Aldus Corporation.

PC Paintbrush is a registered trademark of Z-Soft Corporation.

Post-it Notes is a registered trademark of 3M Corporation.

PostScript is a registered trademark of Adobe Systems.

Print Cache is a registered trademark of LaserTools Corporation.

Tiffany Plus is a registered trademark of Anderson Consulting & Software.

Type Director is a trademark of Agfa Compugraphic, a division of AGFA Corporation.

Ventura Publisher is a registered trademark of Xerox Corporation.

Video Show is a registered trademark of General Parametrics, Inc.

Wingz is a registered trademark of Informix Software, Inc.

WordPerfect is a registered trademark of WordPerfect Corporation.

WordStar is a registered trademark of MicroPro International Corporation.

Getting Started with Word for Windows

In This Chapter

- ▶ *Using a mouse*
- ▶ *Starting Word for Windows*
- ▶ *Working with Word's menus, commands, and dialog boxes*
- ▶ *Getting help with Word*
- ▶ *Quitting Word for Windows*

This chapter introduces you to the Word for Windows workbench and its state-of-the-art tools for working with documents. You'll take a tour of Word's *menus*—the tool racks from which you select commands to perform your word processing tasks. In addition, this chapter explains how to use dialog boxes and Word's built-in help system.

The Word for Windows Environment

Microsoft Word for Windows operates within the Microsoft Windows environment. In other words, before you can use Word for

Windows, you must have Microsoft Windows installed on your computer system. Of course, you must have Word for Windows installed too. If you do not have Word for Windows installed, see Appendix A for installation instructions.

The use of *windows* (frames containing programs or files on your screen), pull-down command menus, *dialog boxes* (for changing command settings and interacting with programs), and *icons* and *buttons* (on-screen symbols used to execute commands) are all standardized features of Microsoft Windows. This friendly, graphical environment substantially improves your ability to master applications by providing a consistent interface among applications.

Windows owes its name to the fact that each program runs inside a separate window, called a *program window*. Microsoft Windows uses the metaphor of a *desktop*, where the screen represents the top of a desk and the desk can have several program windows open at one time. Within a program window, one or more files can be displayed, each within its own window. In Word for Windows, these file windows are called *document windows*.

Using a Mouse

A *mouse* is a pointing device that you move on a flat surface. As you move the mouse, the *mouse pointer* on the screen moves in tandem with the mouse. A mouse is an indispensable tool for Word's graphical point-and-shoot environment of buttons and icons (on-screen symbols). Simply by pointing to a button or icon with the mouse pointer and then clicking a mouse button, you can execute a command. While Word for Windows can be used without a mouse, we strongly recommend using one. Many tasks are far easier to perform with the mouse than with the keyboard.

The mouse pointer takes on different shapes depending on the kind of action being performed. For example, it appears as an outlined arrow when you're selecting commands from a menu, an hourglass when Word is processing a command, or an I-beam when you're entering text. The mouse has its own lingo. Table 1.1 describes basic terms used throughout this book to define mouse operations. Using the mouse becomes second nature. As you become more proficient with Word, you'll integrate various keyboard shortcuts with the use of your mouse to perform many Word for Windows tasks.

> **Tip:** If you don't have a mouse, we recommend that you purchase the Microsoft 400 PPI (pixels per inch) mouse. Its state-of-the-art mouse technology offers superior, user-adjustable sensitivity—which translates into less mouse movement required to move the pointer.

Table 1.1 Mouse Function Terms

Term	Meaning
Click	Quickly press and release the left mouse button while the mouse pointer is on an object such as a menu command, icon, or button.
Double-click	Quickly click the left mouse button twice while the mouse pointer is on an object such as a menu command, icon, or button.
Drag	Move the mouse pointer to an object on the screen. Then press and hold down the left mouse button while moving the mouse.
Point	Move the mouse pointer directly over a specific location on the screen, such as a menu command, icon, or button, by sliding the mouse on a flat surface.

3

> **Note:** In Word for Windows, most mouse functions are performed using the left button on your mouse.

Starting Word

The way you start Word for Windows depends on whether you're starting from within Windows or from the DOS command prompt. If Windows isn't displayed on your screen, at the DOS prompt type

```
cd \winword
```

and press Enter to change to the Word for Windows directory. To start Word for Windows, type

```
winword
```

To start Word for Windows from within Microsoft Windows, have the Windows Program Manager window displayed on your screen, as shown in Figure 1.1. Move the mouse pointer to the Windows Applications icon and double-click the left mouse button. Using the keyboard, press Alt,W,2. Word displays the Windows Application window. Next, move the mouse pointer to the Microsoft Word icon and double-click the left mouse button. Using the keyboard, press the Right or Left Arrow key to highlight the Microsoft Word icon and then press Enter. You can also start Word for Windows from the Program Manager window by using the File/Run command. The Quick Steps explain how.

4

 Starting Word for Windows by Using the Run Command

1. In the Program Manager window, choose the File/Run command or press Alt,F,R.

   Word displays the Run command dialog box.

2. In the Command Line text box,type `winword`.

3. Choose the OK button or press Enter.

   The Word for Windows program is activated. ☐

The *first* time you start Word for Windows, a dialog box asks you to enter your name. Type your name in the Name text box. Use the Backspace or Del keys to correct mistakes. As you type your name, Word extracts the initials from your name and fills in the Initials text box. After you've entered your name, click on the OK button or press Enter. The dialog box disappears. Word saves the name and initials you've entered and uses them as a name stamp for documents. You now see the Word for Windows program window in full-screen size.

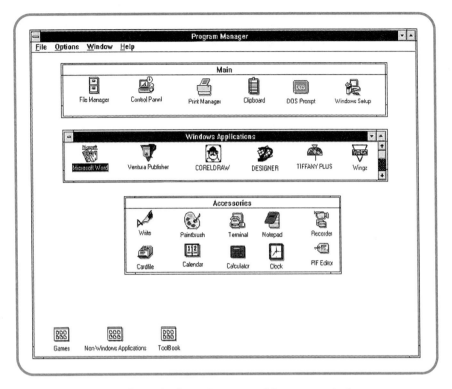

Figure 1.1   The Windows Program Manager window.

5

The Word for Windows Program Window

Initially, Word displays the Word program window and a new document window in full-screen size. A window that is displayed in full-screen size is called *a maximized* window. Figure 1.2 labels the main components of the Word screen. The *title bar*, at the top of the screen, displays the program name (`Microsoft Word`) and the document filename (`Document1`). The `Document1` filename is the default filename assigned to a new document. The *Word Control menu box*, located on the left side of the title bar, provides a menu of commands for manipulating the Word program window. The *Document Control menu box*, located directly below the Word Control menu box, provides a menu of commands for manipulating the document window.

Menu bar   Title bar   Minimize button

Word Control menu box

Document Control menu box

Insertion point

Endmark

Restore button

Thumb

Scroll bar

Text area

Arrow button

Status bar

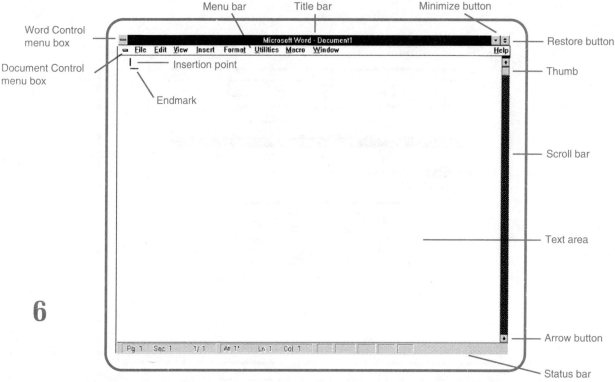

6

Figure 1.2   The Word for Windows program window.

The *Minimize* and *Restore buttons*, shown in Figure 1.2, provide shortcuts for manipulating the Word for Windows program window.The Minimize button allows you to close the Word for Windows program window to an icon on the Windows desktop. The Restore button restores the maximized (full-screen size) Word program window to a smaller size.

The area that occupies the bulk of the screen is the *text area* of the new document window. The *document window* is where you create, edit, format, and view your document files. The blinking vertical bar is called the *insertion point.* It indicates where text is to be entered into a document. The insertion point also specifies the point at which you want to select or edit text, as explained in Chapter 2. The horizontal line to the right of the insertion point is called an *endmark,* and it identifies the end of a document. The *mouse pointer* (not shown) appears in the shape of an I-beam when it is in a document window's text area. Directly below the title bar is the menu bar, which contains Word's command menus.

The Scroll Bar

At the far right side of the screen in Figure 1.2, you can see the vertical *scroll bar* with two arrows inside it. The vertical scroll bar is part of the document window. Clicking on the Arrow buttons, located at the top and bottom of the vertical scroll bar, scrolls the document in the direction of the respective arrow, one line at a time. The box within the scroll bar is called the *thumb*, and its position on the scroll bar indicates your position in the document. By dragging the thumb with the mouse, you can move up or down through your document.

The Status Bar

At the bottom of the Word program window is the *status bar*, shown in Figure 1.3. It provides information regarding the status of the document you're working on and also displays other information provided by the Word program.

7

Figure 1.3   The status bar.

Within the status bar are three sections of status information. The first section displays information about your location in a document, based on the position of the insertion point. It shows the current page number, the section number (sections are specially formatted parts of a document, explained later in Chapter 6), and the current page number followed by a slash and the total number of pages in the document.

The middle section of the status bar displays the precise location of the insertion point. It shows the distance (in inches) from the top edge of the page to the insertion point, followed by the insertion point's line and column number. A *column* is a character width across the screen. A *line* is one character in height up or down the screen.

The third section (furthest right) indicates when certain Word features or modes are active. For example, if you have the Num Lock key activated on your keyboard, NUM is displayed. This indicator disappears when you turn off the Number Lock by pressing the Num Lock key again. Other common indicators are CAPS for the Caps Lock key and OVR (overtype) for the Ins key.

The status bar also displays messages and other information as you're working. For example, as you move through menu commands, each command you select brings up a short descriptive message in the status bar about the command's function. These messages temporarily replace the normal contents of the status bar and disappear when you close the menu.

By default, the status bar is displayed. However, you can turn it off to view more of your document. Choose the View menu and the Status Bar command. Notice that the Status Bar command has a check mark next to it, showing that the status bar is turned on. To turn it off, click the mouse with the pointer on the Status Bar command. To turn off the status bar from the keyboard, press Alt then *V* and *S* (Alt,V,S). To turn the status bar back on, choose the View menu and the Status Bar command (Alt,V,S) again.

8

A Tour of Word's Menus

The *menu bar*, directly below the title bar, displays pull-down menus that organize families of commands for working with documents. Word's menus provide a logical structure for commands, with similar commands clustered together. For example, the File menu contains a group of commands that manipulate your document files (such as the Open/Close commands that open and close document files) and another group of commands, separated by a horizontal line, that preview and print document files.

By opening each menu and looking at its contents, you can get a good overview of Word's features. To get an idea of what each command does, use the Up or Down Arrow or drag the mouse up and down within a menu to highlight its commands. As you highlight commands, Word displays a short message in the status bar stating the function of the highlighted command.

Word provides two modes for displaying your menus: *Short* and *Full*. The Short menu mode, the initial mode, displays the most common commands. The Full menu mode displays all the commands available in Word. To change from Short to Full mode, click on the <u>V</u>iew menu; then click on the Full <u>M</u>enus command. Using the keyboard, press Alt,V,M; Word changes to the Full menu mode. This menu option is a toggle. So, to display the Short menu mode again, choose the <u>V</u>iew menu and then the Short <u>M</u>enus command in the same way you choose the Full <u>M</u>enus command. The menu mode that is active when you end your current work session will be the mode Word begins subsequent sessions with until you change it.

The following sections briefly describe the contents of each menu in the Full menu mode, beginning with the Control menu and the Document Control menu. Figure 1.2 showed the menu boxes for these two menus as two bars at the upper-left corner of the screen. Figure 1.4 shows Word's eight command menus in the Full menu mode.

> ▶ **Tip:** Use the Full menu mode because it's easier to have all the commands displayed. We assume you're using the Full menu mode when we explain menu topics.

9

The Word Control Menu

The Word Control menu box (Figure 1.2) is located at the left side of the Word window title bar. It provides a menu of commands for manipulating the Word program window. Using these commands, you can perform such tasks as resizing, moving, or closing the Word program window. The Run command (explained in Chapter 2) provides access to the Windows Control panel for changing setup controls, such as screen colors, and access to the Clipboard, a special editing tool. You can access the Word Control menu from either the mouse or the keyboard. From the mouse, simply click with the pointer on the menu box. From the keyboard, press Alt-Spacebar.

The Document Control Menu

The Document Control menu box (Figure 1.2) is located below Word's Control menu box, directly at the beginning (left side) of the menu bar. It provides commands similar to those in Word's Control menu, but the commands are for manipulating the document window. When you change the size of the document window from its full-screen size (restoring a maximized window), the Document Control menu box moves to the document window's title bar, as shown in Figure 1.5. To activate the Document Control menu, click on the Document Control menu box or press Alt-Hyphen.

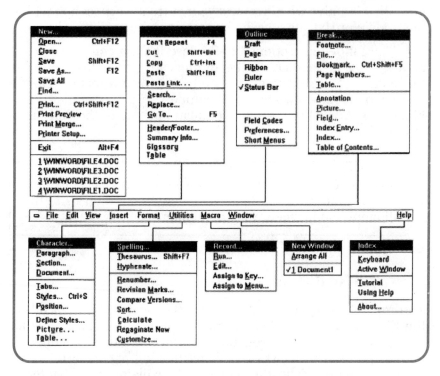

Figure 1.4   Word's command menus in Full menu mode.

The File Menu

The File menu provides commands frequently used for document file management, such as opening a new document window, saving your work, closing a document window, and searching for a document file. Another group of commands is available for previewing and printing your documents. The File menu also includes the Exit command, which closes all documents and quits the Word program window, returning you to Windows. The last four menu options in the File menu (the first menu in Figure 1.4) are shortcut commands to quickly open any of the last four document files that you worked with in Word. The most recently opened document is the first filename on the list.

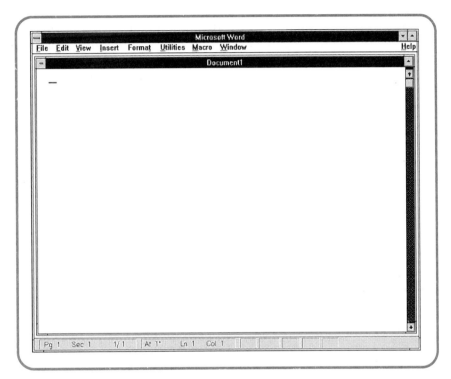

Figure 1.5   A resized document window.

The Edit Menu

The Edit menu contains tools to copy, cut, and paste selected text in your document. The Copy, Cut, and Paste commands are dimmed because you must select text before you can choose these commands. The Undo command allows you to undo your last editing change—which is handy when you suddenly realize you've made a mistake. The Edit menu also includes Word's powerful text search and replace features that allow you to search and replace text and formatting in a document. With the Go To command, you can quickly jump to a specific location in a long document.

11

Additional commands in the Edit menu include the Header/ Footer command for creating headers and footers; the Glossary command (dimmed) for storing frequently used text to be pasted in documents; the Table command (dimmed), which allows you to edit tables created using the Table command in the Insert menu; and the Summary Info command, which displays a dialog box for entering information about your document, such as a title and subject for your document. The Summary Info command also allows you to display statistics about your document, including the number of characters and words it contains and the amount of time spent working on the document.

The View Menu

The View menu provides options for displaying your documents on-screen. Table 1.2. describes the most commonly used options.

12

Table 1.2   Word's Commonly Used View Options

Option	Display
Draft	A stripped-down version of a document that excludes many formatting options and pictures so that you can more quickly manipulate text.
Page	Full-size pages displayed similarly to the way they'll look when printed.
Outline	A skeleton structure of your document in outline form. In order to effectively use this option, the document must have been created by using the heading styles explained in Chapter 7.

The Ribbon, Ruler, and Status Bar commands allow you to display various formatting features on-screen. For example, the Ruler command displays a ruler with a bar of buttons for common paragraph formatting commands. The Ruler appears under the title bar of a document window. The Ribbon command displays a control panel of buttons for character formatting. It is located below the menu bar in the Word window. The Status Bar, as explained earlier, is turned on by default.

Other commands in the View menu display special areas for working with footnotes, annotations, and field codes. The Preferences command lets you set various display preferences, such as the viewing of Word's formatting marks. The Short Menus command, as explained earlier, toggles between Word's Full or Short menu modes.

The Insert Menu

The Insert menu commands provide an array of tools for inserting various items into your documents. These tools include commands for inserting page, column, and section breaks; footnote and annotation references; the contents of another file into your current document; and tables and pictures. This menu also contains the commands necessary to compile and insert a table of contents and an index. In addition, it has commands for inserting special codes into your documents called *fields*, as well as for inserting *bookmarks*, which allow you to mark sections of your documents.

13

The Format Menu

The Format menu commands control the layout and appearance of your text and documents. These commands cover formatting characters, paragraphs, sections, and the entire document. The Tabs command allows you to set tabs. The Styles command lets you define a mix of character and paragraph formats to be automatically applied to one or more selected paragraphs. With the Position command, you can place a paragraph, picture (or graphic), or table anywhere on a page and have text automatically flow around it.

The Utilities Menu

The Utilities menu provides a broad range of supporting tools for proofing your documents. Word's powerful Spelling Checker and Thesaurus are accessed through this menu. With the Hyphenate command, you can improve the appearance of your document by hyphenating text you've already created. The Customize command allows you to change the defaults for various features, such as the frequency of reminders to save your documents, units of measure for documents, and whether you replace selected text when you type a character. Additional features include

▶ Paragraph numbering.

▶ Entering revision marks mode to identify editing revisions from original text.

▶ Comparing two versions of a document.

▶ Sorting and calculating information in documents.

▶ Repaginating documents.

The Macro Menu

The Macro menu provides commands for creating, editing, and running macros. A *macro* is a recorded set of actions that you can play back at any time by either using assigned keys or choosing the macro from a list. Macros are timesavers used to quickly execute multiple commands you frequently perform.

14

The Window Menu

The commands in the Window menu allow you to create new windows to view different parts of the same document or navigate between multiple document windows. This menu also allows you to quickly arrange multiple windows on your screen to view all the windows you have open.

The Help Menu

The Help menu provides access to Word's extensive on-line help and tutorial features. Four of the commands on this menu—Index, Keyboard, Active Window, and Using Help—display a Help window that contains information related to the last editing operation. The Tutorial command accesses Word's interactive tutorial program, if it has been installed on your system. The About command displays a dialog box containing the Word program version number and the amount of available memory and disk space.

Using Word's Menus

You can choose commands from the menu bar by using either the mouse or the keyboard. To open a menu by using the mouse, simply click on the appropriate menu name in the menu bar. The menu name is highlighted and the menu drops down, allowing you to view available commands. To choose a command, click the left mouse button with the pointer on the command name.

To open a specific menu by using the keyboard, press Alt and then the underlined letter in the menu name. For example, to view the File menu, press Alt,F or choose the Edit menu and press Alt,E. To choose a command within the opened menu, use the Up Arrow or Down Arrow to highlight the command you want and then press Enter, or simply type the appropriate underlined letter for the command. For example, in the File menu, type *S* to execute the Save command.

You can execute a command by pressing the Alt key, then the underlined letter for the menu, followed by the underlined letter for the command. For example, to choose the File/Save command from the keyboard, press Alt,F,S.

15

> **Tip:** Word provides keyboard shortcuts that let you execute many commands without going through the menu. For example, in the File menu, you can execute the Exit command directly from the keyboard by pressing Alt,F4. If a keyboard shortcut is available for a command, it appears to the right of the command in the menu.

As you highlight each menu command, notice that Word displays a brief message in the status bar describing the command's function. Pressing Alt by itself places you in the menu bar where you can use the Right Arrow or Left Arrow to highlight a menu name; then press Enter to open the menu. Once you're in the menu bar with a menu opened, you can move through the menus, opening each menu by using the Right Arrow or Left Arrow. Any time you want to exit a menu without selecting a command, click on the menu name again or press the Alt key.

If a command cannot be chosen without first performing another action, Word displays the command as dimmed. For example, the Cut, Copy, and Paste commands in the Edit menu, as shown in Figure 1.6, are dimmed because you must select text before Word can execute these commands. Chapter 2 explains how to select text.

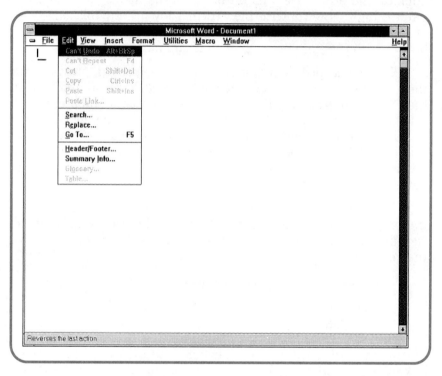

Figure 1.6   Dimmed commands in the Edit menu.

As you view Word's menus, notice the ellipsis (. . .) immediately after some of the commands. An ellipsis indicates that a *dialog box* will appear when you choose the command. A dialog box is a pop-up window in which you can change control settings related to the command, as explained in the next section.

The View menu has several special *toggle* commands. These commands are turned on and off, like a light switch, by performing the same mouse or keyboard action. For example, choosing the View/Ruler command turns it on, and a check mark appears to the left of the command indicating that it is on. When you choose the Underline-View/Underline-Ruler command again, it's turned off. Toggle commands remain in the on or off mode you last selected.

Using Dialog Boxes

Recall that commands followed by an ellipsis (. . .) display a dialog box after you choose the command. For example, selecting the Format/Paragraph command displays the dialog box with control settings, shown in Figure 1.7. Notice that some controls are already set or have text entered. These are Word's default settings, which you can change. Control settings vary, depending on the type of information Word needs to activate a feature. Each control setting has a label that identifies it. Related control settings are usually grouped together and placed inside a box with a group label. One control setting is always active in a dialog box. The active control either has a dotted rectangle around the button label or has the highlight inside of it.

17

Notice that in each label, with the exception of the OK, Cancel, and Close command buttons, one letter is underlined. The underlined letter is the letter you press in conjunction with the Alt key to activate the control setting. Press Tab to move through the control settings in order from upper left to lower right in the dialog box. Press Shift-Tab to move through the options and controls in the opposite direction. A control setting can also be chosen by using the mouse to move the pointer and clicking on the setting.

When a label for a setting, group of settings, or buttons is dimmed, it means that item is not available. When a control setting is available, it is black. You must either choose the OK button (or press Enter) to save your setting changes or choose the Cancel button (or press Esc) to cancel the command before choosing another command or typing text in a document. If you try to do something outside of the dialog box, Word beeps to remind you to close the dialog box first.

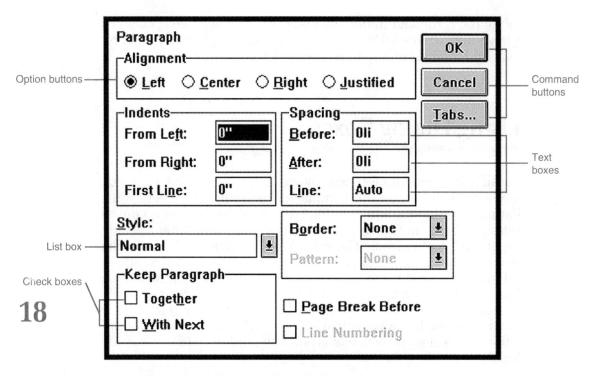

Option buttons —

Command buttons

Text boxes

List box —

Check boxes

18

Figure 1.7   The Format Paragraph dialog box.

Dialog Box Control Settings

The Dialog box control settings allow you to converse with Word by specifying how you want Word to affect your text. Word provides five different types of control settings: the option button, check box, text box, list box, and command button, as shown in Figure 1.7. Table 1.3 describes each of these settings.

Table 1.3   Dialog Box Control Settings

Control Setting	Description
Option button	Displays a dot in the center when turned on or is blank when turned off. Option buttons are grouped for selecting one out of a group of options.
Check box	Displays an x when the feature is turned on and blank when turned off. Check boxes often are clustered in groups but, unlike option boxes, choosing one doesn't exclude choosing others.

Control Setting	Description
Text box	Used to enter text, such as a filename or measurement specification. When you move the mouse pointer to a text box, it changes to an I-beam, indicating that you can insert text. When you select a text box, the selected text is replaced when you type in new text.
List box	Includes a text box with a list of options displayed under the text box. The pop-up list box has a Down Arrow displayed to the right of the text box. When the Down Arrow is chosen, a list of available options appears. The pop-up list box is commonly used in Word for Windows to save space in dialog boxes. Some list boxes always display the list of options. If the list is longer than the list box, a scroll bar appears at the right side of the list box. Many of the list boxes allow you to either type your own entry or choose an option from the list. Some list boxes, however, don't allow you to enter your own option, requiring you to choose from the options in the list.
Command button	Instructs Word to perform the appropriate task or display additional information. For example, the OK button saves your control setting changes and exits the dialog box. If the name in the command button has an ellipsis (...) after it, choosing that button either opens up another dialog box related to that command and closes the first dialog box, or opens a dialog box related to that command while leaving the first dialog box open. When the second dialog box is closed, you can continue to select options in the first dialog box. If the command button is labeled `Options` and is followed by two chevrons (>>), choosing that button expands the current dialog box to display additional options. The active command button has a dotted rectangle around its label.

19

Choosing the OK button instructs Word to accept your changes and execute the command. The Cancel button allows you to cancel any changes you've made in the dialog box and returns you to what you were working on without choosing the command. In some dialog boxes, Word first displays the Cancel button, but after you press a command button that does not close the dialog box, the Cancel button changes to a Close button because you can't cancel the previous action.

To choose the OK button to save your changes, move the mouse pointer on the OK button and click the mouse button, or press Tab to move to the button, if necessary, and then press Enter. To choose a Cancel or Close button, click the mouse with the pointer on the Cancel or Close button or press Esc.

Word's Ribbon and Ruler

20

Two time-saving Word features are the *Ribbon* and *Ruler*. On the Ribbon and Ruler, commonly used character and paragraph formatting commands are graphically displayed as buttons and list boxes. The Ribbon is always displayed on top because it remains with the Word program window, while the Ruler is part of the document window. All the commands displayed in the Ribbon and Ruler are also available using the Format menu commands, but working from the Ribbon and Ruler is easier. The Ribbon and Ruler are not displayed when you initially start Word. However, once turned on they will be displayed the next time you use Word, unless you turn them off before quitting Word.

The Ribbon

The controls displayed on the Ribbon, as shown in Figure 1.8, are used to affect the appearance of characters in your documents. To display the Ribbon by using the mouse, click on the View menu and then click on the Ribbon command. Using the keyboard, press Alt,V,B.

The Font list box offers different typefaces. The Pts (points) list box controls the size of characters. These two list boxes appear when you display the Ribbon. The eight typeface command buttons allow you to add bold, italic, small capitals, underlining of words and spaces, underlining of words only, double underlining, superscripts, and subscripts to characters. The Show All command button (the asterisk) makes normally invisible characters, such as tabs and paragraph marks, visible for easier editing. To apply a typeface feature, such as underlining, you click the underline button. Word displays the 3-D button as pressed, indicating that it is turned on. The text is underlined as you type. To turn off the underlining command, simply click on the underline button again. As you move the insertion point through the text in your document, the Ribbon reflects the formatting applied to your text.

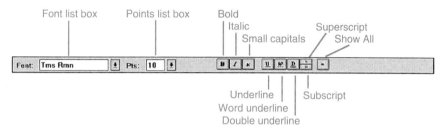

Figure 1.8.   The Ribbon.

21

The Ruler

The Ruler, shown in Figure 1.9, is used to control the appearance of paragraphs in Word documents. A *paragraph* in Word is any group of text ended by pressing the Enter key. To display the Ruler using the mouse, click on the <u>V</u>iew menu; then click on the Ruler command. Using the keyboard, press Alt,V,R. The measure, which by default is in inches, displays the available text area width, indent markers, and tab settings.

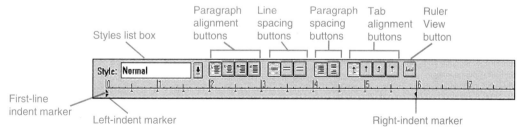

Figure 1.9.   The Ruler.

The Style list box is used to select styles to apply to a selected paragraph or paragraphs. A *style* is a collection of character and paragraph formatting instructions that are commonly used together. Word comes with several premade styles and allows you to create your own, as explained in Chapter 9. Word displays the Normal style in the Style list box, which is the default.

The Paragraph Alignment command buttons allow you to control how you want to indent your paragraphs; the default is flush left. The Line Spacing command buttons allow you to control the line spacing from the default single space to either one-and-a-half or double line spacing. The Tab command buttons, indicated by thin Up Arrows, let you set tab stops. Notice that the default tab settings are set at every half inch on the measure. The Ruler View command button changes the Ruler to show paragraph indents, page margins, or column widths. Similar to the Ribbon, the Ruler displays any applied settings as you move the insertion point through your document.

Getting Help

Word has an extensive help system for commands, dialog box controls, and other features. There are two ways to bring up the Help window in Word. First, you can search through Word's help information by using commands on the Help menu. Second, you can get context-sensitive help by pressing F1 or Shift-F1. *Context-sensitive* means that the Help window displays information directly tied to what you were working on immediately before you requested help.

To display the Help menu by using the mouse, click with the pointer on Help in the menu bar. Using the keyboard, press Alt-H. Word displays the Help menu, as shown in Figure 1.10. The Index command displays an index of available help topics. The Keyboard command displays information about keyboard-specific topics, such as a listing of important keys. The Active Window command displays an index of window help information for the active window. The Tutorial command starts Word's on-line tutorial (if you've installed the tutorial lessons on your system). The Using Help command displays instructions about using the help system. The About command displays Word's version number and information about the disk space and memory available on your computer.

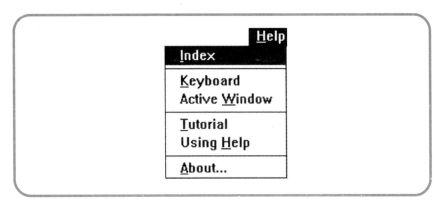

Figure 1.10.   The Help menu.

The Help Window

When you select any Help menu command, with the exception of the About command, Word displays the Help window with the requested help information. Figure 1.11 shows a Help window displayed after choosing the Index command. The Help window includes standard window features, such as a title bar, control menu, menu bar, and a scroll bar.

23

The Help window menu bar lists several command menus, which you choose in the same way as the menu bar. The File menu allows you to print a help topic or close the Help window. The Edit menu copies help information to a Word file. The Browse menu allows you to move around within the help files to find the information you're looking for. The Bookmark menu marks a section to allow for quick access of specific help information, and the Help menu provides information about how to use the help system.

The Help window can be moved anywhere on the screen by moving the mouse pointer to the Help window's title bar, pressing the mouse button, and dragging the mouse. When you've positioned the Help window where you want it, release the mouse button.

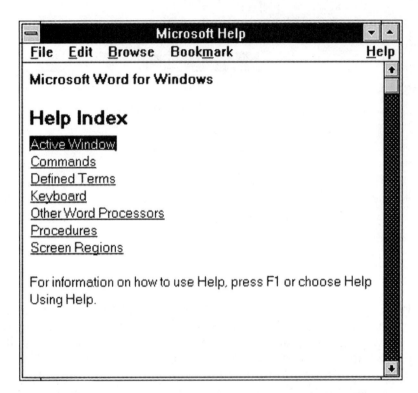

Figure 1.11   *The Help window displaying the Help Index.*

> ▶ **Tip:** If you plan to use the Help window frequently, don't close the Help window. Instead, click on the Minimize button (the Down Arrow at the right of the title bar), click anywhere in the Word window, or press Esc. You can then quickly redisplay the Help window by pressing Alt-Tab.

Getting Context-Sensitive Help

Word provides two different methods for accessing context-sensitive help. The first involves selecting a command, bringing up a dialog box, or generating a message, using either the keyboard or mouse, and then pressing F1. Word brings up the help information

24

for the last active command, dialog box, or message. If you don't activate a command, dialog box, or message before pressing F1, Word displays the Help Index.

The other method for accessing context-sensitive help is to first press Shift-F1. When you do this, the mouse pointer changes to an arrow/question marker. Move the mouse pointer and click on the command or on most areas of the screen for which you want to obtain help. Using this method gives you more latitude in obtaining help about specific areas of the screen, such as window features. For example, pressing Shift-F1 and moving the question mark pointer to the window title bar displays information about the title bar. This information would be unavailable using the F1 method.

Using Definitions and Jump Terms

Two types of cross referencing help are available using the Help window: *definitions* and *jump terms*. Definitions have a dotted underline, and jump terms have a normal underline, as shown in Figure 1.12. The mouse pointer becomes a pointing hand when it's on one of these special items.

To display a *definition* of a term, use the mouse or arrow keys to highlight the definition and then hold down the Enter key, or point to the definition and then hold down the left mouse button to display a definition window. When you release the Enter key or the mouse button, the definition window disappears. To *jump* to a new topic with a jump term, use the arrow keys to highlight the underlined jump term and then press Enter, or click with the pointer on the jump term to jump to the new topic. To jump back, press the F9 key or choose the Backtrack command from the Browse menu.

The Word Tutorial Program

Word for Windows has a tutorial program that includes a set of lessons and practice sessions designed to teach rudimentary Word for Windows skills. To use the tutorial program, you must install it when you set up Word for Windows. If the Word tutorial isn't in your WINWORD directory, Word displays a message box when you choose the Help Tutorial command, indicating that the tutorial file, WINWORD.CBT, cannot be found. If the tutorial is not installed on your system, you'll need to install it using the Word for Windows Setup program, as explained in Appendix A.

25

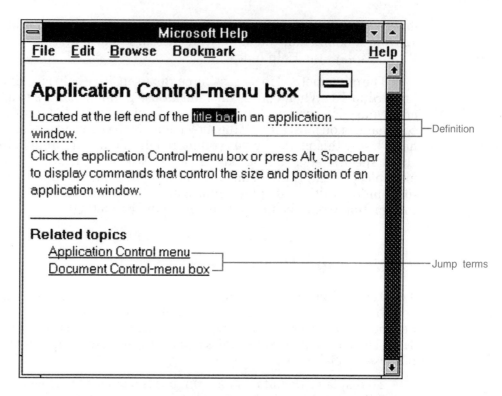

Figure 1.12   Definitions and jump terms.

To activate the Word for Windows tutorial program, choose the Help/Tutorial command. Using the mouse, click on the Help menu and then click on the Tutorial command. Using the keyboard, press Alt,H,T. Word displays the Word for Windows tutorial introduction screen, which asks if you want the lessons to include both mouse and keyboard techniques or just keyboard procedures. After selecting the option you want, Word displays the tutorial's main menu screen, as shown in Figure 1.13. Select the lesson you want by pressing the appropriate lesson number. Word leads you through the lesson. To exit the tutorial program, press *X*.

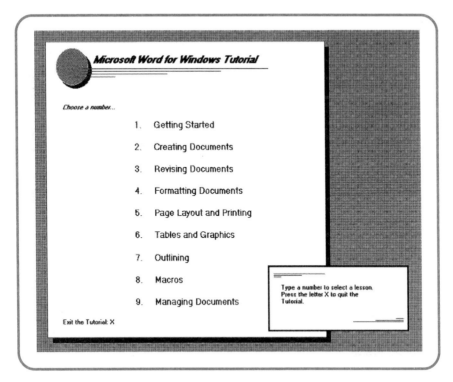

Figure 1.13   The Word for Windows table of tutorial lessons.

27

Closing Word for Windows to an Icon

You can close the Word for Windows program window to an icon on the Windows desktop, as shown in Figure 1.14. This allows you to set aside the Word program without quitting Word so that you can work on other programs. The easiest way to close the Word program window to an icon is to click on the Minimize button (the Down Arrow button located on the right side of the window's title bar or press Alt-F9. The Word program window closes to an icon on the Windows desktop. To quickly return to the full-screen display of Word for Windows, double-click on the Word icon or press Enter if the icon is highlighted. If the icon is not highlighted, press Alt-Esc until the Word icon is highlighted and then press Enter.

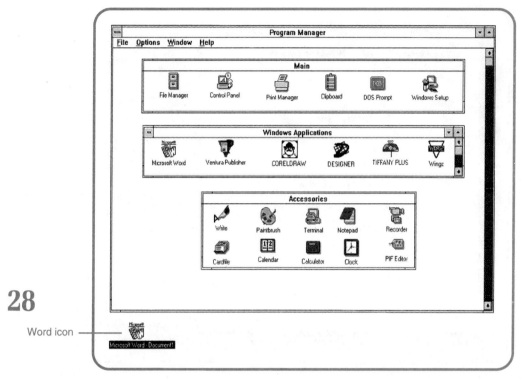

Word icon —

Figure 1.14   The closed Word icon on the Windows desktop.

Quitting Word for Windows

To quit the Word for Windows program and return to Windows, choose the File/Exit command or press Alt,F,X. Double-clicking on the Word Control menu box (located in the upper left corner) or pressing Alt-F4 also quits the Word for Window program. If you change your mind about quitting the current session, choose the Cancel button or press Esc.

If you've made any changes to a document, Word displays a dialog box asking if you want to save your changes to disk. If you don't want to save the changes you made, choose the No button or press N. Your Word session ends without the changes being saved, and you are returned to Windows. If you want to save your work, choose the Yes button or press Y or Enter.

If the document you're working on is a new document, Word displays the Save File Name dialog box for entering the path and filename for your document file, as shown in Figure 1.15. Type a path and filename in the Save File Name text box, for example, c:\winword\memos\fired. Filenames can have up to eight characters, and they follow DOS filename conventions. After entering the path and filename for your document file, choose the OK button or press Enter. Word then displays the Summary Info dialog box, which allows you to enter information about your document. After entering any optional summary information, choose the OK button or press Enter to finish saving your document file.

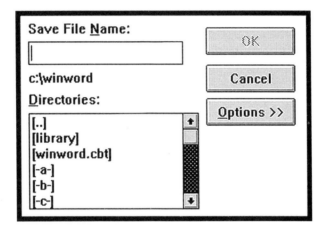

Figure 1.15   The Save File Name dialog box.

29

Quitting Word for Windows and Saving a New Document

1. Double-click on the Word Control menu box or press Alt-F4.

   Word displays a dialog box asking if you want to save the changes you've made to a document.

2. Choose the Yes button or press Y.

   Word displays a Save File Name dialog box, as shown in Figure 1.15.

3. Type the filename for your new document (up to eight characters) in the Save File Name text box.

   The OK button darkens, indicating it's now available.

4. Choose the <u>D</u>irectories list box or press Alt,D.

   The first item in the <u>D</u>irectories list box is highlighted.

5. Choose the path where you want to store the file by double-clicking on the drive and/or directory you want. Using the keyboard, press the Down or Up Arrow key to highlight the drive and/or directory you want and then press Enter.

   You can drag the scroll box or click on the Up or Down Arrow button to view any additional directories or drives not visible. The path statement you've specified is displayed directly above the <u>D</u>irectories list box.

6. After entering the path and filename, choose the OK button or press Enter.

   Word displays a Summary Info dialog box.

7. Choose the OK button or press Enter.

   The new document is saved to the drive and/or directory you specified. Word ends the session, returning you to Windows. □

30

What You Have Learned

▶ Before you can use Word for Windows, you must have Microsoft Windows installed on your computer system. See Appendix A if you need to install Windows.

▶ Using a mouse will improve your productivity. Mouse actions include pointing, clicking, double-clicking, and dragging to manipulate graphical objects on the screen.

▶ To start Word for Windows from the DOS command prompt, type `cd\winword` and press Enter. Next, type `winword` and press Enter.

▶ To start Word for Windows from within Windows, use the <u>F</u>ile/<u>R</u>un command in the Program Manager window or double-click on the Windows Applications icon in the Program Manager window and then double-click on the Microsoft Word icon.

► The main components displayed in the opening Word for Windows screen are the text area, menu bar, status bar, title bar, Word and Document Control menu boxes, scroll bar, insertion point, endmark, and Minimize and Restore buttons.

► The menus displayed on the menu bar include the Word Control and Document menu boxes, the File menu, the Edit menu, the View menu, the Insert menu, the Format menu, the Utilities menu, the Macro menu, the Window menu, and the Help menu. To activate a pull-down menu, click on the menu name or press Alt followed by the underlined letter in the menu name.

► Dialog boxes can include five types of control settings: option button, check box, text box, list box, and command button.

► Word offers two time-saving Word features—the Ribbon and Ruler. They graphically display commonly used character and paragraph formatting commands by using buttons and list boxes. Choosing the View/Ribbon command or pressing Alt,V,B toggles the Ribbon command on or off. Choosing the View/Ruler command or pressing Alt,V,R toggles the Ruler on or off.

► Word provides an extensive on-line help system. Choosing the Help/Index command or pressing Alt,H,I displays the index of available help topics. To get context-sensitive help, select the command and then press F1, or press Shift-F1 and then move the mouse pointer to the command or area of screen you want help with and click the mouse button.

► The easiest way to exit Word is to double-click on the Word Control menu box or press Alt-F4. Anytime you have unsaved work, Word asks if you want to save it before quitting. The previous Quick Steps explain how to quit Word and save a new document as a file.

31

Creating, Editing, and Saving Documents

In This Chapter

▶ *Understanding Word's text definitions*
▶ *Navigating a document*
▶ *Entering, selecting, editing, copying, and moving text*
▶ *Saving and retrieving documents*

Now that you're comfortable with the Word for Windows workbench and the location of your tools, you're ready to master the essential tools for creating and editing documents.

The New Document Window

When you start Word for Windows, Word automatically opens a document window for you. Any text that you enter into this document window can be stored in a file with a name that you specify. Word gives this file the default filename of Document1. In Figure 2.1 you can see the document window with the default filename appearing on the first line of the window. To start working with Word quickly, leave `Document1` as the filename and then rename the file later when you save it.

Before working with Word, turn on the Ribbon and the Ruler, as shown in Figure 2.1. To turn on the Ribbon, choose the View/Ribbon command by pressing Alt,V,B. To turn on the Ruler, choose the View/Ruler command by pressing Alt,V,R.

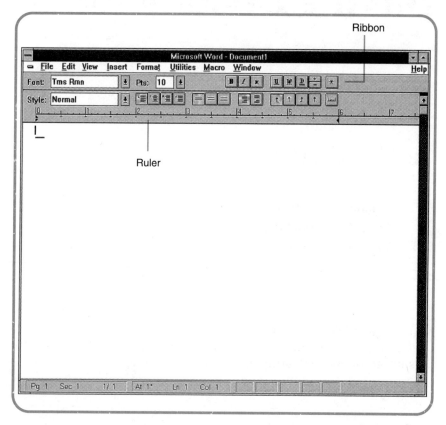

Figure 2.1   The new document window with the Ribbon and Ruler.

Entering Text

As soon as you see the new document window displayed on your screen, you can begin entering text. Try entering some text now. Notice the blinking vertical line at the top left corner of your screen. This is the *insertion point*. It indicates where text you type will be inserted in your document. As you enter text, several things happen: the mouse pointer disappears, the insertion point moves to the right, and the text that you have typed is displayed to the left of the insertion point.

> ⊘ **Caution:** It's easy to confuse the mouse pointer, which is displayed as an I-beam in the text area, with the insertion point. Remember, text you type is always entered at the insertion point, indicated by a blinking vertical line.

Word arranges the lines of text within the text area of your document according to the margin settings. A *margin* is the blank area of the page outside the main body of text. Word's default margin settings are 1 inch at the top and bottom of the page, and 1.25 inches left and right. When the line of text you're typing reaches the right margin, and there isn't enough room for a complete word without hyphenating it, Word automatically begins a new line and moves the whole word to the new line. This feature, called *wordwrap*, works regardless of where in the line you insert text. However, as you'll learn later, you can add hyphens manually to split words, and you can even out the ragged right edge of your text.

Text that you enter is *left justified*, meaning that the text is flush against the left margin and ragged on the right margin. You can change the left-justified alignment to a different alignment, as explained in Chapter 4, "Essential Formatting."

You can delete characters quickly in two different ways. Press the Backspace key to delete a character to the left of the insertion point, or press the Del key to delete a character to the right of the insertion point. Besides deleting one or more characters, you can delete whole sections of text. Selecting and deleting sections of text is covered later in this chapter.

> ⃠ **Caution:** When you are entering text, don't press Enter at the end of each line. Unlike a typewriter, Word for Windows will automatically move to the next line. Press Enter only when you come to the end of a paragraph.

Inserting and Overtype Text

There are two modes for entering text: *overtype* and *insert*. When you first begin using Word, you're in the *insert* mode. Insert mode causes text to be inserted to the left of the insertion point and pushes any other text to the right of the insertion point. The *overtype* mode allows you to type over existing characters, with the new text erasing the previous text. Turn the overtype mode on or off by pressing the Ins key. Word displays OVR in the status line when you're in the overtype mode.

36

A Word About Fonts

The term *font* refers to a family of typeface designs. Figure 2.2 shows examples of different fonts. When you enter text, Word initially displays it in the default font—Times Roman. The Ribbon shows Tms Rmn in the Font list box. You can choose another font (typeface) by clicking on the arrow button to the right of the Font list box and then clicking on a font name. To use the keyboard, press Ctrl-F and then press Alt-Down Arrow to display the list of available fonts. You can then use the Up or Down Arrow to highlight the font you want and press Enter to begin using it. Chapters 4 and 5 cover the subject of fonts in great detail.

The Pts (Points) list box, shown to the right of the Font list box in the Ribbon, displays the point size of the font selected. The term *points* refers to a measurement system for fonts in which 72 points equals one inch in height. The default setting is 10 points for the Times Roman default font. You can select a point size from a list of available point sizes for a particular font by clicking on the Down Arrow button to the right of the Pts list box or by pressing Ctrl-P and then Alt-Down Arrow. You can also enter a number directly in the Pts text box after activating the Pts text box.

```
Courier  7 points
```

Lineprinter 8.5 points

Times Roman   10 points

Optima   12 points

Souvenir   16 points

Melior   18 point

Figure 2.2   Font samples.

▶ **Note:** In Word you can have fonts displayed on your screen but not printed by your printer, and vice versa. Chapters 4 and 5 explain more about fonts and how to work with them.

37

Text Viewing Modes

Word for Windows provides three primary modes for viewing text: Normal, Page, and Draft. In *Normal* mode, which is the default, you can view pictures and most formatting marks on your screen, as shown in Figure 2.3. The *Page* mode, shown in Figure 2.4, displays your text in the manner it will appear on the printed page.

The *Draft* mode, shown in Figure 2.5, displays only the most basic formatting marks on the screen, such as paragraph marks; other features, such as pictures, do not appear. The Draft mode is not true *WYSIWYG* (What You See Is What You Get) but instead is designed for fast text entry and printing. It enables you to concentrate on the text in your document and not worry about the appearance of the pages. Working with documents in the Draft mode is faster than in the Normal mode because the Normal mode requires more memory and slows down screen updating. To switch to the Draft mode using the mouse, click on the View menu and then click on the Draft command. Using the keyboard, press Alt,V,D. Word redisplays your document in the Draft mode. You can turn off the Draft command in the same way you turned it on.

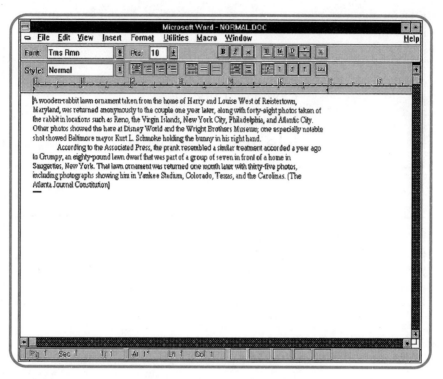

Figure 2.3   Text displayed in the Normal mode.

 Note: The Normal mode is automatically used by Word and is activated if all other view modes are off.

How Your Printer Affects the Viewing of Text

Viewing text in Normal or Page mode takes into account the capabilities of your printer. Choosing the View/Preferences command displays a dialog box that allows you to choose whether your document will display as printed. The Display as Printed check box is turned on by default. This setting limits what is displayed on your screen by what your printer can actually print. Therefore, if your printer has limited font and picture-printing capabilities, the setting will limit certain fonts and font sizes.

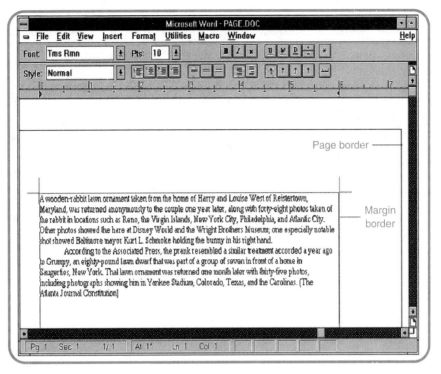

Figure 2.4   Text displayed in the Page mode.

39

In addition, depending on your printer and the font point size assigned to your document, the lines of your text may extend beyond the right side of your screen. This doesn't mean that the text goes beyond the margin of your page. Rather, it reflects the fact that your printer can fit more characters on a line than can be displayed on your screen. Navigating in a document in this situation is cumbersome, requiring you to scroll horizontally to view the ends of lines.

If the printer you've selected causes this situation, Word allows you to change the text display on your screen in two ways. The easiest way is to choose the View/Draft command, which provides a standard font for all text, regardless of the printer selected. While switching to Draft mode solves the problem, remember that it limits your display to a single font and shows only basic formatting marks. The other way is to turn off the Display as Printed check box setting in the View Preferences dialog box. Doing this provides a variety of screen fonts and keeps lines within the confines of your screen view, but you lose the WYSIWYG feature.

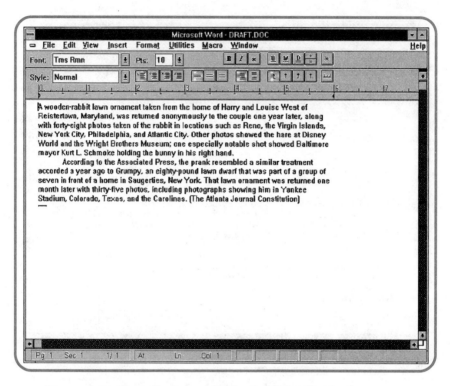

Figure 2.5   Text displayed in the Draft mode.

40

Q Turning Off the **D**isplay as Printed Feature

1. Choose the **V**iew/**P**references command by pressing Alt,V,E.

    Word displays the View Preferences dialog box, as shown in Figure 2.6.

2. Click on the **D**isplay as Printed check box or press Alt-D.

    The setting is toggled off, and the x disappears from the box.

3. Click on OK or press Enter.

    This closes the dialog box. You can turn the **D**isplay as Printed feature back on by performing the same procedure. □

> **Tip:** With the Display as Printed setting turned off, you can format and enhance documents with features your printer cannot handle. This gives you the power to create documents that can be printed on other printers. For example, you could create a document with a dot matrix printer but print it on a laser printer.

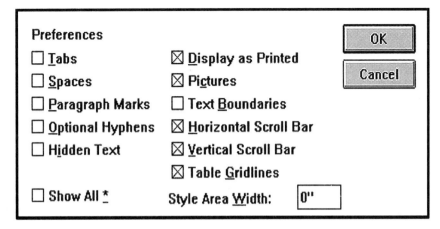

Figure 2.6   The View Preferences dialog box.

Word's Text Definitions

Before you begin selecting, editing, and formatting text in your document, you should understand how Word defines units of text, such as characters, words, sentences, and paragraphs. The most basic element of text in your Word document is a character. A *character* can be any item you enter onto the screen: a blank space, letter, number, punctuation mark, or any other special mark. Words, sentences, and paragraphs are predefined combinations of characters. Table 2.1 describes each of Word's text definitions.

41

Table 2.1   Word's Text Definitions

Unit	Definition
Word	Any group of characters separated by spaces, tabs, hyphens, or punctuation
Line	Any series of characters stretching from margin to margin, including new line or paragraph marks
Sentence	Any group of characters ending with a punctuation mark and a space
Paragraph	Any group of characters in which you press Enter after the characters
Block of text	All the text within a defined area
Document	All the text contained in a document file

Paragraphs, New Lines, and Hyphens

A *paragraph* in Word is the fundamental formatting unit. The paragraph mark stores all the formatting information for the characters in the paragraph. To create a paragraph in Word, simply press Enter after you have typed the last character that you want to include in the paragraph.

Unlike a paragraph mark, the *new line* feature does not begin a new paragraph but allows you to circumvent wordwrap and insert a separate line of text within a paragraph. The new line is still part of the paragraph it's in. If you want to create a new line in a paragraph, hold down Shift and press Enter. Figure 2.7 shows a paragraph with new lines inserted.

Because of wordwrapping, a long word that doesn't fit on a line is automatically placed at the beginning of the next line. This may result in a large space at the end of the previous line. Word allows you to insert a special hyphen, called an *optional hyphen*, in the long word. The optional hyphen allows you to break up words to even out the right edge of your document. If the text is realigned later so that both parts of the hyphenated word are on the same line, Word automatically removes the optional hyphen. To insert an optional hyphen, place the insertion point where you want the hyphen and press Ctrl-Hyphen.

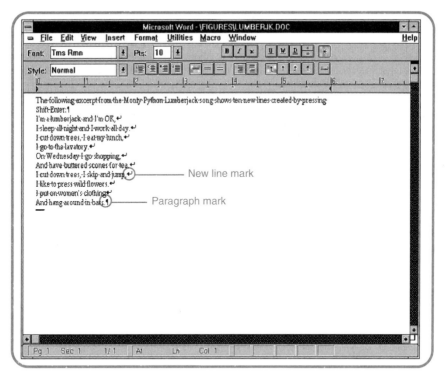

Figure 2.7   A paragraph containing new lines.

> ▶ **Note:** Use the optional hyphen (Ctrl-Hyphen) rather than a regular hyphen (press the Hyphen key) to hyphenate a word. A regular hyphen can cause problems if you later add text or if you change margins or indents. The hyphen remains in the word even though the word may no longer be at the end of a line.

A *nonbreaking hyphen* is used when you have hyphenated words that you don't want Word to break at the end of a line, for example, words like *seventy-five* or *ill-fated*. Nonbreaking hyphens keep the words together on a line. To insert a nonbreaking hyphen, make sure the insertion point is between the words you want to hyphenate and press Ctrl-Shift-Hyphen.

43

Page Breaks

When you're entering text in a document, Word automatically calculates where page breaks will occur. These page breaks are based on the paper size and the top and bottom margin settings. The default paper size setting is 8 ½ by 11 inches, with a top and bottom margin setting of 1 inch from the edge of the paper. Word displays a page break as a dotted line across your screen, as shown in Figure 2.8. When the insertion point is moved below the page break line, the new page number is noted in the status bar. Word creates page breaks automatically. However, you can force a page break (called a *hard page break*) to occur by pressing Ctrl-Enter. To remove a hard page break, move the insertion point below it and press the Backspace key.

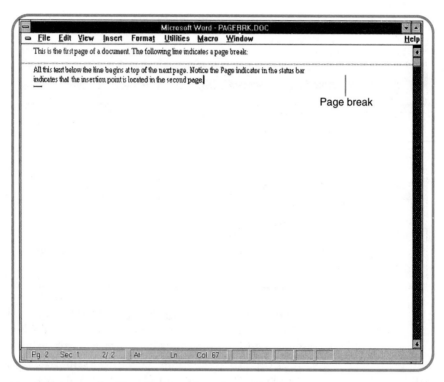

Figure 2.8   Word's page break mark.

Word's Special Marks

Word inserts special marks into your document every time you press Enter to create a paragraph, press Tab to indent the first line of a paragraph, or press Spacebar to add a space between words. When you first start Word, these special marks are not displayed. However, you can instruct Word to display these marks by clicking on the asterisk in the Ribbon or using the View/Preferences command. This is helpful when you want to see how these nonprinting characters affect your text. Table 2.2 shows the most common special marks and their on-screen symbols.

 Displaying Word's Special Marks with the View Menu

1. Choose the View/Preferences command or press Alt,V,E.	Word displays the View Preferences dialog box.
2. Choose the Show All * check box or press Alt-*.	An X appears in the check box.
3. Click on the OK button or press Enter.	The asterisk is pressed in the Ribbon, and Word now displays all special marks in your document. □

45

Table 2.2   Common Special Marks

Special Mark	Key(s) to Press	On-screen Symbol
New line	Shift-Enter	↵
Nonbreaking hyphen	Ctrl-Shift-Hyphen)	—
Optional hyphen	Ctrl-Hyphen	¬
Paragraph	Enter	¶
Space	Space	•
Tab	Tab	→

Navigating Your Document

Word provides two ways to move around in a large document. The most common way is *scrolling*. Scrolling moves your document file through the text area window, bringing successive sections into view, like reading a roll of parchment. The other common way involves jumping from page to page or jumping to the top or bottom of a document. Word also provides ways to move horizontally across a document when lines extend beyond the edge of your screen. We'll discuss each of these ways in turn and show you how to use them from the mouse and the keyboard.

Navigating a Document by Using the Mouse

46

As you'll recall from Chapter 1, the vertical bar with arrow buttons (at the top and bottom to the right of your document's text area) is called a *scroll bar*. The scroll bar is designed for navigating your document with the mouse. In most cases the scroll bar provides the easiest route for quickly scrolling or jumping around your document. The arrow buttons at each end of the scroll bar are used to scroll through your document, one line at a time, in the direction of the arrow you click on.

Notice that the mouse pointer changes to a left-angled arrow when you move it anywhere on the scroll bar. If you press and hold down the left mouse button with the pointer on an arrow scroll box, the document automatically scrolls through your document in the direction of the arrow.

In Figure 2.9 find the box without the arrow, located on the scroll bar between the two arrow boxes. This box is called the *thumb*. It moves in the corresponding direction as your arrow, but the insertion point remains at its original location until you click a mouse button. The thumb shows your relative position in the document, with the scroll bar representing the length of your document. The longer the document, the less distance the thumb moves as you scroll through it.

To move through your document a full screen at a time, click in the gray area of the scroll bar above the thumb to move up a page or below the thumb to move down a page. Notice that Word carries two lines over to the top of the next screen to help you get your bearings.

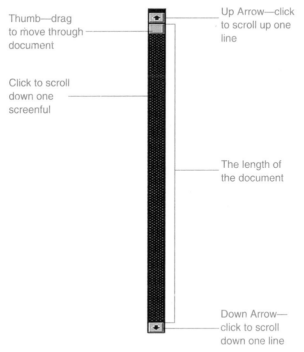

Thumb—drag to move through document

Click to scroll down one screenful

Up Arrow—click to scroll up one line

The length of the document

Down Arrow—click to scroll down one line

Figure 2.9   The scroll bar.

Thumbing lets you move to any place in your document by dragging the thumb in the scroll bar to the approximate location you want and releasing the mouse button. Using this method, Word does not display the text as you drag the thumb. Instead, the text that was displayed when you began the thumbing remains on the screen until you release the mouse button; then the text at the new location is displayed. Dragging the thumb to the very top or bottom of the scroll bar places you at the top or bottom, respectively, of your document.

> ▶ **Tip:** To quickly return to the insertion point after scroll-ing through a document by using the scroll bar, press Shift-F5. Word returns you to the insertion point.

47

Navigating a Document by Using the Keyboard

Word provides extensive keyboard commands for navigating through your document. Many of the keys used in Word for Windows are standard keys used for navigating in other Windows programs. Table 2.3 lists the available keyboard commands for navigating in Word for Windows.

Table 2.3 Document Navigation Commands from the Keyboard

To Move the Insertion Point to the	Press Key(s)
Beginning of the document	Ctrl-Home
End of the document	Ctrl-End
Next character	Right Arrow
Previous character	Left Arrow
Next line	Down Arrow
Previous line	Up Arrow
Beginning of line	Home
End of line	End
Next screen	PgDn
Previous screen	PgUp
Next word	Ctrl-Right Arrow
Previous word	Ctrl-Left Arrow
Top of window	Ctrl-PgUp
Bottom of window	Ctrl-PgDn
Next paragraph	Ctrl-Down Arrow
Previous paragraph	Ctrl-Up Arrow

The Go To Command

The Go To command is handy for quickly jumping to a specific page in a multipage document. You can go directly to the top of a specific page by choosing the Edit/Go To command or by pressing Alt,E,G. Word displays the Go To dialog box, as shown in Figure 2.10. Enter the page you want to move to in the Go To text box; then click on the OK button or press Enter. A shortcut for activating the Go To command is to press F5. The prompt `Go to:` appears in the bottom left corner of the status line. Enter the page number you want to move to and press Enter.

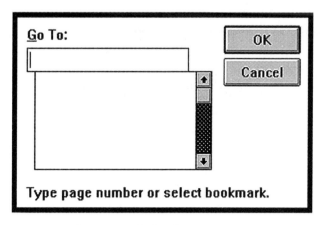

Figure 2.10   The Go To dialog box.

49

You can press Shift-F5 to return to the location where you last made a change. Word remembers the three previous insertion points where you made changes. If you press Shift-F5 immediately after opening a document, Word moves to the section displayed when you last saved your document.

> ▶ **Note:** To quickly move to a location in your document containing a specific section of text, use the Edit/Search command, explained in Chapter 3.

Horizontal Scrolling

Horizontal scrolling means moving the document from side to side in the window. When a document is wider than the window, you may want to scroll horizontally so that you can see what is out of sight. By default, Word's horizontal bar is not displayed. To display the horizontal scroll bar, choose the View/Preferences command or press Alt,V,E. In the Preferences dialog box, choose the Horizontal

Scroll Bar check box or press Alt-H; then click with the pointer on the OK button or press Enter. Word displays the horizontal scroll bar, as shown in Figure 2.11.

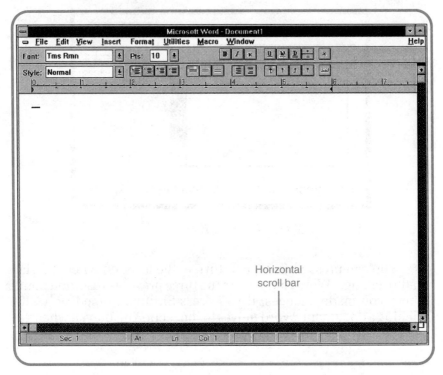

Figure 2.11   The horizontal scroll bar.

Horizontal scrolling is similar to vertical scrolling, except that the distance you travel when you drag the thumb in the horizontal scroll bar is constant. Word allows you to create text up to 22 inches wide. If you drag the thumb to the far right, the insertion point appears at the 22" mark. If you drag the scroll bar to the middle, the horizontal thumb appears at the 11" mark.

Selecting Text

The basic technique for editing is to first select the text you want to affect and then apply the appropriate editing or formatting command. For example, you select a paragraph and then you press the Del key to delete it. You can select text with the mouse or the keyboard. The text you select can be a word, sentence, line, paragraph, block, or the entire document.

Selecting Text by Using the Mouse

The mouse provides the easiest methods for selecting large sections of text. You can select text in any direction from the insertion point. The insertion point serves as the pivot or anchor point for one end of your selection.

51

The quickest way to select text is to move the pointer directly before the character you want to select; then hold down the left mouse button and drag the mouse either forward or backward to include the text you want to select. When you release the mouse button, the characters you've dragged across are displayed in reverse video. For example, if the normal display is black characters on a white background, the reverse video would be white characters on a black background. If the text you want to select is not completely displayed, drag the mouse to the upper or lower window border in the direction of the text you want to select. Word selects the text as it scrolls up or down the screen.

To select a word, place the insertion point anywhere on the word you want to select; then double-click the left mouse button. Word selects the word and any spaces to its direct right. If you double-click on a word followed by a punctuation character, only the word is selected.

To select a line of text, first move the mouse pointer to the selection bar. The *selection bar* is the blank column located between your text and the left page border on your screen. When you move the pointer in the selection bar, the mouse pointer changes to a right-pointing arrow, as shown in Figure 2.12. When the mouse pointer is in the selection bar, point to a line you want to select and click. If you want to select multiple lines, move the pointer to the line you want to start or end your selection, and drag the mouse pointer up or down in your document. To select a paragraph, move the mouse pointer in the selection bar to a position opposite the paragraph you want to select; then double-click the mouse button.

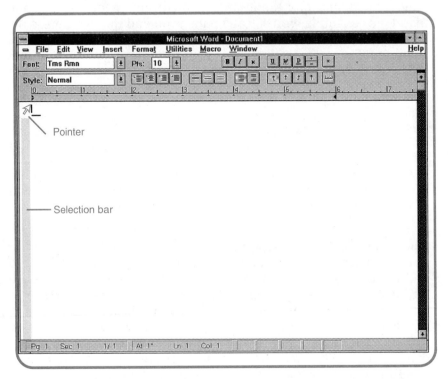

Figure 2.12   The pointer in the selection bar.

The best way to select a large block of text is to move the pointer to the beginning of the text you want to select and click the left mouse button. Then move the pointer to the end of the text you want to select, hold down the Shift key, and again click the left mouse button. To select the entire document, simply move the mouse pointer to the selection bar and press Ctrl; then click the left mouse button.

 Selecting a Large Block of Text with the Mouse

1. Move the mouse pointer to the location where you want to begin the selection.

   The insertion point appears at the location of the mouse pointer.

2. Click the left mouse button.

3. Move the mouse pointer to the last character of the text you want to select.

Word selects the text between the insertion point and the mouse pointer.

4. Hold down the Shift key and click the left mouse button.

5. Choose a command for Word to perform on the selected text or click outside the selection.

If you click outside the selection, Word turns off the selection.

□

To select a column with the mouse, position the pointer at the corner of the text column you want to select. The corner can be anywhere you want. Press the right, not the left, mouse button, and drag the pointer to the opposite corner of the block you want to select. Word considers any character more than half selected to be part of the selection. Table 2.4 lists the different ways to select standard text with a mouse.

53

Table 2.4   Selecting Text with the Mouse

Selection	Action
Block of text	Drag the pointer over the text.
Character	Click with the pointer on the character.
Line	In the selection bar, click next to the line.
Paragraph	In the selection bar, double-click next to the paragraph.
Column	Press the right, not the left, mouse button beginning at the top right corner of ˙ column you want to select. Drag tʰ pointer to the last character of thʲ column and release the mouse ⊦
Large block of text	Click at the beginning of the bˡ release the mouse button, hoˡ Shift, and click at the end of
Entire document	Move the mouse pointer to bar, press Ctrl, and click tʼ button.

Selecting Text by Using the Keyboard

To select text by using the keyboard, press F8. Word enters the Extend Selection mode and remains in this mode until you perform an editing action or until you press Esc to turn off the Extend Selection mode. Pressing F8 and then pressing a direction key (an Arrow key or Home or End) selects the amount of text that the direction key normally scrolls. For example, pressing F8 and then pressing the Right Arrow key selects one character to the right of the insertion point.

Pressing F8 and then pressing a character key extends the selection to the next instance of that character. The number of times you press F8 also affects the amount of text selected. For example, pressing F8 twice selects the word that the insertion point is on; pressing F8 three times selects the sentence; four times selects a paragraph; and five times selects the entire document. To shrink a selection, press Shift-F8. Shrinking backtracks through the selection process until all text is deselected.

Holding down Shift and using a direction key selects the amount of text that the direction key normally scrolls, beginning at your insertion point. For example, holding down Shift and pressing End selects text from the insertion point to the end of the current line. Using the Shift key, however, doesn't put you in the Extend Selection mode. You can quickly deselect text by releasing the Shift key and pressing any direction key, such as the Up Arrow or End key.

> ▶ **Tip:** To quickly select your entire document using the keyboard, press Ctrl-F5.

 Selecting Text with the Keyboard

1. Press F8.   Word displays EXT in the
                                      status line, indicating that
                                      the Extend Selection mode
                                      is toggled on.

2. Use the direction keys to
   select text.

3. When the selection contains the text you want, press Esc.

Word turns off the Extend Selection mode.

4. Perform the edit command you want on the selected text.

□

Selecting a Column of Text by Using the Keyboard

When you select text by using the F8 key, Word automatically follows the wordwrap feature, selecting entire lines of text at a time. Use the column selection key combination, Ctrl-Shift-F8, to enter the Column Selection mode and override selecting text this way. Any rectangular block of characters can be selected by using the Column Selection mode. A column selection may or may not include the text between the left and right margins. Notice that when you press Ctrl-Shift-F8, Word displays COL in the status bar, indicating that you're in the Column Selection mode. Figure 2.13 shows an example of a selected column of text.

55

 Selecting a Column of Text with the Keyboard

1. Position the insertion point at the upper corner of the block of text you want to select.

2. Press Ctrl-Shift-F8.

Word displays COL in the status line, indicating you're in the Column Selection mode.

3. Position the insertion point on the last character of the column you want to select.

Word selects the column from the starting point to the end of the block.

4. Choose an editing command or action to perform on the selected text or press Esc or Ctrl-Shift-F8 to toggle the Column Selection mode off.

Word turns off the Column Selection mode, and the letters CS disappear from the status line.

□

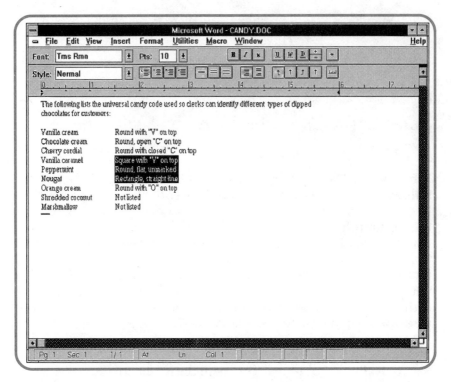

The following lists the universal candy code used so clerks can identify different types of dipped chocolates for customers:

Vanilla cream	Round with "V" on top
Chocolate cream	Round, open "C" on top
Cherry cordial	Round with closed "C" on top
Vanilla caramel	Square with "V" on top
Peppermint	Round, flat, unmarked
Nougat	Rectangle, straight line
Orange cream	Round with "O" on top
Shredded coconut	Not listed
Marshmallow	Not listed

Figure 2.13   A selected column of text.

Moving, Copying, and Deleting Text

Word for Windows provides two ways to move, copy, or delete text in your documents. The first uses a special tool called the *Clipboard*. The Clipboard is a temporary storage area designed to accept text and graphics so that you can transfer them to and from documents and other Windows applications. The second way performs these tasks without using the Clipboard to store your selected text. This way can be helpful if you're running low on memory and don't want to tie up the extra memory required by the Clipboard.

The commands used for moving, copying, and deleting text by using the Clipboard are located in the Edit menu. The Cut command is used to cut (remove) selected text from the document, holding it on the Clipboard. The Copy command copies the selected text onto the Clipboard, leaving your document's text intact. Notice that both of these commands are dimmed, meaning they are unavailable until you select text. The Paste command is used to paste (insert) the contents of the Clipboard into your document, beginning at the insertion point. The Clipboard can hold only one piece of text at a time.

Once you have cut or copied text onto the Clipboard, you can paste it as many times as you like. The text will stay on the Clipboard until it is replaced by cutting or copying new text. Try cutting a selection of text and viewing the contents of the Clipboard.

Q Viewing the Contents of the Clipboard

1. Select text.

   The text appears in reverse video.

2. Choose the Edit/Cut command, press Shift-Del, or press Alt,E,T.

   Word removes the selected text from your document and stores it in the Clipboard.

3. Click on Word's Control menu in the top left corner of the title bar, or press Alt-Spacebar.

   The Word Control menu is displayed.

4. Choose the Run command or press U.

   The Run dialog box appears, as shown in Figure 2.14.

5. Make sure that the Clipboard option button is selected, and choose the OK button or press Enter.

   The Clipboard containing your cut text is displayed, as shown in Figure 2.15. □

57

▶ **Tip:** Because the Clipboard is a window, you can perform any window operation with it. You can hide the Clipboard behind the Word window by pressing Alt-Tab and redisplay it again by pressing Alt-Tab. To close the Clipboard, click outside of the Clipboard area or press Alt,Spacebar,C. For more information on using windows, see Chapter 8.

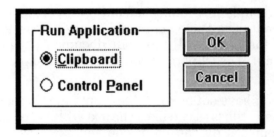

Figure 2.14   The Run Application dialog box.

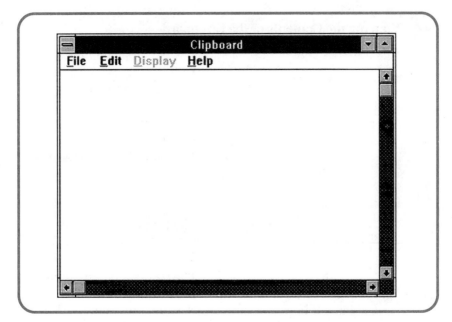

Figure 2.15   The Clipboard window.

Moving Text

When you move text, you cut (delete) it from your document and store it in memory so that you can move the insertion point and paste (insert) the cut text at a new location. You can use the Clipboard to move text, as you did previously when viewing the contents of the Clipboard. Select the text to be cut from your document; then choose

the Edit/Cut command or press Alt,E,T. The keyboard shortcut is
Shift-Del. When you delete text with the Cut command, the text is
stored on the Clipboard. After you've cut the selected text, move the
insertion point to the spot where you want the cut text to appear.
Then choose the Edit/Paste command or press Alt,E,P. The keyboard
shortcut for pasting text is Shift-Ins.

To move text without storing it on the Clipboard, first select the
text you want to move and then press F2. Word prompts you with the
message `Move to where?` in the status line. Move the insertion
point, which is now displayed as a dotted vertical line, to the
location where you want to move the text. Press Enter and the
selected text is moved from the old location to the new location,
beginning at the insertion point.

⊘ **Caution:** Be careful when cutting text using either the
Clipboard or the Move F2 key. If you delete anything in
the moving process, the text you've deleted as part of the move
process is replaced. If you realize your error before pressing any
other keys, press Alt-Backspace to recover (undo) the previously deleted text.

59

Ⓠ Moving Text by Using the Clipboard

1. Select the text you want to move.

   The Cut command becomes available in the Edit menu.

2. Choose the Edit/Cut command or press Alt,E,T.

   The selected text is re-moved from the document and stored on the Clip-board.

3. Move the insertion point to the location in the document where you want to insert the Clipboard text.

4. Choose the Edit/Paste command or press Alt,E,P.

   Word inserts your text at the new location of the insertion point. □

Copying Text

Copying text using the Clipboard is similar to moving text, except that text isn't removed from your document. To copy text, first select the text and then choose the Edit/Copy command or press Alt,E,C. The keyboard shortcut is Ctrl-Ins. Word copies the selected text onto the Clipboard.

You paste the copied text exactly as you did when moving text. To paste the copied text from the Clipboard, move the insertion point to the spot where you want to insert the copied text, and choose the Edit/Paste command or press Alt,E,P. The keyboard shortcut to paste text is Shift-Ins.

Word provides another option to copy text that bypasses the Clipboard. First, select the text you want to copy; then press Shift-F2. Word displays the message prompt `Copy to where?` in the status bar, and the insertion point changes to a dotted vertical line. Move the insertion point to the spot where you want the copied text to appear and press Enter.

Deleting Text

In many cases, you'll want to delete text without using the Clipboard. To delete text, select the text to delete and press Del. To delete a character to the right of the insertion point, simply press Del. To delete a character to the left of the insertion point, press Backspace. If you accidentally delete text, you can undo your deletion by choosing the Edit/Undo command (Alt,E,U) as long as you choose it before performing another editing operation. Table 2.5 summarizes the deletion keys.

 Tip: A keyboard shortcut for issuing the Edit/Undo command is Alt-Backspace.

To delete text using the Clipboard, first select the text you want to delete; then choose the Edit/Cut command or press Alt,E,T. A shortcut is to press Shift-Del. Your text is cut from your document and stored in the Clipboard until you perform another move, copy, or delete operation. If you change your mind, move the insertion point back to the spot where you cut the text and choose the Edit/Paste command by pressing Alt,E,P to restore the text to your screen, or simply press Shift-Ins.

Table 2.5   Deletion Keys

To Delete	Key(s) to Press
A character	F8 to select the character and then Del
A character to the right of the insertion point	Del
A character to the left of the insertion point	Backspace
A word to the right of the insertion point	Ctrl-Del
The current word or the word to the left of the insertion point	Ctrl-Backspace

61

Using Word's Spike

The *Spike* is a special tool similar to the Clipboard. It has one big difference. Instead of replacing text stored in the Spike, each new selection of text that is cut or copied is *appended* to the Spike's existing text. The Spike is especially useful for collecting text from various locations and inserting the various pieces as a group at another location. When you insert the contents of the Spike into a document, all the text in the Spike is inserted at once, and the Spike is left empty.

 Using the Spike Feature

1. Select the text.   The text is highlighted in reverse video.

2. Press Ctrl-F3.   The selected text is cut from the document.

3. Move to the next section of text that you want to append to the Spike and repeat steps 1 and 2.

4. Move the insertion point to the spot where you want to insert the contents of the Spike.

5. Press Ctrl-Shift-F3.   The contents of the Spike are inserted at the insertion point.   □

Undoing or Repeating an Action

One of the most helpful commands is the Edit/Undo command. The Undo command is *context-sensitive*, meaning that it changes to reflect your last editing or formatting action. The Undo command displays the last type of editing operation in the command. For example, if you've just entered text, the Undo command is displayed as `Undo Typing` in the Edit menu. The keyboard shortcut for undoing an editing operation is Alt-Backspace. Once you select the Edit/Undo command, Word undoes the last executed command.

To repeat an action, choose the Edit/Repeat command. Like the Undo command, the Repeat command is context-sensitive and changes to reflect your last typing, editing, or formatting action. For example, Word remembers the last characters you typed, and you can move to another location in your document and choose the Edit/Repeat Typing command. The keyboard shortcut for repeating an editing operation is F4.

Word stores your typing or editing actions in a memory buffer. When you move the insertion point to a new location and start typing or when you begin another edit operation, Word clears your buffer.

 Tip: Remember, the Repeat F4 key repeats only the last edit that changed your text, not navigational commands.

Saving Your New Document

A *new document* is a document created by using the File/New command. When you initially start Word for Windows, remember that a new document window is automatically opened for you with the default filename of Document1. When you save a file, Word takes the information in your computer's memory and writes it to a hard or floppy disk.

Q Saving Your New Document

1. Choose the File/Save command or press Alt,F,S or use the keyboard shortcut, Shift-F12.

Word displays the Save File Name dialog box, as shown in Figure 2.16. The drive and directory displayed directly below the Save File Name text box are the drive and directory to which the document file will be saved unless you specify otherwise. The drive and directory displayed are determined by the drive and directory from which you started Word for Windows. In Figure 2.16 they are shown as c:\winword.

2. If the directory displayed is the one to which you want to save your document, enter the filename for your document directly into the Save File Name text box.

3. Click on the OK button or press Enter.

□

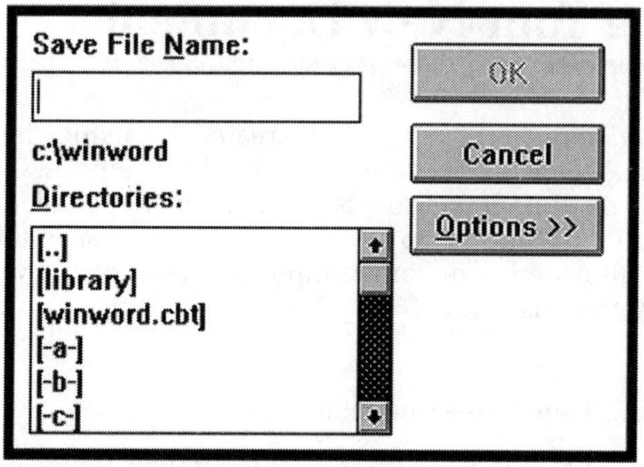

Figure 2.16   The Save File *Name* dialog box.

When naming your Word document files, you must follow the file naming conventions of DOS. A Word document filename can have no more than eight characters and can contain only letters, numbers, and the symbols ! @ # $ % & ( ) [ ] _ { }. Word automatically adds the filename extension .DOC to your filename unless you give it a different extension.

To save your document to another drive and/or directory, type the path and filename directly into the Save File Name text box or use the Directories list box. The Directories list box provides a scrolling list of drives and directories available on your system from which you can select. To activate the Directories list box, click anywhere in the list box, or press Alt-D. Using the mouse, you can then choose the drive and/or directory you want by double-clicking with the mouse pointer on the drive or directory in the list you want. Using the keyboard, press the Up or Down Arrow key to select the drive and/or directory you want and press Enter to change to the selected directory.

Notice that the first entry in the scrolling list is two dots—unless you started Word for Windows at the C:\ (root) directory. These dots indicate the *parent directory*, that is, the directory directly above the current directory. After selecting a drive and/or directory from the Directories list box and entering the new filename in the Save File Name text box, click on the OK button or press Enter. Word displays a Summary Information dialog box, as shown in Figure 2.17.

64

> ► **Tip:** We recommend that you allow Word to automatically add the .DOC extension to your document file. This makes retrieving document files easier.

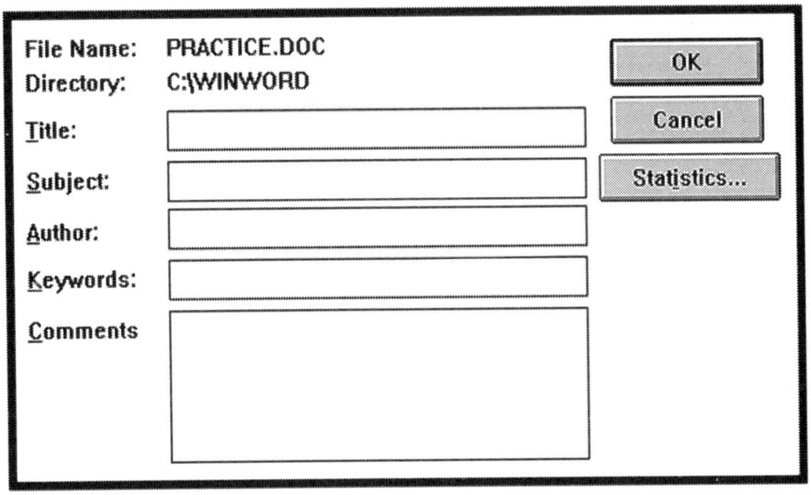

Figure 2.17   The Summary Information dialog box.

The Summary Information dialog box allows you to enter additional information about your document that can be used to sort and find your document files. Entering this information is optional. You can enter information into the Summary Information dialog box at any time by choosing the Edit/Summary Info command. When you choose the OK button or press Enter, Word saves your new document file. The document remains displayed on your screen, but the new filename is displayed in the title bar.

After you've saved a document file, you can exit Word by choosing the File/Exit command or by pressing Alt,F,X or by using the shortcut Alt-F4. Any time you attempt to exit Word or close a document with unsaved changes in your document, Word displays a warning and prompts you to save your changes, as shown in Figure 2.18.

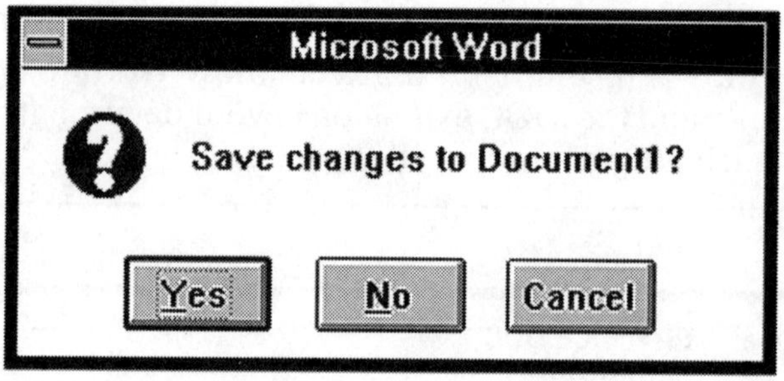

Figure 2.18   The Save Changes dialog box.

> ► **Tip:** You can turn off the Summary Information dialog box so that it does not display every time you save a new file. Choose the Utilities/Customize command or press Alt,U,U and click on the Prompt for Summary Info check box or press Alt-O.

Saving Changes As You Work

Earlier we explained that changes you make to a document are stored in your computer's memory until you save the changes to disk. Because you invest a lot of work in your documents, the last thing you want is to lose your work from a power outage or other disruption. Get into the habit of saving your work often to protect yourself from losing it. Word provides several important tools to help you save your changes as you work.

Using Word's Autosave Feature

As you're working on a document, you can periodically save your work by choosing the File/Save command (press Shift-F12). This approach to saving your work, while easy, requires you to remember to do it on a regular basis. Fortunately, you can turn on Word's autosave feature, which remembers for you. You can set the frequency of the reminders by using the settings described in Table 2.6.

Table 2.6   Autosave Reminder Option Buttons

Autosave Option Buttons	Frequency of Save Reminder
Never	No automatic saves
High	Every 10 to 30 minutes
Medium	Every 20 to 45 minutes
Low	Every 30 to 60 minutes

These save intervals vary depending on the amount of editing you are doing. Heavy editing causes the Autosave dialog box to occur more frequently within the range of the setting you've selected. Once the Autosave feature is turned on, Word automatically displays the Autosave dialog box as you work. By default, the Save Now Yes option button is selected. Choose the OK button to save your work, the Cancel button to skip saving and continue working, or the Postpone option button to delay a save operation, as shown in Figure 2.19.

67

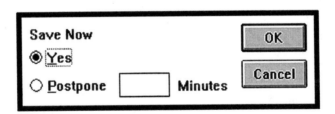

Figure 2.19   The Autosave dialog box.

If you click on the Postpone option button, the number 5 is automatically entered in the Minutes text box to delay the save operation for five minutes. Any number you type after clicking on the Postpone option button is entered in the Minutes text box. When you click on the OK button or press Enter, the save operation is performed or postponed, depending on the option button chosen. The following steps explain how to set up Word's Autosave feature.

 Setting Word's Autosave Reminder by Using the High Option Button

1. Choose the Utilities/Customize command or press Alt,U,U.

   Word displays the Customize dialog box, as shown in Figure 2.20.

2. Choose the High option button by clicking on it or pressing Alt-H in the Autosave Frequency box.

You will see a dot displayed in the setting button you have chosen.

3. Click on the OK button or press Enter.

Word will now periodically remind you according to the setting you've selected. □

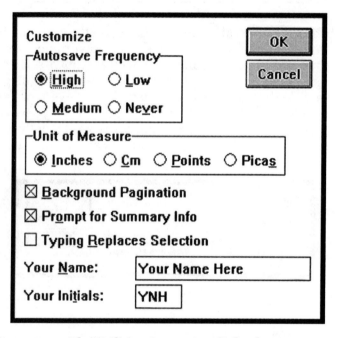

Figure 2.20   The Utilities Customize dialog box.

 Tip: For the best protection against the loss of your editing changes, use the High setting.

Word's Fast Save Feature

The first time you save a document, Word saves the entire file to disk. If you later save the document during the same Word session, Word uses the *fast save* feature. The fast save feature saves only the changes you made since the last save, appending them to the document's disk files. This makes saving to disk much faster than saving the entire document each time.

Word uses the fast save feature automatically when you use the File/Save command more than once on a document. It continues to use the fast save method, resaving the entire document to incorporate all your changes. Word displays Fast saving, followed by your document's filename in the status bar, and shows the percentage of the file saved. When Word finishes saving your document, the number of characters saved is briefly displayed.

To turn off the fast save feature, which by default is turned on, choose the File/Save As command and then choose the Options >> command button in the Save dialog box. Choose the Fast Save check box by clicking on it or by pressing Alt-S.

Creating Backup Files

69

The File/Save command saves your changes by replacing the previous version of your document file with the new version. However, choosing the File/Save As command, the Options >> button, and then the Create Backup check box from the expanded File/Save As command dialog box instructs Word not to overwrite the existing document file. Instead, Word changes the previously saved version's file to a .BAK extension. Word then saves the updated version of your file with the standard .DOC extension. Both files have the same filename. When you retrieve or save the document again, Word again saves the old version with a .BAK extension.

As you continue to save your document, Word continues swapping the two document files so that you always have two versions of your document: the most recently saved version (.DOC) and the previous version (.BAK). You can always open the file with the .BAK extension to retrieve the version of your document that doesn't contain changes. Remember, the backup option saves only the next to last version of your document.

 Note: You cannot use the Create Backup and the Fast Save features simultaneously.

Activating Word's Create Backup Feature

1. Press F12 or choose the File/ Save As command.

   Word displays the Save dialog box.

2. Click on the Options >> button or press Alt-O.

   Word displays an extended Save As dialog box, as shown in Figure 2.21.

3. Click on the Create Backup check box or press Alt-B.

   Word displays an x in the box and removes the x in the Fast Save check box.

4. Click on the OK button or press Enter.

□

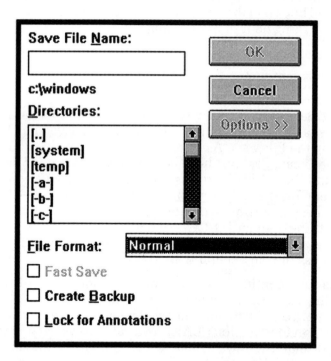

Figure 2.21   The extended Save As dialog box.

Retrieving a Document File

Retrieving an existing document file is called *opening* a document file. Word provides two ways to open existing documents. If the file you want to open is one of the last four document files you've worked on with Word, you can quickly open the file by selecting it from the File menu. The last four items in the File menu, as shown in Figure 2.22, are the paths and filenames of the last four document files you've worked on. To open any of these document files, simply click on the filename or press the appropriate underlined number to retrieve the file you want.

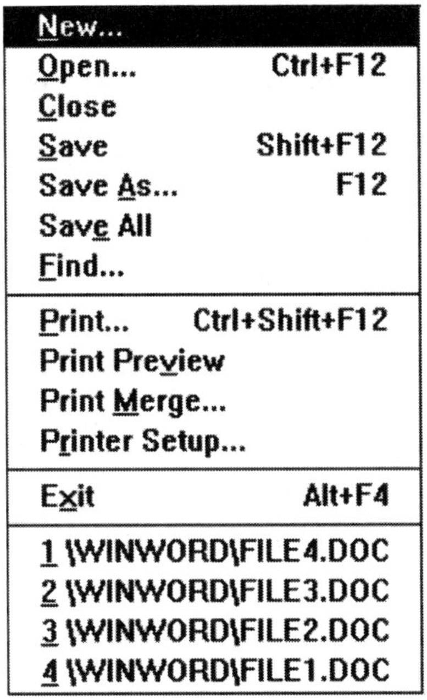

New...
Open...   Ctrl+F12
Close
Save   Shift+F12
Save As...   F12
Save All
Find...
Print...   Ctrl+Shift+F12
Print Preview
Print Merge...
Printer Setup...
Exit   Alt+F4
1 \WINWORD\FILE4.DOC
2 \WINWORD\FILE3.DOC
3 \WINWORD\FILE2.DOC
4 \WINWORD\FILE1.DOC

Figure 2.22   In the File menu, a list of the last four documents edited.

Retrieving Documents Using the Open Command

If the file you want to edit isn't one of these four files, choose the File/Open command. Word displays the Open File dialog box shown in Figure 2.23. The Open File Name text box at the top of the dialog box lets you specify the name of the document file you want to open. The default entry in this text box is `*.DOC`, telling Word to list all the files with a .DOC extension (.DOC files are document files saved in Word format). If the filename you want appears in the Files list box, choose the file by double-clicking on the filename or by pressing Alt-F and the Down Arrow key to highlight the filename you want; then press Enter. The Open File dialog box disappears, and Word displays the selected document file on your screen.

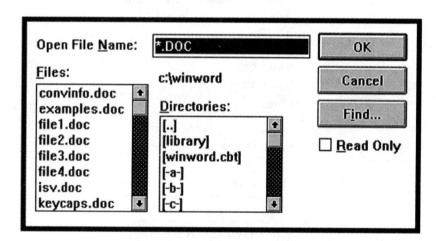

Figure 2.23   The Open File dialog box.

If the document file you want to open does not appear in the Files list box, you'll need to change the current directory. Word lists the name of the current directory just below the Open File Name text box. Notice that the current directory in the dialog box in Figure 2.23 is `c:\winword`.

Changing the Current Directory

1. Double-click on the appropriate directory, or press Alt-D to choose the Directories list box.

   The current directory name appears above the Directories list box.

2. Use the Down Arrow key to highlight the directory you want and then press Enter.

   Word displays the new directory name above the Directories list box. ☐

If your document file is stored in a directory that is located up a level or two on the current disk drive, select the double dots, . ., in the Directories list box. Choosing these dots moves you up one level in the directory structure. If you need to specify a directory located on a different disk, first select the name of the appropriate disk drive in the Directories list box and then choose the appropriate directory. As you step through the directories on your disks, Word will keep the default entry *.DOC in the Open File Name text box so that you can view the Word files stored in each directory.

73

You can also open a Word document by typing the full name of the document file and its path into the Open File Name text box instead of selecting it in the Directories and Files list boxes. For example, if you have a file named LETTER.DOC, and you've stored it in a directory named MAIL on your C drive, you would type `c:\mail\letter.doc` in the Open File Name text box and then press Enter or click the OK button to open the LETTER document file.

 Retrieving a Document by Using the Open Command

1. Choose the File/Open command or press Alt,F,O.

   Word displays the File Open dialog box.

2. If the filename for the file you want to open is not displayed in the Files list box, change to the directory containing the file by using the Directories list box.

3. Double-click on the filename in the Files list box you want to open, or press Alt-F and use the Down Arrow key to select the file to open and press Enter.

   Word displays the file's contents in the text area.

What You Have Learned

▶ You can enter text by using one of two modes: insert mode or overtype. The insert mode is the default mode. To turn on the overtype mode, press the Ins key.

▶ To change from the default Normal view to Page view or Draft mode, choose the Page (Alt,V,P) or the Draft (Alt,V,D) command from the View menu.

▶ By clicking on the asterisk in the Ribbon, you can display Word's special hidden marks, such as paragraphs and tabs.

▶ You can navigate your document by using the mouse or the keyboard, as well as the Edit/Go To (Alt,E,G) command.

▶ With either the mouse and the selection bar or with the F8 key, you can select text by the word, line, or paragraph.

▶ The F2 key lets you copy, move, and delete text without the Clipboard.

▶ The Spike is a handy tool for collecting text from various locations and inserting the pieces as a group at another location.

▶ You can save a new document with a filename you specify by using the File/Save (Alt,F,S) command or the shortcut method of pressing Shift-F12.

▶ Using the File/Save As (Alt,F,A) command and the Options >> button, you can automatically save your work in a backup file.

▶ To retrieve one of the last four document files, use the files listed at the bottom of the File menu.

74

Searching, Replacing, and Correcting Text

In This Chapter

► *Searching for and replacing text, special marks, and charac-ter formats*

► *Using Word's Spelling Checker to check the spelling of a single word, a block of text, or the entire document*

► *Using Word's Thesaurus to find synonyms*

► *Viewing your document's statistics*

After entering text and making basic editing changes, you're ready to apply finishing touches to your text. In this chapter, you'll learn to operate Word's powerful tools for improving the quality of your writing.

Searching for and Replacing Text

Two of the most powerful tools for improving the quality of your writing are Word's Search and Replace commands. Using these commands, you can search a document for words, phrases, punctuation, and formatting and then make changes to them. (Chapter 4 explains searching for and replacing character and paragraph formats.)

The Edit/Search command finds each occurrence of text that you specify, at which point you can make your changes, if needed. The Edit/Replace command, like the Search command, also finds text that you specify. However, it automatically replaces each occurrence of search text with the replacement text that you specified before you executed the Edit/Replace command. For example, suppose you want to replace each occurrence of the word *gold* with the word *silver* in your document. Using the Edit/Replace command, you instruct Word to search for the word *gold* and at each occurrence to replace it with *silver*. You can instruct Word to ask for confirmation each time it finds an occurrence, or you can have the replacement performed automatically without confirmation.

76

The Search Command Dialog Box

To display the Search dialog box, as shown in Figure 3.1, choose the Edit/Search command or press Alt,E,S. In the Search For text box, enter the text you want to search for. The OK button is dimmed until you enter text in the Search For text box. Entering more than 37 characters causes the text to scroll out of view. To view the nondisplayed text, use the Left Arrow, Right Arrow, Home, or End keys. The normal text editing keys will work in the Search For text box. For example, you can use the Backspace or Del key to erase text.

> **Tip:** Before activating the Edit/Search command, you can cut or copy text onto the Clipboard and then, by pressing Shift-Ins, you can paste it into the Search For text box.

Choosing the Whole Word check box or pressing Alt-W restricts the search to entire words that match your search text. Focusing your search this way saves time. For example, suppose that you are searching for the word *able*. By choosing the Whole Word check box, you instruct Word to find only the word *able* and to skip words such as *enable* or *dependable*.

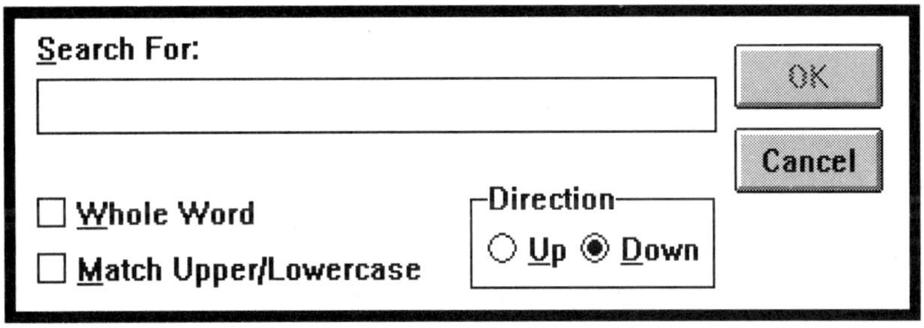

Search For:

[   ] OK

Cancel

☐ **Whole Word**

☐ **Match Upper/Lowercase**

┌─**Direction**─────┐
│ ○ Up ◉ Down │
└────────────────┘

Figure 3.1   The Search dialog box.

By default, the Search command finds each occurrence of your search text regardless of whether characters are upper- or lowercase. Choosing the Match Upper/Lowercase check box or pressing Alt-M instructs Word to match the upper- and lowercase letters of your search text. Like turning on the Whole Word check box, turning on the Match Upper/Lowercase check box focuses your search to save time.

The Direction option buttons control the direction of your search. The default direction is down, meaning Word searches from the insertion point to the end of your document or selected text. Clicking on the Up option button or pressing Alt-U instructs Word to search from the insertion point to the beginning of the document. To switch to the downward direction, click on the Down option button or press Alt-D.

77

▶ **Note:** If you're not sure of the spelling of a word, use the question mark, *?*. The question mark is a *wildcard character* that represents any character in the search text. For example, if you enter `M?RRY`, Word locates each instance of *MERRY* and *MARRY*. To locate a question mark by itself, enter a caret (^) before the question mark, for example, `Are you sure^?`.

Using the *Search* Command

After entering text and setting any controls in the Search dialog box, click on the OK button or press Enter to start the search. Clicking on the Cancel button or pressing Esc exits the Search dialog box. When you start a search, Word either finds and highlights the first occurrence of your search text, or displays a dialog box with the message `Search text not found`. If Word locates your search text, you can make changes to the text or continue searching for the next occurrence by pressing Shift-F4. When Word reaches the top or bottom of the document, depending on the Direction setting you've selected, it displays a dialog box asking you if you want to continue the search from the opposite end of the document.

When performing a search, Word doesn't remember where the insertion point was located when you activated the Edit/Search command. To ensure that your entire document is searched, press Ctrl-Home to move the insertion point to the beginning of your document before you choose the Edit/Search command. Selecting a block of text prior to issuing the Search command does not confine the search to that selection.

 Searching an Entire Document for Specified Text

1. Press Ctrl-Home.

   The insertion point moves to the beginning of the document.

2. Choose the Edit/Search command or press Alt,E,S.

   Word displays the Search dialog box.

3. Type the text you want to search for in the Search For text box.

   The OK button becomes boldfaced indicating that you can choose it.

4. Choose the Whole Word (Alt-W) and/or the Match Upper/Lowercase (Alt-M) check boxes, if needed.

   Make sure the Down option button is chosen.

5. Click on the OK button or press Enter.

   Word begins the search and highlights the first occurrence of the search text.

6. Edit the highlighted text as needed.

7. Press Shift-F4.
Word continues the search and highlights the next occurrence of the search text. When Word reaches the end of your document, it asks if you want to resume the search from the beginning of your document.

8. Choose the No button or press N.
Word ends the search session. ☐

> ▶ **Tip:** To repeat a search using the previous search text and settings, position the insertion point where you want to start the search; then press Shift-F4.

79

The Replace Command Dialog Box

To display the Replace dialog box, as shown in Figure 3.2, choose the Edit/Replace command or press Alt,E,E. The Search For text box and the Whole Word and Match Upper/Lowercase check boxes are the same as the controls in the Search dialog box. Unlike the Search command, the Replace command scans only in the down direction. After you enter the search text in the Search For text box, choose the Replace With text box or press Alt-R and enter your replacement text.

The Confirm Changes check box determines whether Word asks for your confirmation before replacing each occurrence of the search text. By default, this check box is on. To turn off the Confirm Changes check box, choose the Confirm Changes check box or press Alt-C.

Using the Replace Command

After entering text and setting any controls in the Replace dialog box, click on the OK button or press Enter to begin the replace session. If you begin a replace session with the insertion point anywhere but at the beginning of your document, Word replaces the text you specified until it reaches the end of your document. At that point, Word prompts you to continue the replace session from the beginning of your document until it reaches the location of the insertion point before you executed the Replace command. To exit the Replace dialog box, click on the Cancel button or press Esc.

If the Confirm Changes check box is turned on, Word displays the Replace window, as shown in Figure 3.3, when the first occurrence of search text is found. Clicking on the Yes button or pressing Y replaces the highlighted text with the replacement text. Clicking on the No button or pressing N leaves the search text unchanged. After choosing one of these options, Word continues to search for the next occurrence of search text. The Confirm Changes check box displayed in the Replace window allows you to change the confirmation setting and automatically change the remaining occurrences of your search text. Clicking on the Cancel button or pressing Esc cancels the current replace session, leaving any changes intact.

80

Search For:		OK
		Cancel
Replace With:		

☐ Whole Word   ☒ Confirm Changes
☐ Match Upper/Lowercase

Figure 3.2   The Replace dialog box.

If the Confirm Changes check box is turned off, Word automatically replaces all occurrences of the search text with the replacement text, without asking you for confirmation. When the replacement session is completed, Word displays the number of changes made in the status bar.

> ▶ **Tip:** You can undo the last Replace command that was performed without confirmation of changes by immediately choosing the Edit/Undo command or by pressing the Alt-Backspace key combination after the replace session.

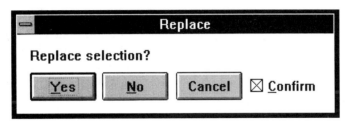

Figure 3.3   The Replace command confirmation dialog box.

 Replacing Text and Using Confirmation

1. Press Ctrl-Home.	The insertion point moves to the beginning of your document.
2. Choose the Edit/Replace command or press Alt,E,E.	Word displays the Replace dialog box.
3. Enter the text you want to search for in the Search For text box.	As you enter text, notice that the OK button becomes active.
4. Choose the Replace With text box or press Alt-R.	The insertion point appears in the Replace With text box.
5. Enter your replacement text.	The text appears in the Replace With text box.
6. Choose the Whole Word and/or Match Upper/Lower-case check boxes, if needed.	An X appears in the check box when the option is turned on.
7. Choose the Confirm Changes check box if it's turned off, or press Alt-C.	An X appears in the Confirm Changes check box, instructing Word to prompt you to confirm replacements.
8. Click on the OK button or press Enter.	Word searches for the first occurrence of the search text. When an occurrence is found, Word displays the Confirm dialog box, as shown in Figure 3.3.
9. Choose the Yes or No button or press Y or N.	Choosing Yes replaces the highlighted text. Choosing No leaves the highlighted text as is. After you select one of these options, Word continues the search.

81

10. Repeat step 9 for each additional occurrence of search text.

When the replace session is completed, the Confirm dialog box disappears and Word displays the number of changes made in the status bar. □

Searching for and Replacing Special Marks

Besides searching for and replacing text, you can search for and replace Word's special marks, such as paragraph and tab marks. The procedure is similar to that used for text. The only difference is that in the <u>S</u>earch For or <u>R</u>eplace With text box you enter a unique code representing the mark. Table 3.1 lists Word's special marks and their respective codes. Each code starts with the caret (^) symbol (Shift-6).

> ▶ **Tip:** It's a good idea to have the Show All button turned on when searching for and replacing special marks. Turning on this button lets you view the special marks on your screen. To turn on the Show All button, click on the Show All button of the Ribbon or press Ctrl-Shift-*.

Table 3.1   Special Marks and Their Codes

Format	Special Mark	Key Code
New line	↵	^n
Nonbreaking hyphen	—	^~
Optional hyphen	¬	^-
Paragraph	¶	^p
Space	•	^w
Tab	→	^t

Using the Replace Command with the Clipboard

You can use the Edit/Replace command together with the Clipboard to replace specified text with new text containing different formats, large blocks of text, tables, or pictures. To instruct Word to replace text with the contents of the Clipboard, first select the text, picture, or table you want to place in the Clipboard. Then choose the Edit/Cut command (Shift-Del) or the Edit/Copy command (Ctrl-Ins). In the Replace With text box located in the Edit Replace dialog box, type ^c (press Shift-6 to type a caret).

 Using the Replace Command with the Clipboard

1. Select the text you want to place on the Clipboard.	The text is highlighted.
2. Press Ctrl-Ins to copy or Shift-Del to cut the selected text.	Word copies or cuts the selected text onto the Clipboard.
3. Press Ctrl-Home.	The insertion point moves to the beginning of your document.
4. Choose the Edit/Replace command or press Alt,E,E.	Word displays the Replace dialog box.
5. Enter your search text in the Search For text box.	
6. Choose the Replace With text box or press Alt-R.	The insertion point appears in the Replace With text box.
7. Type ^c in the Replace With text box.	The ^c (Shift-6, *c*) directs Word to use the contents of the Clipboard as the replacement text. No other text can be entered in the Replace With text box if you use the ^c code.
8. Turn on or off the control setting check boxes, depending on your needs.	The control settings include the Whole Word, Match Upper/Lowercase, and Confirm Changes check boxes.

83

9. Click on the OK button or press Enter.

Word begins the replace session. □

Checking Your Spelling

Word's sophisticated Spelling Checker is an indispensable proofing tool for correcting misspelled words, repeated words, and capitalization errors. The Spelling Checker matches words in your document with words stored in a dictionary file. Word's main dictionary file contains over 130,000 words. The main dictionary can't be altered by adding or deleting words. However, Word provides a default *user dictionary* file, STDUSER.DIC, for including words not found in the main dictionary, such as proper nouns and technical terms. Additional user dictionaries can be created for different professions or topics, such as a dictionary of legal or medical terms. When you activate the Spelling Checker, it automatically checks your document using the main dictionary and the standard user dictionary (STDUSER.DIC). You can use an additional user dictionary, as explained later in this chapter.

You can use the Spelling Checker to check a single word, a block of selected text, or your entire document. The Spelling Checker scans your text from the insertion point to the end of your document or selected text. If you start the Spelling Checker with the insertion point anywhere but the top of your document, the Spelling Checker will display a dialog box when it reaches the end of your document. Word asks if you want to continue checking the spelling from the top of the document. If you choose the Yes button or press Y, Word continues the Spelling Checker session until you reach your starting point.

If you've made the same spelling error more than once in your document, the Spelling Checker remembers the correction you made and automatically corrects subsequent misspellings without notifying you. Remember, the Spelling Checker can't check a document for misused words. For example, if you type *wood* when you mean *would*, the Spelling Checker will not catch it, because *wood* is spelled correctly.

84

The Check Spelling Dialog Box

To begin the Spelling Checker, you must first display the Check Spelling dialog box, as shown in Figure 3.4, by choosing the Utilities/Spelling command or by pressing Alt,U,S. This dialog box provides you with options to start the Spelling Checker, check the spelling of a single word, or expand the Check Spelling dialog box for setting Spelling Checker controls.

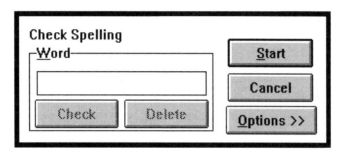

Figure 3.4   The Check Spelling dialog box.

Now display the expanded Check Spelling dialog box, as shown in Figure 3.5, by clicking on the Options >> button or by pressing Alt-O. You will see the Word text box, where you enter a word to check its spelling. The Check and Delete buttons, which are dimmed, are used with the Word text box to check the spelling of the word or to delete the word from a user dictionary. To activate the Spelling Checker, click on the Start button or press Enter. Clicking on the Cancel button or pressing Esc exits the Check Spelling dialog box.

The two Dictionaries list boxes display the dictionary files used by the Spelling Checker. The English (US) (the main dictionary file), displayed in the Main list box, and the STDUSER.DIC (the standard user dictionary), displayed in the Supplemental list box, are Word's default dictionaries. After creating other user dictionaries, you can choose them by using the Supplemental list box, as explained later in this chapter.

The Ignore All CAPS check box, initially turned off, instructs the Spelling Checker to ignore words in all capital letters. Turning this feature on can save you time if your document contains a number of acronyms, such as NASA, ASCII, or EPA. Choose the Ignore All CAPS check box or press Alt-I to turn it on.

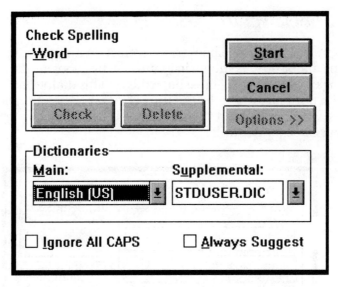

Figure 3.5   The expanded Check Spelling dialog box.

The Always Suggest check box, initially turned off, instructs the Spelling Checker to display suggested spellings for misspelled words. Choose the Always Suggest check box or press Alt-A to turn it on. Both Ignore All CAPS and Always Suggest check box settings remain in effect until you change them again. The Ignore All CAPS and Always Suggest check boxes can be turned on or off for the current Spelling Checker session from the Spelling window as explained next.

> **Tip:** If you are confident of your spelling abilities, you can speed up the Spelling Checker by turning off the Always Suggest check box. Otherwise, keep the Always Suggest check box turned on to view the list of suggested words.

Checking the Spelling of a Document

After setting the controls in the Check Spelling dialog box, you're ready to perform a Spelling Checker session. Click on the Start button or press Alt-S; Word begins checking your document. If there are no misspelled, repeated, or improperly capitalized words in the document, Word displays the message `Spell check completed` in the status bar. If the Spelling Checker finds a word that is not in its dictionary, or if it finds an uncommon capitalization or a repeated word, the Spelling Checker displays the Spelling window, as shown in Figure 3.6.

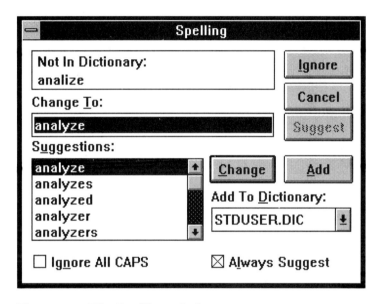

Figure 3.6   The Spelling window.

To use the Spelling window with the Always Suggest check box turned on, follow these steps:

▶ *If the word is misspelled and a word in the Suggestions list box is correct,* double-click on the word you want. By default, the first word in the list is highlighted; if this word is the one you want, simply click on the Change button. If the list is longer than can be displayed in the Suggestions list box, click on the Arrow buttons to scroll through the list. Using the keyboard, press the Down Arrow key to move the high-light to the word you want and press Enter or Alt-C to correct the misspelling.

▶ *If the word is spelled correctly,* click on the Ignore button or press Alt-I to continue. If you want to add the word to the

87

standard user dictionary (STDUSER.DIC), click on the <u>A</u>dd button or press Alt-A.

▶ *If the word is misspelled but not listed in the Su<u>g</u>gestions list box,* type the correct spelling for the word in the Change <u>T</u>o text box. Click on the <u>C</u>hange button or press Enter or Alt-C to correct the misspelling.

▶ *If a repeated word is found,* the Not In Dictionary box changes to a Repeated Word box, with the repeated word displayed in it. Clicking on the <u>C</u>hange button or pressing Enter or Alt-C deletes the repeated word.

▶ *If a word with uncommon capitalization is found,* the Not In Dictionary box changes to the Uncommon Capitalization box, with the word displayed in it. At this point, you can correct the word, click on the <u>I</u>gnore button or press Alt-I to ignore it, or click on the <u>A</u>dd button or press Alt-A to add it to the standard user dictionary.

To exit the Spelling Checker window, click on the Cancel button or press Esc. Any changes remain intact. Word returns to the insertion point where you first started the Spelling Checker.

▶ **Tip:** The Spelling window can be moved anywhere on your screen. Move the mouse pointer to the window title bar, press the left mouse button, drag the window to its new location, and then release the mouse button.

Checking the Spelling of a Single Word

To quickly check the spelling of a word, place the insertion point within the word or to its immediate right, or select the word, and then press F7. If the word is correctly spelled, Word displays the message `Spell check completed` in the status bar. If the word is misspelled, Word displays the Spelling window where you can correct the word.

Another way to check the spelling of a word is to enter it into the <u>W</u>ord text box located in the Check Spelling dialog box. Use the <u>U</u>tilities/<u>S</u>pelling command to do this. As you enter characters in the <u>W</u>ord text box, the Check and Delete buttons become activated. After entering the word in the <u>W</u>ord text box, click on the Check button or press Alt-C. If the word is correctly spelled, the Spelling Checker displays a dialog box indicating that the word was found in a dictionary. If the word is not found, the Spelling window is displayed. After checking the suggested spellings in the Spelling window, Word returns to the Check Spelling dialog box. Additional words can be checked, or you can exit the Check Spelling dialog box by clicking on the Cancel button or by pressing Esc.

Creating a User Dictionary

If you're working with a large number of terms for different professions or topics, you may find it helpful to create separate user dictionaries. You can create as many additional user dictionaries as you like; however, only one user dictionary can be used with the default standard user dictionary (STDUSER.DIC).

89

 Creating a User Dictionary

1. Choose the <u>U</u>tilities/<u>S</u>pelling command or press Alt,U,S.

    Word displays the Check Spelling dialog box.

2. Click on the <u>O</u>ptions >> button or press Alt-O.

    Word displays the expanded Check Spelling dialog box.

3. Choose the S<u>u</u>pplemental text box or press Alt-U.

4. Type the name of a new user dictionary, up to eight characters, followed by the .DIC extension.

    You must enter the .DIC extension in order for Word to recognize the file as a dictionary file.

5. Click on the <u>S</u>tart button or press Enter.

    Word displays a dialog box with the message `User dictionary not found. Create?`

6. Click on the <u>Y</u>es button or press Y to create the new user dictionary.

    Word begins a Spelling Checker session using your new user dictionary. □

Choosing User Dictionaries

If you want to use another user dictionary with the standard user dictionary (STDUSER.DIC), you must choose it before starting the Spelling Checker. The additional user dictionary you choose remains available until you choose another user dictionary or end your Word session.

To specify a user dictionary, choose the Utilities/Spelling command or press Alt,U,S. Then click on the Options > > button or press Alt-O. Word displays the expanded Check Spelling dialog box. Choose the Supplemental list box or press Alt-U. Then click on the Arrow button or press Alt-Down Arrow to display the list of available user dictionaries. Click on the user dictionary filename you want. If the list of user dictionaries is longer than the list box, click on the Arrow buttons to scroll through the list. Using the keyboard, press the Down Arrow key to highlight the user dictionary file you want. Then click on the Start button or press Enter or Alt-S to begin the Spelling Checker session.

Adding a Word to a User Dictionary

The easiest way to add words to a user dictionary is to add them during a Spelling Checker session by clicking on the Add button or pressing Alt-A. The word is added to the user dictionary displayed in the Add To Dictionary list box. To add the word to the other active user dictionary (if you've chosen one), first choose the Add To Dictionary list box or press Alt-D; then click on the Arrow button or press Alt-Down Arrow to display the user dictionary filenames. Next click on the other user dictionary filename displayed in the Add To Dictionary list box.

Using the keyboard, press the Up or Down Arrow key to highlight the user dictionary file you want. Choose the Add button or press Alt-A to add the word to the dictionary.

 Adding a Large Group of Words to a User Dictionary

1. Type the words you want to add to the user dictionary in a document, separating each word by a space.

2. Select all the words.

3. Choose the Utilities/Spelling command or press Alt,U,S.

The Check Spelling dialog box appears.

4. Click on the Options >> button or press Alt-O.

Word displays the expanded Check Spelling dialog box.

5. Choose the Supplemental list box or press Alt-U.

6. Click on the Down Arrow button or press Alt-Down Arrow.

Word displays a list of your user dictionaries.

7. Click or press the Up or Down Arrow key to highlight the dictionary to which you want to save the selected words.

If the list of user dictionaries is longer than the list box, click on the Arrow buttons to scroll through the list.

8. Choose the Start button or press Enter or Alt-S.

The Spelling Checker displays the Spelling window at the first unrecognized word.

91

9. Choose the Add button or press Alt-A for each word you want to add.

☐

Another method of adding words to a user dictionary is to use the Check Spelling dialog box. With this method, you can specify any user dictionary to which you want the word saved. However, because each word must be entered one at a time, this method is slower. Choose the Utilities/Spelling command or press Alt,U,S. Then click on the Options >> button or press Alt-O to display the expanded Check Spelling dialog box. Type the word you want to add to a user dictionary in the Word text box.

To save the word to a different user dictionary than the one displayed in the Supplemental list box, choose the Supplemental list box or press Alt-U. Click on the Arrow button or press Alt-Down Arrow to display the list of all your user dictionaries. Click on the user dictionary filename you want or press the Up or Down Arrow key to highlight the user dictionary filename. If the list of user dictionaries is longer than the list box, click on the Down Arrow button to scroll through the list.

Click on the Check button or press Alt-C, and Word displays the Spelling window. Click on the Add button or press Alt-A. The word is added to the user dictionary you've specified, and Word returns to the Check Spelling dialog box. You can add another word in the same manner, or you can exit by clicking on the Cancel button or pressing Esc.

Deleting a Word from a User Dictionary

To help you manage the words that you add to your user dictionaries, Word allows you to delete any unwanted or incorrectly spelled entries. Choose the Utilities/Spelling command or press Alt,U,S; then click on the Options >> button or press Alt-O. Word displays the expanded Check Spelling dialog box. In the Word text box, type the word you want to delete. The Delete button is activated.

To delete the word from a user dictionary that is different from the one displayed in the Supplemental list box, choose the Supplemental list box or press Alt-U. To display the list of all your user dictionaries, click on the Arrow button or press Alt-Down Arrow. Click on the user dictionary filename or press the Up or Down Arrow key to highlight the user dictionary file you want to use. If the list of user dictionaries is longer than the list box, click on the Down or Up Arrow button to scroll through the list.

After choosing the user dictionary from which you want to delete the word, click on the Check button or press Alt-C. Word displays a dialog box with the message Word was found in User dictionary. Click on the OK button or press Enter to return to the Check Spelling dialog box. When you click on the Delete button or press Alt-D, the word is removed from the user dictionary.

Word's Thesaurus

Word's Thesaurus helps you add variety to your vocabulary and avoid the repetitious use of words. A *thesaurus* provides a cross-referenced collection of *synonyms*, words with similar meanings for a particular word. To quickly activate Word's Thesaurus, position the insertion point anywhere in the word or to the immediate right of the word, or select a word; then press Shift-F7. Choosing the Utilities/Thesaurus command or pressing Alt,U,T also displays the Thesaurus window, as shown in Figure 3.7.

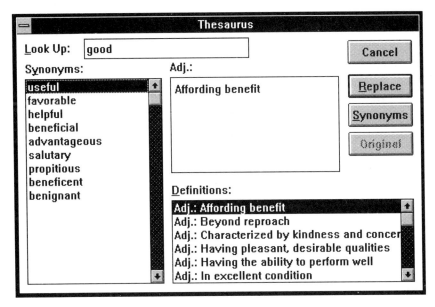

Figure 3.7   The Thesaurus window.

The word you choose appears in the Look Up text box. The Synonyms list box shows words with definitions similar to the word you've chosen. The Definitions list box shows a listing, in truncated form, of the different definitions of the word. Definitions are alphabetical in the Definitions list box according to the usage of the word (noun, verb, adjective, or adverb). Above the Definitions list box is a box that displays the full definition of the highlighted definition in the Definitions list box.

The Replace button replaces the chosen word in the document with the highlighted word in the Synonyms list box. The Synonyms button displays a new list of synonyms for any new word placed in the Look Up text box or when you select a different definition in the Definitions list box. The Original button displays the synonyms list for the word you originally checked. Clicking on the Cancel button or pressing Esc exits the Thesaurus window.

> ▶ **Tip:** You can move the Thesaurus window anywhere on your screen. Move the mouse pointer to the window title bar, press the left mouse button, drag the window to its new location, and then release the mouse button.

Looking Up Synonyms for a Word

You can look up synonyms in the Thesaurus window for as many words as you want, one at a time, until you choose the Cancel or the Replace button. If the word you've selected is not in the Thesaurus, Word displays the message `No Synonyms` in the Synonyms list box.

To use the Thesaurus window, move the insertion point to a spot in the word or to its immediate right, or select the word for which you want to display synonyms. If you select more than one word, the Thesaurus window is displayed with the Look Up text box empty. Choose the Utilities/Thesaurus command or press Alt,U,T. The keyboard shortcut for activating the Thesaurus is Shift-F7. The Thesaurus window appears with a list of synonyms for the chosen word (unless none are available). The following steps explain how to use the options in the Thesaurus window:

▶ *If one of the synonyms listed in the Synonyms list box is the word you want to use,* double-click on the synonym or use the Down or Up Arrow keys to highlight the word you want. The word is displayed in the Look Up text box. The definitions in the Definitions list box change according to the word you've chosen. Word replaces the selected word when you click on the Replace button or press Alt-R. The Thesaurus window is then closed, returning you to the document.

▶ *To view a synonym's definition,* choose one from the Synonyms list box by double-clicking on the word. The definitions for the selected word are automatically displayed in the Definitions list box. Using the keyboard, press the Down or Up Arrow keys to highlight the word you want; then press Alt-S to choose the Synonyms button.

▶ *To view synonyms based on a definition,* choose the Definitions list box or press Alt-D. Click on the definition you want, or press the Down or Up Arrow keys to highlight the definition you want. As you move the highlight, the associated synonyms are displayed in the Synonyms list box. To scroll through the Definitions list box, click on the appropriate Arrow button for the direction in which you want to scroll.

▶ *To look up synonyms for a word not chosen in your document,* choose the Look Up text box or press Alt-L. Type the word for which you want to display synonyms; then click on the Synonyms button or press Alt-S.

▶ *To return to the original word that was first displayed in the Look Up text box,* click on the Original button or press Alt-O.

After you're finished working in the Thesaurus window, click on the Cancel button or press Esc to return to your document.

Document Statistics

Word keeps track of a variety of data about your document, including such statistics as the number of revisions, the total editing time spent on the document, and the number of characters and words in the document. You can view the statistics for the document you're working on by choosing Edit/Summary Info command or by pressing Alt,E,I. Word displays the Summary Info dialog box. Click on the Statistics button or press Alt-I to display the Document Statistics dialog box, shown in Figure 3.8.

95

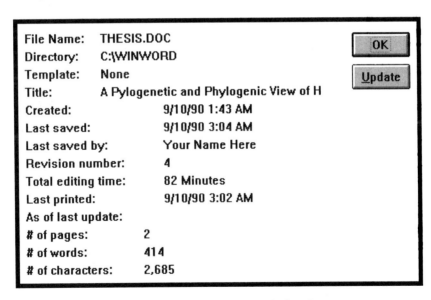

File Name:	THESIS.DOC
Directory:	C:\WINWORD
Template:	None
Title:	A Pylogenetic and Phylogenic View of H
Created:	9/10/90 1:43 AM
Last saved:	9/10/90 3:04 AM
Last saved by:	Your Name Here
Revision number:	4
Total editing time:	82 Minutes
Last printed:	9/10/90 3:02 AM
As of last update:	
# of pages:	2
# of words:	414
# of characters:	2,685

Figure 3.8   The Document Statistics dialog box.

Among the most useful document statistics are the `Revision number`, which displays the cumulative number of times the document has been saved; the `Total editing time`, which displays the cumulative number of minutes the document has been opened; and the `# of words`, which lists the number of words in your document. Each time you save your document to disk, Word automatically updates the `Last saved`, `Last saved by`, `Revision number`, and `Total editing time` statistics. Each time you print your document, Word updates the `Last printed`, `# of words`, and `# of characters` data. If the `# of word` or `# of characters` data is dimmed, it means that characters or words have been added since the document was last printed. Clicking on the Update button or pressing Alt-U updates these statistics.

What You Have Learned

▶ Word's Search command lets you search a whole document or just part of it. You can search for words, phrases, punctuation, and formatting. Once an occurrence of the search text has been found, you can change the text, as needed. To search for text, use the Edit/Search command (Alt,E,S).

▶ The Replace command lets you search for text and then automatically replace the text with your specified replacement text or with the Clipboard contents. You can instruct Word to search and replace a document without asking for confirmation of each replacement, or you can instruct Word to prompt you at each replacement. To search and replace text, use the Edit/Replace command (Alt,E,E).

▶ Word's most powerful proofing tool is its Spelling Checker. The Spelling Checker checks for misspelled words, repeated words, and capitalization errors. To activate it, choose the Utilities/Spelling command or press Alt,U,S.

▶ In addition to Word's main dictionary, you can add your own words to Word's default user dictionary (STDUSER.DIC) or create your own customized dictionaries.

▶ Word's Thesaurus helps you add variety to your vocabulary and avoid the repetitive use of words by providing an extensive collection of synonyms. Pressing Shift-F7 quickly activates the Thesaurus to check any word.

▶ Word keeps track of statistics about your document, such as the number of revisions made and the number of words in your document. To view your document's statistics, choose the Edit/Summary Info command (Alt,E,I) and then choose the Statistics button or press Alt-I.

97

Chapter 4

Essential Formatting

In This Chapter

▶ *Understanding Word's levels of formatting*
▶ *Formatting document pages*
▶ *Formatting paragraphs*
▶ *Formatting characters*
▶ *Setting and using tabs*
▶ *Creating headers and footers*

In this chapter, you'll learn formatting techniques for designing the appearance of your documents. These formatting techniques also provide a foundation for building the skills needed for the more complex formatting tasks explained in Chapter 6.

Formatting in Word

Word's primary formatting tools are the first four commands in the Format menu. These formatting commands are organized into four levels: document, section, paragraph, and character. *Document formatting* is the most general level and involves setting margins, page size, page breaks,and more. *Section formatting* (covered in Chapter 6) allows you to apply different formats to selected parts of your document. A *paragraph* is any string of text ending with a paragraph mark created by pressing Enter. *Paragraph formatting* includes such features as aligning, indenting, and spacing paragraphs. *Character formatting* allows you to change fonts and character sizes, and to emphasize characters.

The best approach to formatting a document is to use the top-down strategy. *Top-down* means starting from the largest formatting level (document) and progressively formatting to the smallest level (characters). Because each of these levels is interrelated, using the top-down approach prevents formatting levels from clashing. This approach is especially helpful when you are formatting more complex documents, such as a newsletter.

100   *Units of Measure in Word*

Many of the controls in the Document, Paragraph, and Character dialog boxes take measurement entries. The settings in these and other dialog boxes, by default, are based on inches. In most cases, staying with the inch unit of measurement is the easiest course. However, Word provides additional units of measurement, including centimeters, points, and picas. You can enter a value based on any of these measurements by typing into any text box requiring a measurement value the abbreviation for the respective measurement unit:

Measurement	Abbreviation That You Type
Centimeters	cm
Inches	" *or* in
Lines	li
Picas	pi
Points	pt

You can change the default unit of measurement for all commands in Word by choosing the Utilities/Customize command. In the Customize dialog box, select the unit of measurement you want by choosing one of the Unit of Measure option buttons. The Ruler changes to reflect the unit of measure you're using as the default. If the value you enter is the same as the default unit of measurement, you don't need to type a unit abbreviation. Use decimal form to enter fractions of a measurement; for example, ¹/₄ inch equals .25, or ¹/₂ inch equals .50.

Document Formatting

To set document formatting controls, choose the Format/Document command or press Alt,T,D. Word displays the Document dialog box, as shown in Figure 4.1.

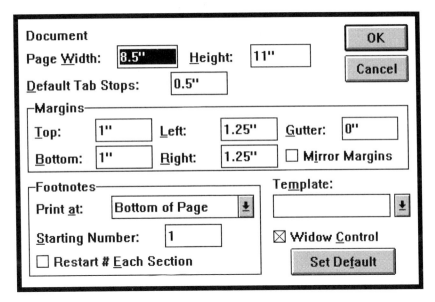

101

Figure 4.1   The Document dialog box.

The *page size settings*—Page Width and Height—define the dimensions of your page. The *margin settings*—Top, Bottom, Left, and Right—define the space between the edge of the page and the text area. Page size and margin settings determine the available text area in a document. Word determines the width of the available text area by subtracting the left and right margins from the page width. Similarly, Word determines the height of your text area by subtracting the top and bottom margins from the height of the paper. When you use Word's default page dimensions and margin settings, the text area on each page is 6 inches wide and 9 inches high, as shown in Figure 4.2.

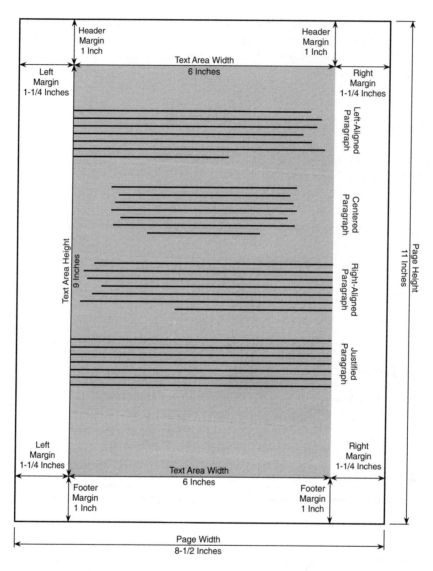

Header
Margin
1 Inch

Header
Margin
1 Inch

Text Area Width
6 Inches

Left
Margin
1-1/4 Inches

Right
Margin
1-1/4 Inches

Left-Aligned
Paragraph

Centered
Paragraph

Text Area Height
9 Inches

Right-Aligned
Paragraph

Page Height
11 Inches

Justified
Paragraph

Left
Margin
1-1/4 Inches

Right
Margin
1-1/4 Inches

Text Area Width
6 Inches

Footer
Margin
1 Inch

Footer
Margin
1 Inch

Page Width
8-1/2 Inches

Figure 4.2   Word's default text area.

The Widow <u>C</u>ontrol check box prevents a single line at a page
break from standing alone at the beginning or end of a page. When
a single line is split from the end of a paragraph and placed at the top
of the next page, it's called a *widow*. When a single line is split from
the beginning of a paragraph and left standing alone at the end of the
preceding page, it's called an *orphan*.

> ▶ **Note:** The settings you change in the Document dialog box affect the current document. However, if you want the settings to affect every subsequent document you create, choose the Set De_f_ault button or press Alt-F.

Setting Page Size

Word's default page size measurements are 8¹/₂ inches by 11 inches, the standard page size, as shown in the Page _W_idth and _H_eight text boxes. If you want to print on a nonstandard page size, such as legal paper, you can easily change the page dimensions settings, provided that your printer supports and is set up for the new page size. (Chapter 5 explains how to change your printer setup.)

Q Changing Page Size Settings

103

1. Choose the Forma_t_/_D_ocument command or press Alt,T,D.

   Word displays the Document dialog box with the Page _W_idth text box highlighted. If you're at another control setting in the Document dialog box, press Alt-W.

2. Type the new page width dimension.

3. Choose the _H_eight text box or press Alt-H.

4. Type the new page height dimension.

5. Choose the OK button or press Enter.

   Word changes the page dimensions as you specified and displays the text to reflect your new text area settings. ☐

Changing Margins

The *margin* is the white space between the edge of the paper and the text area. Word's default top and bottom margins are 1 inch and $1^1/_4$ inches for the left and right margins.

> ⃠ **Caution:** When you are setting margins, keep in mind that most laser printers can't print within $^1/_2$ inch of the paper edge.

Changing Margins by Using the Format/Document Command

1. Choose the Format/Document command or press Alt,T,D.	Word displays the Document dialog box.
2. Choose the Top text box or press Alt-T.	The insertion point moves to the Top text box.
3. Type a top margin value.	
4. Choose the Bottom text box or press Alt-B.	The insertion point moves to the Bottom text box.
5. Type a bottom margin value.	
6. Choose the Left text box or press Alt-L.	The insertion point moves to the Left text box.
7. Type a left margin value.	
8. Choose the Right text box or press Alt-R.	The insertion point moves to the Right text box.
9. Click on the OK button or press Enter.	Word reformats your entire document, reflecting the new margin settings. ☐

To change the left and right margins by using the Ruler, you must have a mouse installed on your system.

Setting the Left and Right Margins with the Ruler

1. If you haven't turned on the Ruler, choose the View/Ruler command or press Alt,V,R.	The Ruler appears at the top of your document window.

2. Click on the Ruler View button located at the far right of the Ruler.	The scale of the Ruler changes to Margin view mode, as shown in Figure 4.3. The brackets indicate the margin settings, reflecting their position relative to the edge of the paper.
3. Drag the left or right margin bracket to the position you want.	The bracket is dimmed as you drag it.
4. Release the mouse button.	Word changes the margin for your entire document to the new setting. ☐

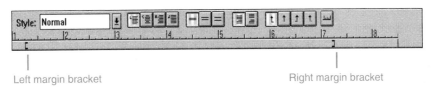

Left margin bracket   Right margin bracket

Figure 4.3   The Ruler in the Margin view mode.

105

Widow and Orphan Control

Recall that *a widow* is a straggling line of text that appears at the top of a printed page, and an *orphan* is a single paragraph line that appears at the bottom of a page. The Widow Control check box, in the Document dialog box, controls both orphans and widows. In most documents you'll want to keep at least two lines of a paragraph on a page. In other words, the first or last line of a paragraph shouldn't stand alone. When you turn on the Widow control check box, Word automatically adjusts your page breaks to ensure that at least two lines of a paragraph appear on a page (unless the entire paragraph is only one line).

Document Repagination

Word's automatic pagination feature, called *background pagination*, is turned on by default. This feature gives you up-to-date page breaks as you work on your document. These page breaks are calculated based on the Height page size and the top and bottom margin settings. In most cases, keeping the background pagination feature turned on is preferred. However, if you're working on a long document, using the background pagination feature can slow down Word's performance. You can turn off Word's automatic pagination feature by first choosing the Utilities/Customize command. Then, in the Customize dialog box, choose the Background Pagination check box or press Alt-B, and then choose the OK button or press Enter.

When you want to repaginate your document, choose the Utilities/Repaginate Now command. Word repaginates your document. If you've turned off the background pagination feature, you can repaginate your document by using the File/Print Preview command and printing the document, or by using the View/Page command.

Viewing Formatting Changes

Word allows you to view your document-level formatting by using the View/Page command or the File/Print Preview command. The Page view mode shows the document's actual page size and formatting. In this mode, you can edit and format the document similarly to the Normal editing view. However, working in the Page view mode is slower than Normal view because of the memory demands for displaying all the document's formats.

To get a bird's eye view of one or two pages of your document, choose the File/Print Preview command or press Alt,F,V. Figure 4.4 shows a two-page document. You *can't* edit the text in the Print Preview mode.

In the Print Preview mode, you navigate through your document by using the scroll bar or PgUp or PgDn keys. Choose the Cancel button or press Esc to return to the Normal view. Choose the Page View button or press Alt-V to display the document in the Page view mode. Chapter 5 explains other features of the Print Preview mode.

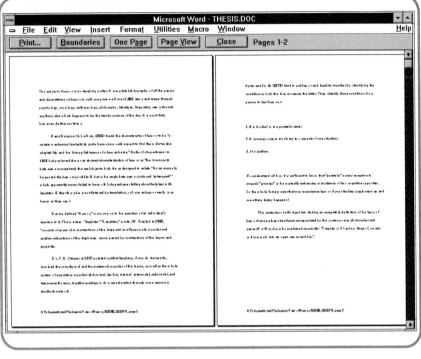

Figure 4.4   A document in the Print Pre_view mode.

107

Paragraph Formatting

Once you've established the page layout of a document, you're ready to move on to formatting paragraphs. Paragraph formatting consists of setting indents, changing alignment, adjusting line and paragraph spacing, and adding a border around a paragraph.

Paragraphs are the basic unit of text in Word. Recall that paragraphs are any string of text defined by pressing Enter. Word uses a paragraph mark ¶ to distinguish a paragraph. This paragraph mark does more than mark the end of a paragraph; it also contains the paragraph's formatting specifications. To show your paragraph marks, click on the Show All button on the Ribbon or turn on the Paragraph Marks check box displayed by choosing the View/Preferences dialog box.

When applying a paragraph format, you can place the insertion point *anywhere* in the paragraph you want to affect. If you want to apply formatting to more than one paragraph at a time, you need to select the paragraphs.

Applying Paragraph Formats

Word provides three ways to apply paragraph formatting: the Ruler, keyboard shortcuts, and the Format/Paragraph command. The Ruler provides a quick way to apply common paragraph formats. Figure 4.5 shows the Ruler and labels its paragraph formatting features. To turn on the Ruler, choose the View/Ruler command or press Alt,V,R. The Ruler also indicates formats for the paragraph containing the insertion point by displaying depressed buttons for each formatting feature applied. If you select two or more paragraphs with differing formats, Word dims all or part of the buttons and indent markers on the Ruler.

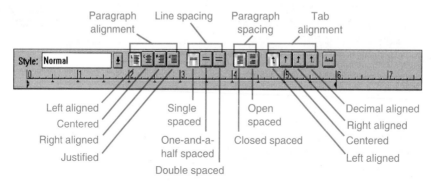

Figure 4.5   Paragraph formatting options on the Ruler.

Some paragraph formatting can be applied only by using the Paragraph dialog box. For example, adding a border around a paragraph requires the Paragraph dialog box. To open the Paragraph dialog box, choose the Format/Paragraph command or press Alt,F,P. Word displays the Paragraph dialog box, as shown in Figure 4.6. Many of the settings are the same as the ones provided in the Ruler. However, using the dialog box allows you to tailor settings.

> **Tip:** To quickly display the Paragraph dialog box, double-click just above the Ruler measurement line.

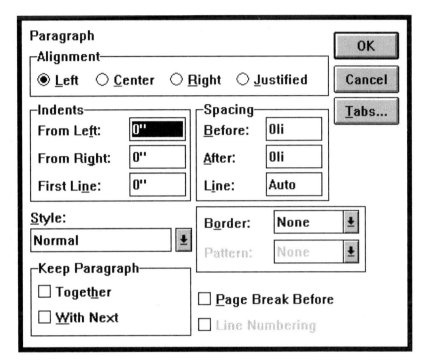

Figure 4.6   The Paragraph dialog box.

Aligning Paragraphs

Word aligns text relative to the indent markers on the Ruler. By default, these markers are positioned at the left and right margins. An *indent* is a relative position from the margin. If the margin moves, the indent moves with it. Word's default paragraph formatting aligns all the text flush against the left margin, as indicated by the depressed Left alignment button in the Ruler.

To change this alignment, place the insertion point in the paragraph or select the paragraphs you want to format and click on an alignment button on the Ruler. The Center alignment button centers the paragraph(s) between the left and right indents. The

Right alignment button aligns the paragraph(s) flush against the right indent. The Justified button aligns the paragraph(s) flush against both indents. When text is justified, Word increases or decreases the width of the blank spaces in your text to keep the left and right text edges even. Figure 4.7 shows text formatted in each of these alignments.

110

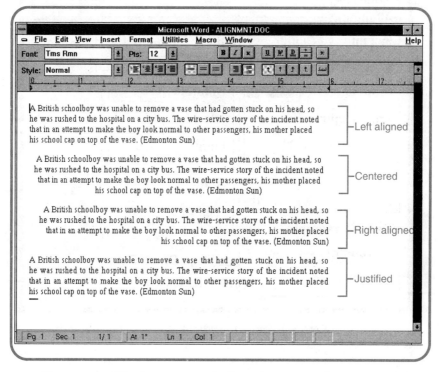

Figure 4.7   The four types of aligned paragraphs.

Besides the Ruler, there are two other methods you can use to align paragraphs: keyboard shortcuts and the Format/Paragraph command. Using the keyboard, place the insertion point in the paragraph you want to format or select the paragraphs you want to affect, and then press one of the following key combinations to align your paragraph:

Paragraph Alignment	Key Combination
Left	Ctrl-L
Center	Ctrl-C
Right	Ctrl-R
Justify	Ctrl-J

The least efficient way to align a paragraph is to use the Format/ Paragraph command. Choosing this command displays the Paragraph dialog box. A quicker method of displaying the Paragraph dialog box is to double-click on the Ruler. Once the Paragraph dialog box is displayed, choose the alignment option button you want and then click on the OK button.

Line Spacing

Line spacing is the blank space between lines in a paragraph. Spaces between lines are directly related to the largest-size font in a line. By taking into account the size of the largest font, Word prevents text lines from overlapping in your document. The three line-spacing buttons, clustered to the right of the paragraph alignment buttons on the Ruler, let you control the amount of space between lines of text in a paragraph. Word defaults to single spacing, as indicated by the depressed single-line button. The second button applies 1 $\frac{1}{2}$ lines of blank space between each line of text. The third and last line-spacing button applies 2 lines of blank space between each line of text.

To apply the single, one-and-a-half, or double line-space settings, place the insertion point in the paragraph or select the paragraphs you want to format; then click on the line-spacing button you want. From the keyboard, you can use these key combinations:

Paragraph Line Spacing	Key Combination	
Single line	Ctrl-1	
One-and-a-half lines	Ctrl-5	(use the 5 key on the top row of the keyboard, *not* the numeric keypad)
Double line	Ctrl-2	

Using the Format/Paragraph command provides more flexibility than using the Ruler or the keyboard to specify line spacing. Choosing this command displays the Paragraph dialog box. The default setting in the Line text box is set to Auto, which automatically sets the line spacing to match the largest font in each line. Choose the Line text box or press Alt-I. Then type the number of blank lines you want to have between each line in your paragraph. Clicking on the OK button applies the new line spacing. If you type 0 (zero), Word automatically defaults to the Auto single-line setting.

> **Tip:** Word considers line spacing to be a paragraph formatting feature. However, the spacing of your entire document can be changed by pressing Ctrl-5 (the 5 key on the numeric keypad) to select the entire document and then applying the line spacing you want.

112

Paragraph Spacing

Paragraph spacing is the blank space used as a visual break between two paragraphs. You can add space before and/or after a paragraph by using Word's Open Space feature. By default, Word creates paragraphs without any extra paragraph spacing.

A common mistake is to create blank spaces between paragraphs by pressing the Enter key several times. This technique is inferior to using the Open Space feature. The main advantage of using the Open Space feature is the time it saves, since you can change the spacing of all your paragraphs at one time. Suppose you decide to increase or decrease the amount of space between paragraphs. Selecting the paragraphs and changing the Open Space setting reformats all the selected paragraphs. Another advantage of this feature over spacing paragraphs by pressing Enter is that the Enter key might add an extra paragraph that could create a gap at the top of the next page. Using the Open Space feature eliminates the blank space before a paragraph when it falls at the beginning of a page.

To add a line space before one or more paragraphs, place the insertion point in the paragraph or select the paragraphs you want to format, and then click on the Open Space button on the Ruler.

Figure 4.8 identifies the Open Space button and shows paragraphs before and after applying this format. Using the keyboard, press Ctrl-O to apply an open space (one blank line) before the selected paragraph. Pressing Ctrl-E eliminates a paragraph space.

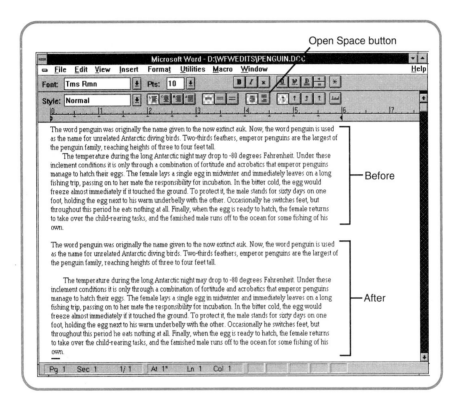

Figure 4.8   Paragraphs before and after applying the Open Space command.

113

Using the Format/Paragraph command provides more flexibility than using the Ruler or keyboard to specify paragraph spacing. Choosing this command displays the Paragraph dialog box. Choose the Before or After text box or press Alt-B or Alt-A. Then type the number of lines you want before or after the paragraph.

Indenting Paragraphs

Indenting paragraphs means positioning the paragraphs between the left and right margins. The space between the edge of your paragraph boundaries and the page margin is called an *indent*. Three indent measurements exist for each paragraph: the left, right, and first line. The *left indent* is the distance from the left margin to the left boundary of the paragraph. Correspondingly, the *right indent* is the distance from the right margin to the right boundary of the paragraph. The *first line indent* is the distance from the left indent to the first character in the line of a paragraph and is one of the most commonly used indents. Indenting the first line of a paragraph makes it easier to distinguish paragraph breaks.

The first line of a paragraph can also be indented in the opposite direction to the left of the paragraph's text. This type of indenting is known as a *hanging indent*. Hanging indents are useful for creating lists, resumes, or bibliographies. Chapter 6 explains how to create lists by using hanging indents.

114

The quickest way to indent paragraphs is to use the indent markers in the Ruler with the mouse. Figure 4.9 identifies each indent marker and shows how it affects paragraphs. To change the first-line indent on the Ruler, drag the first-line indent to the spot where you want to indent the first line, and then release the mouse button. You can change the left and right indents in a similar manner by dragging the left or right indent markers to a new position and releasing the mouse button.

With the mouse, you can create a hanging indent by first using the left indent marker to indent the paragraph to the right and then dragging the first-line indent marker to the left. When you drag the left indent marker, the first-line indent moves in tandem to keep the relationship between the first line and left indents. If you want to drag the left marker without affecting the first-line indent, press the Shift key while dragging the left indent marker.

To indent one or more paragraphs using the keyboard with the Ruler, follow the next Quick Steps.

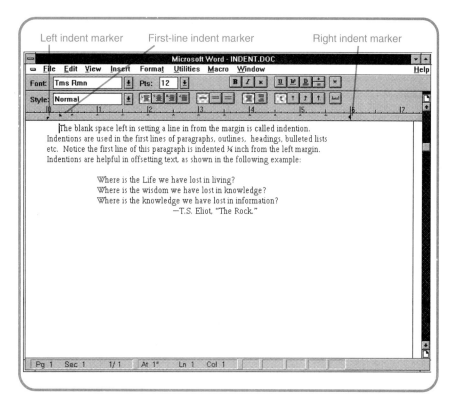

Figure 4.9   Indent markers and their effect on paragraphs.

Indenting Paragraphs by Using the Keyboard with the Ruler

1. Position the insertion point in the paragraph or select the paragraphs you want to indent.

2. Press Ctrl-Shift-F10.

   A ruler cursor appears next to the left indent marker.

3. Press the Right or Left Arrow key to position the ruler cursor where you want the indent to appear.

   Pressing Ctrl and either the Right or Left Arrow key moves the cursor one inch at a time. Pressing End moves the cursor to the right edge of the text column, and pressing Home moves the cursor to the zero position on the Ruler.

115

4. Type *F*, *L*, or *R*.	Use *F* for a first-line indent, *L* for a left indent, and *R* for a right indent. To cancel changes you've made on the Ruler and return to your document, press Esc.
5. Press Enter.	Word indents the paragraph as specified. ☐

Word provides keyboard shortcuts for indenting paragraphs with Word's default tab stops ($1/2$-inch intervals). Pressing Ctrl-N indents a paragraph one tab stop at a time. To unindent a paragraph created using Ctrl-N, press Ctrl-M. Pressing Ctrl-T creates a hanging indent. Every time you press Ctrl-T, all of the paragraph, *except the first line*, moves one tab stop at a time. Every time you press Ctrl-G, all of the paragraph, *except the first line*, moves one tab stop to the left.

116

The least efficient way to indent paragraphs is to use the Format/Paragraph command. Choosing this command or pressing Alt,T,P displays the Paragraph dialog box. To indent the first line of a paragraph, choose the First Line text box or press Alt-N and type the value you want for the first-line indent. Entering a negative value in the First Line text box creates a hanging indent. To left-indent a paragraph, choose the From Left check box or press Alt-F. To right-indent a paragraph, choose the From Right check box or press Alt-G. Type the value you want for the paragraph indent. Remember, to enter fractions of an inch, use decimals, such as .50 for $1/2$ inch. Choose the OK button or press Enter to indent your paragraph.

Adding Borders and Lines to Paragraphs

You can enhance the visual emphasis of a paragraph by adding a border or lines above, below, or on the left side of it. You can select multiple paragraphs. For example, if you select multiple paragraphs and choose a box border, all the paragraphs are placed within a single box.

To draw a border or lines around a paragraph, first place the insertion point in the paragraph you want to affect. Choose the Format/Paragraph command or press Alt,T,P. In the Paragraph dialog box, choose the Border list box or press Alt-O. Display the list of options by clicking on the Arrow button or pressing Alt-Down Arrow. Click on the border option you want or highlight the option by using the Down or Up Arrow key. The following border options are available:

Border Option	Effect
None	Removes a border if one exists
Box	Encloses the paragraph in a box
Bar	Draws a vertical line to the left of the paragraph
Above	Draws a horizontal line above the paragraph
Below	Draws a horizontal line below the paragraph

Once you've selected a border option, Word displays the Pattern list box. Choose the Pattern list box or press Alt-E. Display the list of options by clicking on the Arrow button or press Alt-Down Arrow. Click on the pattern option you want or highlight the option by using the Down or Up Arrow keys. The following pattern options are available:

117

Pattern Option	Effect
None	Removes border or pattern
Single	Draws a single-width line
Thick	Draws a double-width line
Double	Draws two parallel single-width lines
Shadow	Draws a single line with a shadow effect on the bottom and right sides

After selecting the border and pattern options you want, choose the OK button or press Enter. Word applies the border and pattern you've selected. Figure 4.10 shows the different border and pattern option effects.

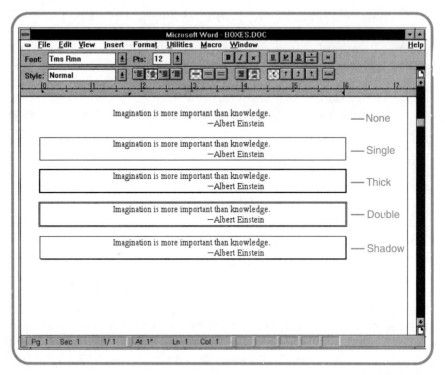

Figure 4.10   Effects of border and pattern options.

Adding a Border to a Paragraph

1. Choose the Format/Paragraph command or press Alt,T,P.

   Word displays the Paragraph dialog box.

2. Choose the Border list box or press Alt-O.

   Word highlights the Border list box.

3. Click on the Arrow button or press Alt-Down Arrow.

   Word displays the list of border options.

4. Click on the border option you want or press Down Arrow to highlight the border option.

   The Pattern list box appears in boldface, indicating that it's now available.

5. Click on the Pattern list box or press Tab or Alt-P.

   Word highlights the Pattern list box.

6. Click on the Arrow button or press Alt-Down Arrow.

   Word displays the list of pattern options.

7. Click on the pattern option you want or press Down Arrow to highlight the pattern option.

8. Choose the OK button or press Enter.

The border and pattern you've selected are added to your paragraph. □

Searching and Replacing Paragraph Formats

The Edit/Search and Edit/Replace commands allow you to change paragraph formats. For example, suppose you want to format all the paragraphs in your document so that they are centered instead of the default left-aligned. In the Replace dialog box's Search For text box, press Ctrl-L—the key combination for left-aligned lines. Next, choose the Replace With text box or press Alt-R. Then press Ctrl-C—the key code for centered lines. Choose the confirmation setting you want and click on the OK button or press Enter. Word begins the replace session according to the confirmation setting you've chosen. You can also enter more than one key code to further refine your search and replace operation. For example, you can enter Ctrl-L, and then enter Ctrl-2 to locate all left-aligned paragraphs that are double-spaced. Table 4.1 shows the key combinations for paragraph formats.

119

Table 4.1   Key Combinations for Paragraph Formats

Paragraph Format	Key Combination
Centered lines	Ctrl-C
Close the space before	Ctrl-E
Double-spaced lines	Ctrl-2
Justified lines	Ctrl-V
Left-aligned lines	Ctrl-L
One-and-one-half-spaced lines	Ctrl-5
Open space before	Ctrl-O
Remove paragraph formatting	Ctrl-X
Right-aligned lines	Ctrl-R
Single-spaced lines	Ctrl-1

> Ⓧ **Caution:** A common mistake is not clearing the para-
> graph formats from the Search and Replace text boxes
> after performing a search or a search and replace operation. If
> one or more paragraph formats appear below a text box, press
> Ctrl-X to remove the formats.

Character Formatting

Character formatting lets you add visual emphasis to text in your document. Character formatting includes the changing of fonts and font sizes, character colors, and the positioning and/or spacing of characters. You can also apply special emphasis features, such as bold, italic, or underline. You can apply character formatting to any text, from a single character to the entire document.

120

Applying Character Formatting

As in paragraph formatting, Word provides three ways to apply character formats: the Ribbon, the Format/Character command, and keyboard shortcuts. Using the Ribbon provides an easy way to apply character formats. Figure 4.11 shows the Ribbon and labels its character-formatting features. To turn on the Ribbon, choose the View/Ribbon command or press Alt,V,R. If a format characteristic is active at the insertion point, its button appears as depressed. If you select text with differing character formats, Word dims all or part of the buttons on the Ribbon.

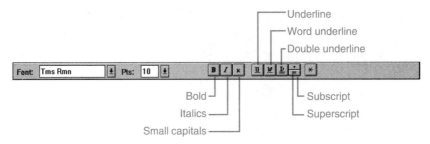

Figure 4.11   The character-formatting features on the Ribbon.

In many cases, the Ribbon offers the quickest and easiest way to format characters, but some character formatting can be applied only by using the Character dialog box or by using keyboard shortcuts. For example, the Hidden text, Color, Position, and Character Spacing controls are available only using the Character dialog box or keyboard shortcuts. To open the Character dialog box, choose the Format/Character command or press Alt,T,C. Word displays the Character dialog box, as shown in Figure 4.12.

Word provides an extensive collection of keyboard shortcuts for many character-formatting functions. Each keyboard shortcut is a combination of the Ctrl key and a letter. These key combinations act as toggle switches; you apply a format using one of these combinations and turn it off by pressing the key combination again.

Character formats can be changed as you're typing. The new format begins at the insertion point. As you begin typing, the text will appear with the formatting characteristics you've chosen. These characteristics don't change until you apply new formats or move the insertion point to another part of your document with different character formats. For example, if you move the insertion point to the middle of a line of boldfaced text, any new characters you type appear boldfaced as well.

121

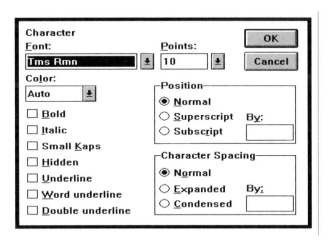

Figure 4.12   The Character dialog box.

> ▶ **Tip:** To quickly display the Character dialog box, double-click anywhere on the Ribbon, except on a button or text box.

Emphasizing Characters

You can emphasize characters by applying character formats to them, such as bold, italic, underline, small caps, and superscript. The easiest way to emphasize characters is by using the Ribbon or keyboard shortcuts. Table 4.2 lists the three methods of applying emphasis to characters and provides a brief explanation of each.

Table 4.2 Methods of Applying Emphasis to Characters

Emphasis	Ribbon Button	Dialog Box	Keyboard Shortcut	Effect
Boldface	B	`Bold`	Ctrl-B	Boldfaces text
Double underline	D	`Double underline`	Ctrl-D	Double-under lines text and spaces
Italic	I	`Italic`	Ctrl-I	Italicizes text
SMALL CAPS	K	`Small Kaps`	Ctrl-K	Turns lowercase letters into small capitals; leaves uppercase letters full height
Subscript	=	`Subscript`	Ctrl-=	Reduces the size of characters and lowers them below the line
Superscript	+	`Superscript`	Ctrl-Shift-+	Reduces the size of characters and raises them above the line
Underline	U	`Underline`	Ctrl-U	Continuously underlines both text and spaces
Word underline	W	`Word underline`	Ctrl-W Under- lines words, excluding spaces

> ▶ **Tip:** To strip any character formats, select the text and press Ctrl-Spacebar.

Word provides eight color options for displaying and printing characters. You must have a color monitor to view character colors or a plotter or color printer to print color formatting. To display or print text in color, choose the Format/Character command or press Alt,T,C. Choose the Color list box or press Alt-L, and then click on the Arrow button or press Alt-Down Arrow to display the list of color options.

Spacing Characters

Word lets you control the amount of space between characters. Tightening space between characters to achieve a more visually pleasing effect is called *kerning*. Tighter kerning means less space between characters, and looser kerning means more space between characters. To change the spacing of your characters, choose the Format/Character command or press Alt,T,C, and then choose either the Expanded or the Condensed option button and enter the measurement to either tighten or loosen your text. When you choose the Expanded or Condensed option button, the By text box displays Word's default values (in points) for the active font.

123

Hiding Text

You can enter text into your document that you don't want printed or displayed on your screen, such as personal notes. This feature is called *hidden text*. Before turning on the hidden text feature, make sure the Show All button on the Ribbon (the asterisk) is depressed. Turning on the Show All button enables you to view hidden text as you enter it.

To enter hidden text, press Ctrl-H to activate the hidden text feature, and then type your text. Word underlines the hidden text to identify it from normal text. To turn off the hidden text feature, simply press Ctrl-H again. The hidden text feature can also be activated by choosing the Format/Character command and turning on the Hidden Text check box.

Changing Fonts and Font Sizes

A *font* is a family of characters that have the same design. Word uses two types of fonts: *printer fonts*, which are directly related to the printer driver file that Word uses to control your printer, and *screen fonts*, which come from Windows. If you want the font you see on the screen to match the font that prints, choose the View/Preferences command and activate the Display as Printed check box. Word may not be able to display your text in all the fonts available to your printer. Unless you purchase and install additional screen fonts, Word displays only six fonts on your screen: Courier, Helvetica, Modern, Roman, Script, and Times Roman (Word's default). If you want to use optional screen fonts, you need to purchase and install those fonts separately.

If you select a printer font that does not correspond to one of Windows' screen fonts, Word substitutes the closest screen font. For example, if you've installed and selected the HP LaserJet Series III printer, one of the fonts available in the Font list box is LinePrinter. If you use this font to format text, Word substitutes Courier in your screen display.

To choose a font, first select the characters you want to change, or move the insertion point where you want to begin the new font. Using the mouse, click on the Arrow button to the immediate right of the Font list box and double-click on the font you want. Using the keyboard, press Ctrl-F and then press Alt-Up or Down Arrow to display the available fonts. Use the Up or Down Arrow key to highlight the font you want, and then press Enter to activate the new font or press Esc to exit without selecting a font. Fonts can also be chosen by using the Format/Character command or by pressing Alt,T,C. Word displays the Character dialog box. You choose a font in the Font list box the same way you choose a font from the Ribbon Font list box.

Fonts come in different heights, measured in points. A point is $1/72$ of an inch. You should always choose a font before you choose its point size. After selecting a font, choose the Pts list box (or press Ctrl-P). Select the point size in the same manner as you did in the Font list box. The Pts list box displays the standard sizes for the selected font. Remember, the options available in the Font and Pts list boxes depend on the printer you've installed. In general, Word will not include any font or point size that your printer is not capable of producing.

> ► **Note:** For more information about working with fonts and different types of printers, see Chapter 5, "Previewing and Printing Documents."

Searching and Replacing Character Formats and Fonts

The Edit/Search and Edit/Replace commands let you change character formats and fonts in your document. For example, suppose you've underlined words in your document and you want them italicized instead. In the Replace dialog box's Search For text box, press Ctrl-U, the key combination for underlined characters. Choose the Replace With text box or press Alt-R; then press Ctrl-I, the key code for italicized characters. Choose the confirmation setting you want and click on the OK button or press Enter. Word begins the replace session according to the confirmation setting you've chosen. Table 4.3 gives the key combinations for character formats.

125

Table 4.3   Key Combinations for Character Formats

Character Format	Key Combination
Boldface	Ctrl-B
Double underline	Ctrl-D
Italic	Ctrl-I
Remove character formatting	Ctrl-Spacebar
Small capitals	Ctrl-K
Subscript	Ctrl-=
Superscript	Ctrl-Shift-+
Underline	Ctrl-U
Word underline	Ctrl-W

To search and replace fonts, choose the Search For text box; then press Ctrl-F. Word displays a font name directly below the text box. Pressing Ctrl-F scrolls you through the list of available fonts, one by one. Pressing Ctrl-Shift-F moves you backward through the font names list. When the name of the font you want to search for is displayed, choose the Replace With text box or press Alt-R. Use this same procedure to select the replacement font. Choose the Confirm Changes check box setting you want and click on the OK button or press Enter. Word begins the replace session according to the confirmation setting you've chosen.

You can also search for and replace font point sizes. Press Ctrl-P in the Search For text box and press Ctrl-P to scroll through the list of available point sizes. Pressing Ctrl-Shift-P scrolls through the Pt size list backwards, showing the previous point size in the list.

> ⊘ **Caution:** It is a common mistake not to clear the character formats or fonts from the Search and Replace text boxes after performing a search or a search and replace operation. If one or more character formats and/or a font name appear below a text box, press Ctrl-Spacebar to remove them.

Understanding Tabs

If you've used a typewriter or another word processor, you're probably familiar with *tab stops*, positions you set within the margins of a document for aligning text. Generally, tabs are used to create aligned columns of text, such as tables. Tabs are sometimes used to indent the first line of a paragraph's text. Working with tabs is a two-step process. First, you need to specify your tab settings on the Ruler. Then you must press the Tab key to position text according to these settings. Each time you press the Tab key, Word moves the insertion point to the next tab stop, creating a tab space. If the Show All feature is on, a tab mark is designated by a right-pointing arrow.

If you press the Tab key without specifying any tab stops on the Ruler, Word will use its default ½-inch tab settings. These default tab stops appear as inverted **T** marks that hang slightly below the ruler line. To change Word's default tab stops, choose the Format/Document command or press Alt,T,V. In the Document dialog box, choose the Default Tab Stops text box or press Alt-D. Enter a new tab interval. For example, if you want tab intervals at every ¼ inch, enter .25 and click on the OK button.

Setting Tab Stops

In Word, you can set up to 50 tab stops. When you create a tab stop, you can choose from the four kinds of tab alignments shown here and illustrated in Figure 4.13:

Tab Alignment	Description
Left	Text is placed to the right from the tab.
Centered	Text is centered at the tab.
Right	Text is placed to the left from the tab until the tab's space is filled; then text extends to the right.
Decimal	Text before the decimal point is placed to the left, and text entered after the decimal point is placed to the right.

127

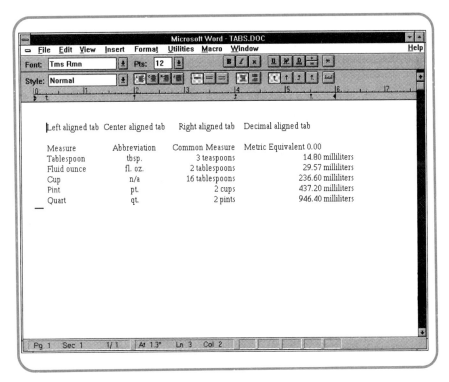

Figure 4.13   Tab stops and their effects.

Before you create a tab stop, place the insertion point in the paragraph you want to format. Next, on the Ruler, click on the tab button you want. Click on the ruler position where you want the tab to appear. For example, if you want to place a left-aligned tab at the $\frac{1}{4}$-inch position on the Ruler, first click on the Left tab button, if it's not already selected, and then click on the $\frac{1}{4}$-inch mark on the Ruler.

When you insert a tab on the Ruler, Word clears all default tab stops that appear to the left of the new tab. For example, if you insert a tab stop at the 2-inch position on the Ruler, Word deletes all the default tab stops at the $\frac{1}{2}$-inch, 1-inch, and 1 $\frac{1}{2}$-inch positions. If you've already formatted the current paragraph by inserting tabs, Word adjusts the text in that paragraph according to the new tab stops. If you need to reposition a tab, drag the tab indicator to its new position. To clear a tab stop, drag the tab indicator off the Ruler.

Choosing the Format/Tabs command (Alt,T,T) or clicking on the Tabs button in the Paragraph dialog box displays the Tab dialog box shown in Figure 4.14. Using this dialog box, you can set tab positions, alignments and leader characters, and you can clear tab settings. In the Tab Position text box, enter the tab position as a numeric measurement. After entering a value in the Tab Position text box, choose the tab alignment option you want from the option buttons in the Alignment box, and then choose the Set button. You can enter additional tab settings in the same manner. After entering all the tab stops you want, choose the OK button or press Enter.

128

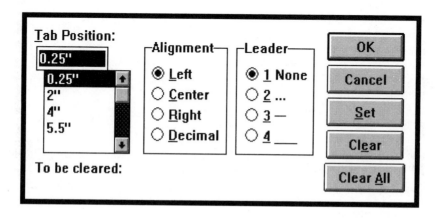

Figure 4.14   The Tabs dialog box.

To clear tab settings, use the Tab dialog box and select the tab setting you want to clear from the Tab Position list box. Then choose the Clear button or press Alt-E. To clear all the tab settings displayed in the Tab Position list box, choose the Clear All button or press Alt-A.

When your text has words that are separated by tab characters, you can set leader characters to fill the spaces between the words. Use the option buttons in the Leader box. Tab leaders draw the reader's eye across a line of specified characters. This visual aid makes it easier for the eye to match up two or more columns of text created by tabs, such as an index or table of contents, as shown in Figure 4.15

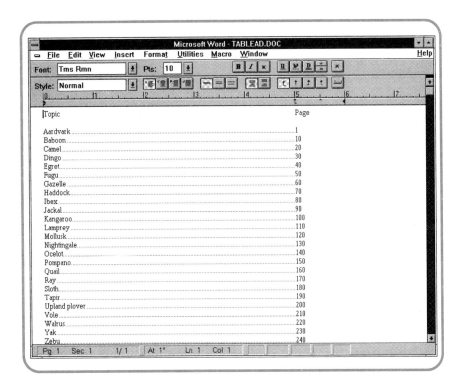

Figure 4.15   Tab leaders.

Headers and Footers

Headers and footers provide information about a document, such as page numbers, document titles, and dates. A *header* is positioned within the top margin area, and a *footer* is positioned at the bottom margin area. Word's default position for headers and footers is ¹/₂ inch from the top or bottom of the page. The procedures for setting up a header or a footer are the same. Headers and footers are not displayed in the Normal or Draft view modes but can be viewed and edited in the Page view mode. You can apply headers and footers to every page, to every page starting with the second page, or other combinations. You can even apply different headers and/or footers for odd and even pages.

Creating a Header or Footer Dialog Box

Choosing the Header/Footer command from the Edit menu or pressing Alt,E,H displays the Header/Footer dialog box, shown in Figure 4.16. The Header/Footer dialog box provides options for specifying the type of header or footer you want to create.

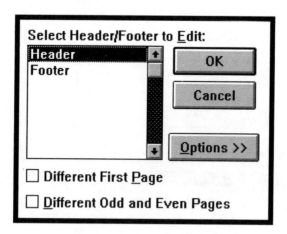

Figure 4.16   The Header/Footer dialog box.

The Select Header/Footer to Edit list box initially shows two entries: Header and Footer. The Different First Page check box allows you to create a separate header and footer for the first page. The

Different Odd and Even Pages check box allows you to create different headers and footers for odd and even pages. Turning on either of these options adds the appropriate header and footer options to the list box. The OK and Cancel buttons are the standard dialog buttons for activating or exiting the command. The Options>> button expands the Header/Footer dialog box, as shown in Figure 4.17. These additional controls allow you to affect page number types, starting point, and header or footer positioning.

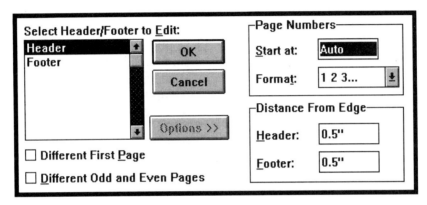

Figure 4.17   The expanded Header/Footer dialog box.

The procedure for creating a header or a footer is the same. The Quick Steps explain how to create a header for your entire document, excluding the first page. Omitting a header/footer from the first page is a commonly used convention.

 Creating a Header

1. Choose the Header/Footer command from the Edit menu or press Alt,E,H.	Word displays the Header/Footer dialog box.
2. Choose the Different First Page check box or press Alt-P.	Word displays First Header and First Footer in the Select Header/Footer to Edit list box.
3. Double-click on the Header option in the Select Header/Footer to Edit list box or press Enter.	Word displays the Header pane at the bottom of the screen, as shown in Figure 4.18. The option you choose

131

from the Select Header/ Footer to Edit list box is noted on the bar of the pane, which in this case is `Header`.

4. Type your header text.

You can apply character or paragraph formats to your header's text.

5. Click on the page number button (#) or press Shift-F10, and then press *P*.

Word adds a page number indicator to your header. You can also add a time (clock button) and date stamp (calendar button) to your header by clicking on the appropriate button or pressing Shift-F10, then *D* for the date and/or *T* for the time.

6. Choose the Close button or press Alt-C.

The Header pane disappears from the screen. □

Customizing Page Numbering

If you add a page number to your header or footer, by default Word begins numbering the pages at page 1. You can start page numbering in headers and footers beginning at a page other than 1. To change page numbering, first open the Header/Footer dialog box and then choose the Options >> button or press Alt-O. Choose the Start at text box or press Alt-S, and type a starting page number. For example, if you wanted the page numbering to start on page 2, enter the number *2*. Word begins printing page numbers starting at page 2, with 2 printed on page two.

The Format list box provides a selection of numbering systems to choose from: the default Arabic numerals (1, 2, 3, etc.), lowercase letters, uppercase letters, lowercase Roman numerals, and uppercase Roman numerals. To select the numbering system you want, first choose the Format list box or press Alt-T. Click on the Arrow button or press Alt-Down Arrow to display the list of numbering options. Choose a number system; then choose the OK button or press Enter.

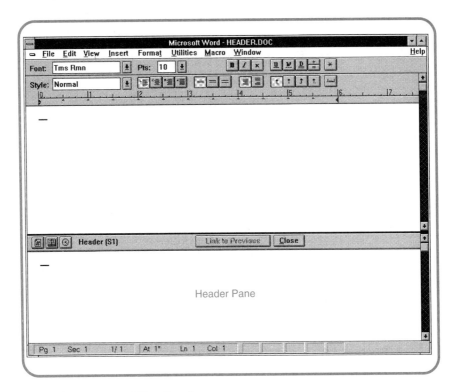

Figure 4.18   The Header pane.

Changing Header and Footer Positions

Word's normal positioning of headers and footers is ¹/₂ inch from the top or bottom of the page. You can change the vertical location of the headers or footers by using the Distance from Edge text boxes in the expanded Header/Footer dialog box. The values you enter measure the distance in inches from the top or bottom of the page to the beginning of the header or footer. For example, if you enter 2 in the Header text box, all headers in the document start 2 inches from the top of the page. Entering 1.5 in the Footer text box positions all footers in the document 1 ¹/₂ inches from the bottom of the page.

> Ø **Caution:** Your header or footer won't print if you're using a laser printer and set the distance of the header or footer for less than ¹/₂ inch, because laser printers can't print within ¹/₂ inch of the page edge.

Inserting Page Numbers

If you want to add page numbers only to the top or bottom of your document, you can use the Insert/Page Numbers command. To insert page numbers, choose the Insert/Page Numbers command or press Alt,I,U. Word displays a dialog box. Choose the Top option button (Alt-T) or the Bottom (Alt-B) option button to indicate where you want the page number inserted. Next, choose either the Left (Alt-L), Center (Alt-C), or Right (Alt-R) option button to horizontally position the page numbers. Choose the OK button or press Enter to insert the page number in your document. If you've created headers or footers in your document, Word displays a message box asking for a confirmation to replace it with the page number.

What You Have Learned

▶ Word has four levels of formatting commands: document, section, paragraph, and character. By starting at the top level (document), you can avoid clashes between levels.

▶ With the Format/Document (Alt,T,D) command, you can change your document's formats. For example, you can change page size and margins, control widows and orphans, and turn off background pagination.

▶ To change the format of one or more paragraphs, use either the Ruler or the Format/Paragraph (Alt,T,P) command. For example, you can align paragraphs, change the line and paragraph spacing, and indent paragraphs.

▶ To change the format of one or more characters, use either the Ribbon or the Format/Character (Alt,T,C) command. For example, you can change fonts and font sizes, emphasize and space characters, and create hidden text.

▶ Tabs let you align columns of text according to measurement settings you specify. To create tabs, use the Format/Tabs (Alt,T,T) command or the Ruler.

▶ Headers and footers let you print information about a document at the top or bottom, respectively, of a page. To create headers and footers, use the Edit menu's Header/Footer (Alt,E,H) command.

135

Previewing and Printing Documents

In This Chapter

- ► *Setting up your printer*
- ► *Previewing your document before printing*
- ► *Printing your entire document or a part of it*
- ► *Printing while working on other documents*
- ► *Downloading and adding fonts*
- ► *Installing a printer*
- ► *Troubleshooting common printer problems*

Now that you've created your document, you're ready to see the tangible results. Word provides comprehensive printing options to take advantage of most printers. In this chapter, you'll learn how to use Word's previewing and printing options to get the most out of Word and your printer.

Setting Up Your Printer

As part of the Word for Windows installation process, the Setup program asks you to identify the printer or printers you'll be using. After identifying your printer(s), Word installs the printer driver file(s) for the printer(s) you've selected. A *printer driver* is a file containing the printing instructions for a specific printer so that the printer can follow Word's formatting and printing instructions. If you have installed one or more printers using the Setup program, you're ready to proceed to the next step: selecting and setting up the printer you want to use. Later in this chapter, you'll learn how to install additional printers.

To select a printer, choose the File/Printer Setup command or press Alt,F,R. Word displays the Printer Setup dialog box, shown in Figure 5.1. The Printer list box shows all the printers you selected when installing Word. The highlighted printer is the active printer, meaning that it's the one for which Word formats your documents and the one that Word prints to. By default, Word displays your document as it will print, based on the active printer. When you choose a different printer, Word reformats the document to reflect the capabilities of that printer.

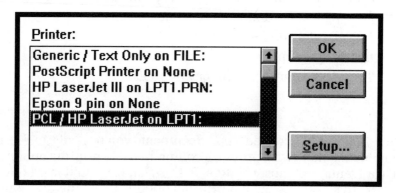

Figure 5.1   The Printer Setup dialog box.

Select a printer from the Printer list box by clicking on the printer name you want or pressing the Down or Up Arrow key to highlight the printer. Then choose the OK button or press Enter. Notice in Figure 5.1 that the `PCL/HP LaserJet on LPT1:` option in the Printer list box is highlighted, indicating that LaserJet is the active printer and that it is printing on the `LPT1:` port, which was assigned when the printer was installed. A *printer port* is an interface or connector between the computer and the printer.

Choosing the Setup button or pressing Alt-S in the Printer Setup dialog box displays the Printer Setup window for the selected printer. This window allows you to control the features of your printer. The control options vary according to the printer you've selected. For example, Figure 5.2 shows a Printer Setup window for an Epson dot matrix printer, and Figure 5.3 shows a Printer Setup window for an HP LaserJet II printer. Table 5.1 lists and describes the available options in the LaserJet II Printer Setup window.

139

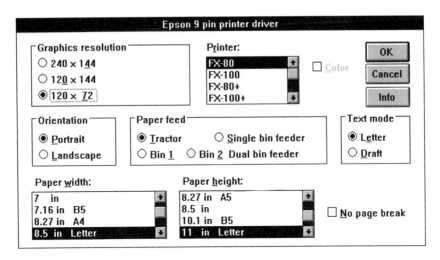

Figure 5.2   An Epson dot matrix Printer Setup window.

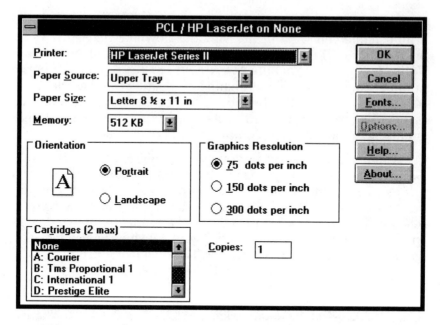

Figure 5.3   The HP LaserJet II Printer Setup window.

Table 5.1   Options for the Printer Setup Window

Option	Description
Printer list box	Displays the selected printer model. Depending on the printer chosen, several other brand names and models may share the same standard printer driver. In these situations, Word lists the other printers in the Printer list box; for example, the LaserJet Series II printer driver is used by a number of laser printers. Choosing a specific printer type from this list enables you to take advantage of any printing capabilities specific to your printer.
Paper Source list box	Defines the paper feed supply source, which for the LaserJet II includes the Upper Tray (the default), Manual, or Envelope feed options.
Paper Size list box	Displays the default paper size, which for the LaserJet II is 8 1/2" by 11". You can choose other paper size options from the list. If you choose a paper size different from the page size defined in

Option	Description
	the Document dialog box, Word displays a message when you exit the Print Setup dialog box, indicating there's a difference.
Memory list box	Specifies the amount of installed printer memory. This option is available only for printers with memory upgrade options.
Orientation option buttons	The Portrait option button, the default setting, prints documents in *portrait mode*—down the length of the paper. The Landscape option button prints documents in *landscape mode*—across the length of the paper. If you change the orientation to landscape, when you exit the Print Setup dialog box Word displays a message box indicating that there are different page dimension settings in the Document dialog box. Choosing the Yes button or pressing Y instructs Word to automatically change the settings in the Document dialog box to match the dimensions for landscape mode.
Graphics Resolution option buttons	Defines the resolution of your graphics. This option doesn't affect the resolution of text. Generally, the higher the resolution, the better the picture, the slower the printing, and the more memory required.
Copies text box	Specifies the number of copies to print. Generally, this option should be left at the 1 copy setting because you can specify the number of copies when you execute the File/Print command.
Cartridges list box	Specifies up to two font cartridges you're using with your LaserJet II printer. Fonts contained in the font cartridges are added as options in the Font list box.
Fonts button	Displays a dialog box for managing soft fonts, as explained later in this chapter.
Help button	Provides useful information specific to the controls in the LaserJet II Printer Setup window.
About button	Displays a message box providing brief information about the printer driver, such as its version number.

141

After setting the printer options you want, choose the OK button or press Enter to save your changes and exit the Printer Setup window. Word returns to the Printer Setup dialog box. Choose the OK button or press Enter to save your changes and exit the Printer Setup dialog box.

Previewing Your Document Before Printing

Word's Print Preview feature provides a bird's eye view of one or two pages of your document as they will appear when printed. Because printing documents can take some time, especially if your document contains a lot of formatting, the Print Preview feature can save time by allowing you to check your document's layout before printing. In addition, you can reposition such formats as margins, headers, and/or footers while in the Print Preview mode. You can't edit or format text in the Print Preview mode. However, you can quickly access the Page view mode from the Print Preview window to make any text changes necessary. To display your document in Print Preview mode, choose the File/Print Preview command or press Alt,F,V. Word displays the Print Preview window, as shown in Figure 5.4.

The bar at the top of the Print Preview window provides command buttons for working in the Print Preview mode. Choose a command button by clicking on it or typing its underlined character; you don't need to press Alt to access these buttons. For example, to choose the Print command button, simply press *P*. Page Preview mode can display one or two pages of your document at a time. Choosing the Two Pages button or pressing *A* changes the screen from a one- to a two-page display, and the button label changes to One Page.

The vertical scroll bar, located at the right of the window, allows you to scroll through your document. Clicking on the Down or Up Arrow buttons in the scroll bar has the same effect as clicking below or above the thumb to move through the document one page at a time. Pressing the PgUp or PgDn keys accomplishes the same thing. The current page numbers are displayed in the upper right corner next to the Cancel button.

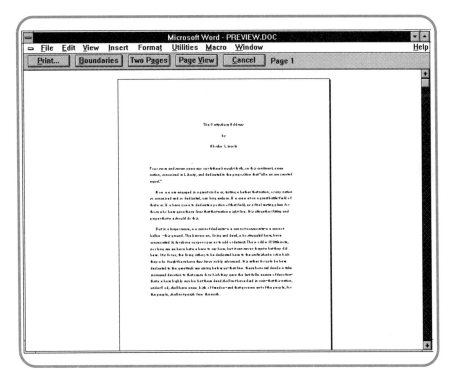

Figure 5.4   The Print Preview window.

143

The Print button activates the File/Print command. The Page View button changes the view of your document from Print Preview to the Page view mode, where you can edit text. Pressing the Cancel button or Esc ends the Print Preview session and returns you to the document. If you make any changes using the Boundaries feature, the Cancel button changes to a Close button. In the Print Preview window, you also have access to several menu commands, such as the Utilities/Repaginate Now and the Format/Document command. Menu commands not available to you in the Print Preview mode are dimmed.

Positioning Margins, Headers, and Footers in the Print Preview Mode

The Boundaries command button in the Print Preview window allows you to change your document's margins, headers, and footers.

Choosing the Boundaries button or pressing *B* displays lines representing your margins and displays rectangles or boxes for other formatting objects, such as headers, footers, and pictures. Any boxed object can be repositioned by moving the mouse pointer anywhere on the rectangle or box and dragging the mouse to the spot where you want to reposition the object. Using the mouse is the most efficient way to work with the Boundaries feature; however, you can also use the keyboard.

 Changing Margins by Using the Boundaries Command and the Mouse

1. In the Print Preview window, choose the Boundaries button or press *B*.

   Word displays the margins as dotted lines, as shown in Figure 5.5. The four dotted lines represent the top, bottom, right, and left page margins. The black square at one end of the margin line is called a *node*.

2. Move the mouse pointer to the node connected to the margin you want to change.

   The mouse pointer changes from an arrow to a crossbar.

3. Drag the node in the direction you want the margin to move.

   As you drag the margin node, notice that the location of the margin is displayed to the right of the buttons at the top of your screen.

4. Release the mouse button after positioning the margin.

5. Repeat steps 2, 3, and 4 for each margin you want to change.

6. Choose the Utilities/ Repaginate Now command or press Alt,U,P.

   Word repaginates your document based on your new margin settings.

7. Choose the <u>C</u>lose button or press *C*.

Word exits the Print Preview mode. The new page margins you create in the Print Preview window can be displayed in the Format Document dialog box after you exit the Print Preview mode. □

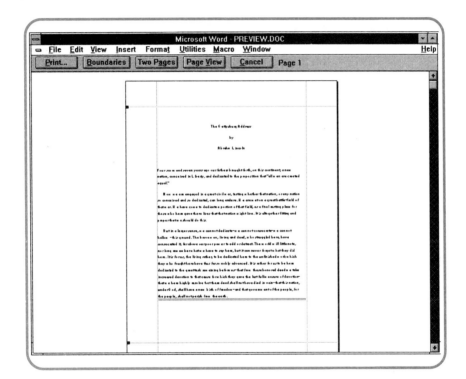

Figure 5.5   Margins displayed in the Print Preview window by using the <u>B</u>oundaries command.

You can reposition margins, headers, and footers in the Print Preview mode by using the keyboard. With the boundaries displayed, press the Tab key to move the highlight from object to object. The highlight is first located at the left margin. When highlighted, the margin disappears from the screen, and the mouse pointer changes to a crossbar indicating you're in reposition mode. Pressing the Tab key moves you to objects in the following order: top margin,

145

right margin, bottom margin, header, footer, page break, and then any other objects, such as pictures. Once you've highlighted the object you want, use the Arrow keys to move the object to where you want to reposition it. After repositioning the object, press Enter. Press *B* or click on Boundaries to leave the Boundaries mode.

Printing Your Document

You have the option of printing your entire document, a selected portion, or a specific range of pages. Word provides a number of additional printing options, such as printing in reverse order or draft mode. When you select the Print command, Word doesn't begin printing instantly. It first processes the document and sends special codes to control your printer; then your document starts printing. Generally, the longer the document and the more formatting it contains, the longer it takes to process and print.

146

If you've already selected the printer you want to use, choose the File/Print command (Alt,F,P) or use the keyboard shortcut, Ctrl-Shift-F12. Word displays the Print dialog box, as shown in Figure 5.6. The selected printer name appears at the top of the dialog box.

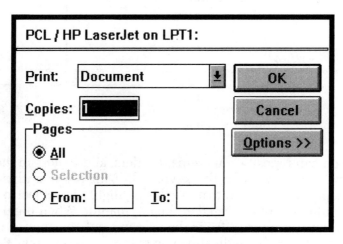

Figure 5.6   The Print dialog box.

To select another printer, first choose the File/Printer Setup command or press Alt,F,R. Word displays the Printer Setup dialog box, as shown in Figure 5.7. Choose the printer you want from the Printer list box by highlighting it, and then choose the OK button or press Enter. The Quick Steps explain how to print your *entire* document by using the File/Print command.

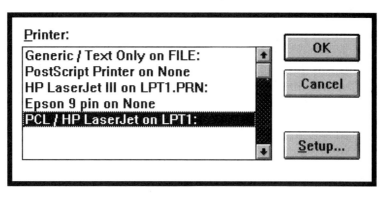

Figure 5.7   The Printer Setup dialog box.

147

Printing an Entire Document by Using the File/Print Command

1. Display the document you want to print. Choose the File/Print command or press Ctrl-Shift-F12 (or Alt,F,P).

    Word displays the Print dialog box. The Print list box by default displays the Document option, instructing Word to print the entire document.

2. Type the number of copies you want to print if different from the number displayed in the Copies text box.

    Notice in the Pages box that the default All option button is activated, indicating the whole document is to be printed.

3. Choose the OK button or press Enter.

    Word begins printing your document and displays a message in the status bar showing the page number currently being printed. Press Esc to cancel the printing request.   □

Printing Selected Parts of Your Document

To print a selected portion of text, select the text and then choose the File/Print command. Word activates the Selection option button in the Print dialog box. If you do not select any text, the Selection option button is dimmed. Choose the Selection option button or press Alt-S, and then choose the OK button or press Enter. Word prints only your selected text.

Word also allows you to specify a single page or range of pages to print. To do this, use the From and To text boxes in the Print dialog box. To print a single page, choose the From option button or press Alt-F. Type the page number you want to print. Then choose the To option button or press Alt-T. Type the same page number again, and then choose the OK button or press Enter. Word prints the single page you specified. If you want to print from a specified page to the end of your document, leave the To text box blank. To print a range of pages, simply type the first page number in the From text box and the last page number in the To text box. For example, to print only pages 5 through 10, enter 5 in the From text box and 10 in the To text box.

Additional Printing Options

Word allows you to specify several additional printing options by choosing the Options >> button or pressing Alt-O in the Print dialog box. Word displays an expanded Print dialog box, as shown in Figure 5.8.

Choosing the Reverse Print Order check box or pressing Alt-R begins the printing backwards, starting at the last page and continuing to the first page. This option is useful for printers that stack the pages face up as they are ejected. Choosing the Draft check box or pressing Alt-D prints the document without text formatting, such as boldface and italics. This option provides a faster way to print a document if you just want to review the text. Choosing the Paper Feed list box or pressing Alt-E allows you to select the paper source and the way paper is fed to your printer. Table 5.2 describes the available options.

148

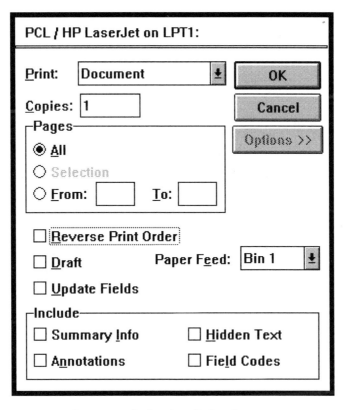

Figure 5.8   The expanded Print dialog box.

**Table 5.2   Printing Options Available from the Expanded
Print Dialog Box**

Option	Description
Auto	Feeds paper automatically (the default setting).This includes laser printers and tractor-feed printers that use continuous paper.
Manual	Stops printing at the end of every page. Depending on the printer you're using, Word may display a message (in the status line) asking you to press Y after inserting another piece of paper.
Bin 1	Designates the first paper bin of the printer as the primary paper source for printing. Usually this bin contains standard paper stock, such as 8 $\frac{1}{2}$" by 11".

(continued)

149

***Table* 5.2**   *(continued)*

Option	Description
Bin 2	Designates the second bin as the paper source for printing.
Bin 3	Designates the third bin as the paper source for printing.
Mixed	Prints the first page on paper from bin 1 and then the remainder of the document on paper from bin 2. This option is useful if you fill bin 1 with letterhead and bin 2 with blank second sheets.

The Include box provides a cluster of check box options for printing additional information from a document. Choosing the Summary Info check box or pressing Alt-I prints the document's summary information on a separate page after the document is printed. Choosing the Hidden Text check box or pressing Alt-H prints hidden text. Choosing the Annotations check box prints annotations at the end of the document. Choosing the Field Codes prints field codes that have been inserted in your document. Chapter 11 explains how to work with annotations and field codes.

150

Printing While Working on Other Documents

If you have the full version of Windows installed, you can take advantage of the Print Manager that controls a spooler. A *spooler* sets aside a memory buffer to store documents and send them to the printer. The spooler works by creating a temporary print file on your disk. It then sends the print file to a memory buffer and then to the printer. Using the Print Manager frees you to work on other documents while one or more files are being printed. For example, you can print several files in the order you've selected them. To cancel printing, press Esc. Besides the memory buffer that is controlled by the Print Manager, your printer most likely has a built-in memory buffer. So when you press Esc, your printing might not stop immediately; it must first clear the text stored in its printer buffer.

Controlling the Print Manager

Normally the Print Manager runs in the background. To view the Print Manager icon, minimize the Word Program window and the Windows Program Manager window after sending a document to the printer. If you double-click on the Print Manager icon, the Print Manager window is displayed, as shown in Figure 5.9. You can return to the Word program window at any time by double-clicking on the Word for Windows icon. The Print Manager window lists the active printer, its status, print jobs, percentage and size of the file sent to the printer, and the time and date the file was sent. To view the Print Manager without printing a file, select the Print Manager icon from the main window of Microsoft Windows.

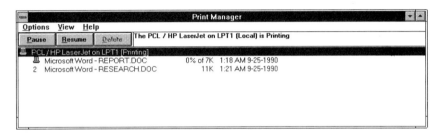

Figure 5.9   The Print Manager window.

The Print Manager window allows you to control the process of sending files to the printer. Three buttons appear above the file list: Pause, Resume, and Delete. The Pause button temporarily halts printing, and the Resume button continues printing. The Delete button is dimmed if the highlight is on the printer name. If you select a file, the Delete button becomes available. Clicking on the Delete button causes Word to display a message box. The message box requests verification that you want to terminate the printing of the selected file. Pressing Enter terminates the current print job.

The Options menu allows you to rearrange the printing order. Once you have several items in the spooler, you can change the print order by dragging up or down in the list the filename that you want to move. When you drag a print job to a new location, the insertion point turns into an arrow. When you release the mouse button, the print job is moved to its new location.

The brain of your computer, the microprocessor, is known as the central processing unit, or *CPU*. The CPU performs tasks so fast that it appears as if you're performing multiple tasks at once. When you use the Print Manager to print documents and use Word to edit another file, both operations are performed at once. To do this, the CPU must juggle between processing the printing requests from the Print Manager and executing the changes you're making to a document. This multitasking capability can slow down Word's response time when editing a file. The Print Manager lets you prioritize the amount of CPU time allocated between printing and working in Word. Here are the three priority options available from the Options menu in the Print Manager window:

Priority	CPU Time Division
Low	Reduces CPU time spent on printing.
Medium	The Word for Windows program and printing get equal CPU time (Windows default).
High	Gives printing the most CPU time.

> ▶ **Tip:** Printing in Word for Windows can be notoriously slow. Several print caching (memory buffer) programs are available that can accelerate printing beyond the speed of the Print Manager. *PrintCache* from LaserTools improves printing speed dramatically and works well with Word for Windows. This program can decrease the time it takes to print your file by two to four times.

The Print Manager allows you to determine how print status messages are displayed. This can be helpful if you want to ignore error messages or want to be alerted while working on another document. Here are the options for displaying or ignoring Print Manager error messages.

Error Message Option	What It Does
Alert Always	Word beeps and displays a dialog box.
Flash if Inactive	The Print Manager icon flashes. If the window is open but not active, the title bar in the window flashes. The Print Manager also sounds a beep to let you know there is a problem.

Error Message Option	What It Does
	When you open the icon or activate the window, the error message appears.
Ignore if Inactive	Printing stops if the Print Manager appears as an icon or if the Print Manager window is inactive.

> ▶ **Tip:** There are two ways to print multiple files: using the Document Retrieval window or using fields. The Document Retrieval window is covered in Chapter 8, "Managing Windows and Documents." Fields are covered in Chapter 9, "Saving Time with Glossaries, Macros, and Fields."

153

Printing to a File

Printing to a file is advantageous if you have one type of printer at home and another at the office, or if you are preparing documents to be laser-printed quickly at a print shop. When you print to a file, Word for Windows sends your file, including any special formatting codes, to a disk. The document can then be sent directly to the printer without using Word for Windows.

 Printing to a File

1. Choose the Control/Run command or press Alt,Spacebar,U.

Word displays the Run Application dialog box.

2. Click on the Control Panel option button or press Alt-P. Then click on the OK button or press Enter.

The Control Panel window appears.

3. Double-click on the Printers icon or press the Down Arrow and press Enter.

You see the Printers window.

154

4. Select the printer that will be used to print the file later by clicking on the printer name in the Installed Printers list box or by using the Arrow keys to move the highlight to the printer you want to use.

   Word highlights the selected printer.

5. Click on the Active option button in the Status box or press Alt-S and then the Up Arrow key.

   Word activates the printer that is highlighted in the Installed Printers list box.

6. Click on the Configure button or press Alt-C.

   Word displays the Printers-Configure window.

7. Click on the `FILE:` option in the Ports list box or use the Arrow keys to move the highlight to the `FILE:` option.

   This highlights the `FILE:` option in the Ports list box.

8. Click on the OK button in the Printers-Configure window or press Enter.

   Word selects `FILE:` as the active port and closes the Printers-Configure window.

9. Click on the OK button or press Enter to close the Printers window.

   The Printers window closes.

10. Choose the Control/Close command or press Alt-F4.

    The Control Panel window closes.

11. Choose the File/Print command or press Alt,F,P.

    Word prints the document to a file named FILE in your WINDOWS directory.   □

To print the file to the printer for which the file was set up, use the DOS COPY command to copy the file to the printer. For example, typing `copy file lpt1:` at the DOS prompt prints your file on the printer connected to the LPT1: port. The file containing the text and formats is copied to the printer as though you were sending the file directly from Word for Windows.

⊘ **Caution:** After printing to a file, make sure that you change the printer setting to another port by using the Control Panel. If you don't, the next time you print, the file named FILE will be overwritten instead of sending your document to your printer.

Using Soft Fonts

Windows comes with various fonts, including Helvetica, Times Roman, Script, Modern, Symbol, and Courier. These fonts are stored on your disk and are sent (downloaded) to the printer before printing. Any font stored on a disk and downloaded to a printer is called a *soft font*. Many companies, such as Adobe, BitStream, Hewlett-Packard, and ZSoft, sell soft fonts. Soft fonts, unlike cartridge fonts, must be downloaded before printing your document. The main drawback to soft fonts as opposed to cartridge fonts is that they take some time to download and they eat up disk space.

155

There are actually two types of printer fonts: bit-mapped and scalable. A *bit-mapped* printer font is made up of minute, dot-by-dot patterns. These patterns are stored in a special format for use by your printer. Bit-mapped fonts are point-size specific. For example, Times Roman 10 point is one font and Times Roman 12 another. A few printers, such as the LaserJet III and PostScript printers, can handle scalable printer fonts.

Scalable fonts save disk space and give you greater flexibility because, not being point-size specific, they contain a description of a character's design in mathematical form. When you download a scalable font, an outline of the characters is created according to the point size you indicate and then the characters are filled in. Many point sizes can be chosen from one scalable font. Word can scale most fonts from 4 to 127 points, which should be a suitable range for most documents.

Viewing and Adding Fonts

As mentioned earlier, there are two types of fonts: screen fonts and printer fonts. To see a list of your printer fonts and view their screen font equivalents, first choose the Control/Run command or press Alt,Spacebar,U. Next, choose the Control Panel option button or press Alt-P and then Enter to display the Control panel. Choosing the Fonts icon or pressing Right Arrow and then Enter displays the Fonts window, as shown in Figure 5.10. The Installed Fonts list box shows the available printer fonts. In the box at the bottom of the window, you can see samples of screen fonts that Word uses to display the selected printer font. Remember, if a screen font isn't available, Word uses one of its own screen fonts that most closely matches the printer font. The words All res that appear next to some fonts mean that the font can be displayed in any size from 4 to 127 points. If you are using the full version of Windows, you can add or remove fonts by using the Fonts window.

156

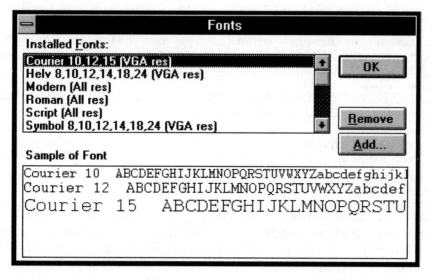

Figure 5.10   The Fonts window.

Adding a Font

1. Choose the Control/Run command or press Alt,Spacebar,U.

   The Run Application dialog box appears.

2. Choose the Control Panel option button or press Alt-P and then choose OK or press Enter.

   Word displays the Control Panel.

3. Double-click on the Fonts icon or use the Arrow keys to highlight the Fonts icon; then press Enter.

   The Fonts window appears as shown in Figure 5.10.

4. Click on the Add button or press Alt-A.

   You see the Add Font Files window.

5. Type the path name of the directory containing the font you want to add and press Enter.

   If you're adding a font from a disk, first insert the disk in a drive and then click on the drive name in the Directories list box.

6. Select the font from the list of fonts and click on the OK button or press Enter.

   The font is added. If the font is already installed, Word displays the message `Font already installed.` □

157

Deleting a font is done in the same manner, but instead of using the Add button, choose the Remove button.

> ⊘ **Caution:** Don't remove the fonts named `Helv` (short for Helvetica) or `System`. These fonts are used to display the characters in dialog boxes on your screen.

Permanently Downloading Fonts

Before printing your document, Word searches it for any text that is formatted using soft fonts. If Word finds a soft font, it downloads the font into your printer's memory before printing your document. This saves time so that Word can quickly print your document rather than loading fonts each time it comes across one. You can add a font so that it is downloaded when you first start your computer, rather than each time you print a document, as explained in the following section.

Downloading soft fonts for the current printing job only, is known as *temporarily* downloading fonts. You can download fonts *permanently*, too. Then, every time you turn on your computer (after turning on your printer), the fonts are sent and stored in your printer's memory, until you turn off your printer. Permanently downloading fonts in Word changes your AUTOEXEC.BAT file (a file that initializes your computer). The next time you start your computer, you're asked whether to download the fonts to your printer. Pressing Y for Yes copies the fonts to your printer's memory.

158

⊘ **Caution:** Not all font packages work in conjunction with Word for Windows Font Installer. If downloadable fonts do not appear in the Fonts window, check the documentation that accompanied your downloadable fonts program.

🅠 Downloading a Soft Font Permanently

1. Choose the File/Printer Setup command or press Alt,F,R.

   The Printer dialog box appears.

2. Make sure that the printer to which you want fonts automatically downloaded is highlighted. Then choose the Setup button or press Alt-S.

   Word displays the Printer window.

3. Choose the Fonts button or press Alt-F.

   The Printer Install Fonts window appears.

4. Click on a font name in the list box, or use the Up or Down Arrow key to move to a font you want to download permanently. To highlight the font, press Ctrl-Spacebar from the keyboard.

   Select only one font at a time.

5. Click on the <u>P</u>ermanent option button or press Alt-P.

A dialog box appears, identifying the number of the permanent font selected. The Permanent option button is darkened, and a tiny x appears before the selected font.

6. Choose the E<u>x</u>it button or press Alt-X.

You see a dialog box with two check boxes: Download <u>n</u>ow and Download at <u>s</u>tartup. Keep both options turned on (checked).

7. Choose the OK button or press Enter for each remaining window and dialog box.

Word prints a list of the permanently downloaded fonts. The next time you start your computer, you're asked whether to download the permanent fonts.   □

159

Copying Fonts from One Port to Another

When you set up a LaserJet or compatible printer, a button labeled <u>F</u>onts appears in the Printer Setup window. Choosing this button displays the Printer Font Installer window. This window displays the option <u>C</u>opy between ports. Remember, fonts are directly related to the printer driver you're using. When you use any font installation program, you are asked which port your printer is using. The printer driver is either created or updated to handle the new fonts. If you add fonts to one printer on printer port LPT1:, and you have different fonts on a printer using the port LPT2:, the fonts are available only for the port for which you created the printer driver. If you want another printer driver to have access to a font available on a different printer driver, highlight the fonts you want to copy and choose the <u>C</u>opy between ports option. The Copy between ports window is displayed. In the Select <u>p</u>ort list box, choose the port you want to copy to and choose the OK button or press Enter.

Installing an Additional Printer

During the Word for Windows installation process, the Setup program installed the printer drivers for the printers you specified. You can add other printers for use with Word for Windows. If a printer driver is not available in the list provided with Word, you cannot print through either Windows or Word except by using a generic printer driver. In Word, the generic printer driver is TTY.DRV. Using this printer driver means that most formatting in a document will not print. If your printer can emulate other printers, such as IBM ProPrinter or Epson for dot matrix printers, you can select these options if your printer isn't listed.

 Installing a Printer

1. Choose the Control/Run command or press Alt,Spacebar,U.

   Word displays the Run Application dialog box.

2. Choose the Control Panel option button or press Alt-P and click on the OK button or press Enter.

   Word displays the Control Panel.

3. Double-click on the Printers icon or use the Arrow keys to highlight the Printers icon and then press Enter.

   Word displays the Printers window.

4. Choose the Add Printer >> button or press Alt-A.

   Word displays the expanded Printers window, as shown in Figure 5.11.

5. Click on the scroll bar to move through the list, and then click on the printer you want to install, or press the Down or Up Arrow key to highlight the printer you want to install.

   The printer name is highlighted.

6. Click on the Install button or press Alt-I.

Word displays a dialog box indicating which original Windows or Word for Windows disk contains the printer driver file for the printer you've selected. Word suggests the name of a drive to insert the disk into. If the suggested drive is incorrect, change it by typing the new drive, such as B:\.

7. Insert the specified disk in the drive indicated and choose the OK button or press Enter.

Word copies the printer driver to your Windows or Word for Windows direc-tory. The printer is then displayed and highlighted in the Installed Printers list box. Don't exit the Printers window until you configure your printer, as explained in the following section. □

161

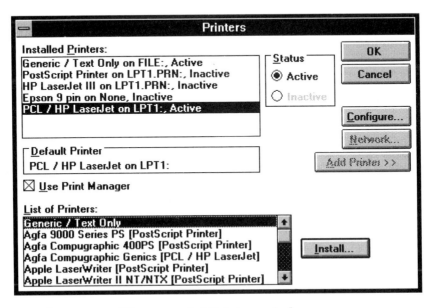

Figure 5.11   The expanded Printers window.

Configuring and Activating Your Printer

Once you've installed a printer driver, you're ready to configure and activate it. To configure a printer, you need to assign a printer port to it. Word provides several printer port options. A *printer port* is an interface (connector) between your computer and your printer.

There are two types of printer ports: parallel and serial. Parallel ports are designated as LPT, which stands for line printer. Serial ports are designated as COM, which stands for communications. Because most computers have more than one of either of these types of ports, each port is assigned a number by DOS, for example, LPT1, LPT2, or COM1, COM2. Most dot matrix printers are parallel printers connected to an LPT port. Laser printers come in both parallel (LPT) and serial (COM) configurations. Word allows you to connect multiple printers. You can assign multiple printers to the same printer port; however, only one can be active at a time.

162

Q Configuring and Activating Your Printer

1. In the Printers window, choose the Configure button or press Alt-C.

   Word displays the Printers-Configure window, as shown in Figure 5.12.

2. Click on the printer port to which you want your printer output sent, or press the Down or Up Arrow key to highlight the printer port.

   Remember, you can assign multiple printers to a port, but only one printer can be active on a port at a time. The Timeouts (seconds) options affect error message response time and don't need to be changed.

3. Choose the OK button or press Enter.

   Word redisplays the Printers window.

4. If your installed printer is inactive, choose the Active option button in the Status box or press Alt-S and then press Up Arrow.

   Word changes the status of your installed printer to active and changes to inactive the former active printer sharing the same printer port.

5. Choose the OK button or press Enter.

   Word completes the configuration of your printer.

6. Choose the Control/Close command or press Alt-F4 (or Alt,Spacebar,C).

The Control Panel window closes. You can now return to the Word program window and use the File/ Printer Setup command to set up your printer. □

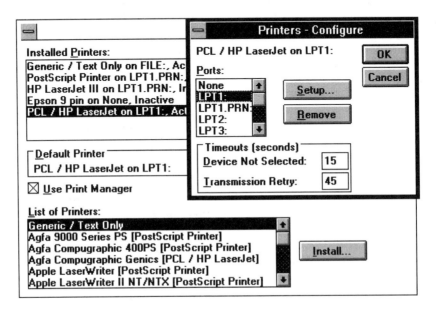

Figure 5.12   The Printers-Configure window.

Removing a Printer

You can remove an installed printer driver by first highlighting the printer driver you want to remove in the Installed Printers list box in the Printers window. Next, choose the Configure button or press Alt-C. Word displays the Printers-Configure window. Choose the Remove button or press Alt-R. Word displays a message box asking for confirmation to remove the printer driver. Choose the Yes button or press Alt-Y to delete the printer driver. Choose the No button if you decide you *don't* want to remove the driver. Word returns to the Printers window. If you've deleted a printer driver and want to restore it, choose the Cancel button in the Printers window or press Esc.

163

Troubleshooting Common Printer Problems

Many of the problems that beginning users of Word for Windows have are printer problems. If Word displays a message that your printer is printing and nothing seems to be happening, use the following checklist to troubleshoot the problem:

1. First check to make sure that your printer is plugged in and that the cables are connected to both your computer and your printer.

2. Make sure your printer's On-line light is on. If not, press the button or switch that toggles your printer on- or off-line.

3. Make sure there is paper in your printer and that it isn't jammed. If you are using a daisy wheel printer, make sure that the print wheel is mounted correctly and that you're not out of ribbon. If you're using a laser printer, make sure there is a toner cartridge installed. Also, make sure the printer cover is in place; most printers cannot print with their covers lifted.

4. Make sure you have selected the correct printer driver for your printer. Printer drivers are not interchangeable. If you are printing on a dot matrix printer, you cannot use a laser printer driver.

5. Check the printer setup to make sure the correct printer and port are active. If the Printers Setup dialog box indicates that the printer is on the port None, your printer will not work until you change it to the correct port. If you are using a Serial printer connection, double-check your CONFIG.SYS file to make sure that it contains the correct MODE settings. (For more information on the MODE command, see your DOS manual or any good book on DOS.)

6. Many printers perform self tests that print out a sample of available fonts. Try running the self test to see whether Word for Windows is causing the problem or whether your printer is. If your printer works fine, try printing from DOS. If you're using a parallel connection, try using the following command to test your printer. At the DOS prompt, type `dir>lpt1:`. If your current directory prints, then your problem is in Word for Windows.

7. If you're using a dot matrix printer and you can print from DOS but not from Word for Windows, try configuring your printer using the OS/2 option in the Ports list box of the Printers-Configure window. The OS/2 port sends text to your printer through DOS and may solve the problem.

8. Check to make sure that your AUTOEXEC.BAT file includes the line SET TEMP=C:\ or that the TEMP variable is set to another available drive. If this line does not appear in your AUTOEXEC.BAT file, use Word for Windows to open the AUTOEXEC.BAT file and choose OK to select the default Text option when opening the file. Be sure to accept the default conversion Text file. If you select another format, your machine will not boot (start) correctly. Once the file is displayed, add the line and save the file by using the File/Save command. Word saves the file in a Text format.

9. Turn off the spooler by displaying the Control Panel and choosing the Printers icon. Click on the Use Print Manager check box setting, or press Alt-U so that the check box appears empty.

10. If you don't have enough printer memory, Word gives you a message telling you that Word for Windows cannot print. If this happens, make sure no other programs are running except Windows and Word for Windows, and try again. There also must be enough disk space available for the Print Manager to spool your file to disk. If Word displays a message stating that there isn't enough disk space to print your document, delete some unused files and try again.

165

What You Have Learned

▶ To set up a printer, use the File/Printer Setup command.

▶ To get a bird's eye view of how your document will print, use the File/Print Preview command. In Print Preview mode, you can reposition margins, headers, and footers by using the Boundaries command.

▶ Using the File/Print command, you can print your entire document, a selection, or a range of pages.

▶ The Print Manager lets you control your printing jobs. For example, you can rearrange the print order of your documents or stop documents from being printed.

▶ By choosing the FILE: option in the Ports list box, located in the Printers-Configure window, you can print to a file. This is handy when you later want to print using another type of printer.

▶ You can permanently download soft fonts by choosing the File/Printer Setup command (Alt,F,R), choosing the Setup button (Alt-S), and then choosing the Fonts button (Alt-F).

▶ To install, configure, or activate additional printers, use the Control Panel's Printer window.

166

Chapter 6

More Formatting Features

In This Chapter

- ► *Adding special characters to your document*
- ► *Creating bulleted or numbered lists*
- ► *Inserting and working with footnotes*
- ► *Automatically inserting hyphens in your document*
- ► *Inserting and formatting sections of your document*
- ► *Numbering paragraphs and lines*
- ► *Adding gutter and mirror margins to documents*

In Chapter 5 you learned basic formatting techniques. In this chapter you'll expand your formatting skills so that you can further enhance and refine the appearance of your documents.

Adding Special Characters

A *character set* is a grouping of alphabetic, numeric, and other characters that match the design of the selected font. The characters might include special symbols such as math symbols, editing marks, and foreign characters. A typical character set has 190 to 256 characters; that is more characters than appear on your keyboard.

To enter these additional special characters, hold down the Alt key, press 0 (zero) on the numeric keypad, and then enter a three-digit number that indicates the character you want. For example, to insert the copyright symbol into your document, type 0169 on the numeric keypad while holding down the Alt key.

To view a listing of the default (ANSI) character set and each character's corresponding decimal number, check the User's Reference Guide that comes with Word. Table 6.1 lists some of the characters that are most useful in embellishing a document.

168

Table 6.1   ANSI Codes for Adding Special Characters

Description	Code	Character
Single open quotation	0145	'
Single closing quotation	0146	'
Double opening quotation	0147	"
Double closing quotation	0148	"
Bullet	0149	•
Em dash	0150	—
En dash	0151	–
Cent sign	0162	¢
Copyright symbol	0169	©
Registered trademark	0174	®
Degree sign	0176	°
One-quarter	0188	$\frac{1}{4}$
One-half	0189	$\frac{1}{2}$
Three-quarters	0190	$\frac{3}{4}$

Q Adding Special Characters to Your Document

1. Press the Num Lock key.   NUM appears in the status bar.

2. Hold down the Alt key.

3. Press 0 (zero) on the numeric keypad.	The zero isn't displayed in your document.
4. On the numeric keypad, type the character's decimal number.	The numbers aren't displayed in your document.
5. Release the Alt key.	The special character appears in your document. □

> **Tip:** Included with Word is a file that lists special symbols that can be added to a document. To view this assortment of characters and to see which key to press for a symbol, open the KEYCAPS.DOC file located in the WINWORD directory.

To add fonts not in the default (ANSI) character set, you need a separate font package and a printer driver file that contain the necessary font instructions to print the additional characters. If you want to display these characters, you'll also need to install the additional screen fonts. Refer to the documentation that accompanies your additional fonts to determine which key inserts the character you want.

169

Creating Bulleted or Numbered Lists

In Chapter 4 you learned about hanging indents and tabs. These are the principal elements used to create bulleted or numbered lists. To set a hanging indent, first select the paragraph and choose the Format/Paragraph command or press Alt,T,P. Then, in the From Left text box, type a measurement for the left indent. Next, in the First Line text box, type a measurement less than the left indent. This specifies how far the first line will "hang" to the left over the rest of the text. Finally, choose OK or press Enter to apply the hanging indent format to the selected paragraph. Figure 6.1 shows sample bulleted and numbered lists. The Quick Steps explain how to create a bulleted list by using a combination of mouse and keyboard techniques.

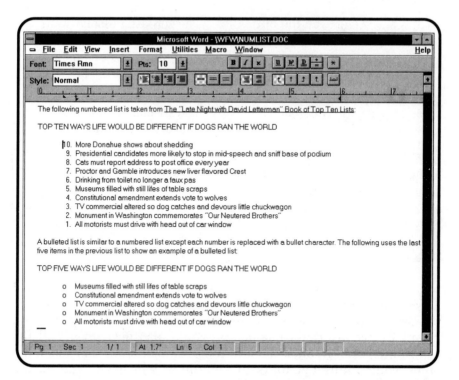

Figure 6.1   Sample bulleted and numbered lists.

Creating a Bulleted List

1. Choose Format/Paragraph or press Alt,T,P.

   Word displays the Paragraph dialog box.

2. Choose the First Line text box or press Alt-N. Enter .50" and choose the OK button or press Enter.

   The first line indent appears at the .50-inch mark on the Ruler.

3. On the Ruler, click on the Left Align Tab button (the first Up Arrow) and then click just below the ³/₄-inch mark on the Ruler to set the tab.

   The left indent mark is aligned with the left align tab at the ³/₄-inch mark on the Ruler.

4. Hold down the Shift key and drag the left indent marker (the lower indent marker) to the $^3/_4$-inch mark (on top of the left-aligned tab).

Word indents the text following the hanging indent, aligning it with the first-line text that follows the tab, as shown in Figure 6.1.

5. With Num Lock active, hold down the Alt key and type 0149 (on the numeric keypad).

Releasing the Alt key inserts a bullet.

6. Press the Tab key.

Word leaves space between the bullet character and your text.

7. Type your text.

Your text appears to the right of the bullet.

8. Press Enter and repeat steps 5 through 7 for each additional item in the bulleted list.

Word adds the additional bullets and text to your list.

9. Press Enter and then press Ctrl-X.

Word returns you to your normal paragraph format. □

171

> **Tip:** You can create a bulleted list by typing a bullet (Alt-0149), pressing Tab, pressing Ctrl-T, and entering the rest of the text for the bulleted list. Word uses the first default tab for the indent unless you've set another tab. You can extend the indent to the next tab by pressing Ctrl-T. To decrease the amount of the indent, press Ctrl-G.

Footnotes

Footnotes are statements that amplify a remark in a document or provide a reference for verification. Footnotes are separated from the main text to avoid interrupting the flow of the subject matter. A *footnote marker* is inserted in the main body of text to inform the reader that a footnote exists related to the preceding text. The footnotes are usually sequentially numbered and placed at the bottom of the page, or they can be placed collectively at the end of a chapter or document.

Word, by default, uses numbered footnote markers and places footnotes at the foot (bottom) of the page. If there is not enough space on the page for all the footnote text, Word continues printing the footnote at the bottom of the next page. To separate footnote text from the document text, Word prints a line 2 inches long between them called a *separator*. When footnote text spills over to the next page, Word prints a margin-to-margin line called a *continuation separator* line. Word provides a number of options for working with footnotes and customizing footnote markers, separators, and the placement of footnote text. To view the positioning of your footnotes, use the File/Print Preview command.

Inserting Footnotes

172

Inserting a footnote involves two steps: inserting a footnote marker in the text and then typing the footnote text. You insert a footnote marker in the text where you want to reference the footnote. When you insert a footnote mark, Word displays the Footnote pane if you're using the Draft or Normal view modes, as shown in Figure 6.2. The Footnote pane is where you enter your footnote text. If you're using the Page view mode, Word doesn't display a Footnote pane. Instead, Word places the insertion point at the bottom of the page for entering the footnote text. The Quick Steps explain how to insert footnotes in your document by using the Footnote pane and Word's default settings.

Q **Inserting Footnotes in Your Document**

1. Position the insertion point where you want to insert the footnote marker in your text.

2. Choose the Insert/Footnote command or press Alt,I,N.

   Word displays the Footnote dialog box, as shown in Figure 6.3.

3. Choose the OK button or press Enter.

   Word inserts a footnote marker and opens the Footnote pane.

4. Type and format your footnote text.

   You can apply paragraph and character formats to footnote text in the same way that you do in documents.

5. To add additional footnotes, press F6 or click in the document window. Repeat steps 1 through 5 for each additional footnote you want.

6. After entering footnotes, choose the View/Footnotes command or press Alt,V,F to close the Footnote pane.

Word closes the Footnote pane. You can also close the Footnote pane by dragging the split box to the top or bottom of the scroll bar. The split box is located just above the Up Arrow button in the Footnote pane's scroll bar. Remember, to view the positioning of your footnotes, choose the File/Print Preview command. □

173

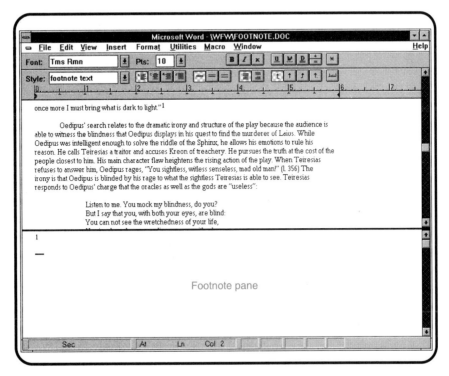

Figure 6.2 The Footnote pane.

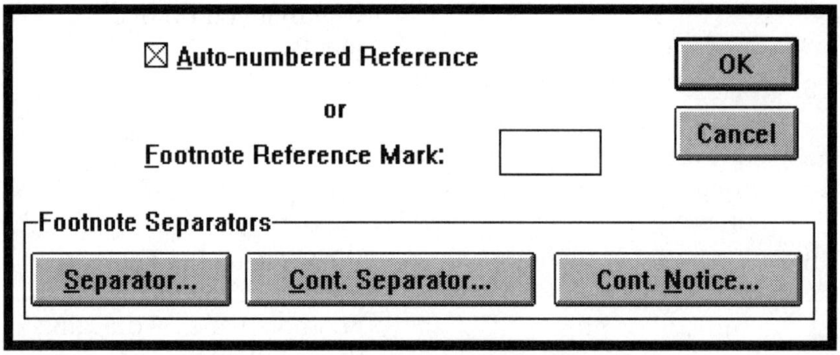

Figure 6.3   The Footnote dialog box.

When you type footnote text, the font size of the footnote text is the same as the font size of your document, unless you change it. You may want to shrink the size of your footnote font so that more text can be fit into the footnotes and so that the footnotes can be easily distinguished from the document text. To quickly change the font size of all the footnotes in your document, move the mouse pointer in the selection bar of the Footnote pane (between the left margin and your text). Hold down the Ctrl key and click the left mouse button. Then choose a smaller font size from the Pts list box on the Ribbon.

Working with Footnotes

Word provides a number of tools to make working with footnotes a smooth process. Choosing the View/Footnotes command or pressing Alt,V,F displays the Footnote pane that displays all the footnotes. In the Footnote pane, you can scroll through your document's footnotes. As you scroll through footnote text, the document text automatically scrolls to match the location of the footnote marker in your document. You can edit the footnote text as you would any text in the document.

To search for a specific footnote marker in your document, choose the Edit/Go To command, press Alt,E,G, or simply press F5. In the Go To text box, enter F followed by the number of the footnote you want to find, and then choose the OK button or press Enter. If you press F5, the Go To prompt appears in the Status bar. For example, entering F10 and pressing Enter instructs Word to jump to the number 10 footnote marker.

To delete both the footnote marker and the footnote text at the same time, select the footnote marker in your document and then press the Del key. Word deletes the marker and the associated footnote text. Word automatically renumbers your footnotes to reflect the deleted footnote. If you delete the text of a footnote in the Footnote pane, the footnote mark remains in your document until you remove it.

To move a footnote, select the footnote marker and then remove the marker by choosing the Edit/Cut command (Alt,E,T) or by pressing Shift-Del. Move the insertion point to the spot where you want to reposition the footnote, and then choose the Edit/Paste command (Alt,E,P) or press Shift-Ins. Word automatically renumbers your footnotes to reflect the change. To copy a footnote, select the footnote marker and then choose the Edit/Copy command (Alt,E,C) or press Ctrl-Ins. Position the insertion point at the spot where you want the copied footnote to be, and then choose the Edit/Paste command (Alt,E,P) or press Shift-Ins. Word automatically renumbers your footnotes to reflect the additional footnote.

175

Setting Footnote Printing Locations

By default, Word prints your footnotes at the bottom of the page where they're referenced. However, Word provides other choices for positioning your footnotes. To select footnote position options, choose the Format/Document command. Then choose the Print at list box, shown in Figure 6.4. Here are the options for footnote locations:

Footnote Location Options	Description
Bottom of Page	Prints the footnote at the bottom of each page within a fixed space allocated by Word, ending at the bottom margin (the default setting).
Beneath Text	Prints the footnote directly beneath the text in the document until the footnote text reaches the bottom margin.
End of Section	Prints the footnote at the end of each section regardless of where the section ends.

End of Document

Prints all the footnotes from your document at the end of the document after the text.

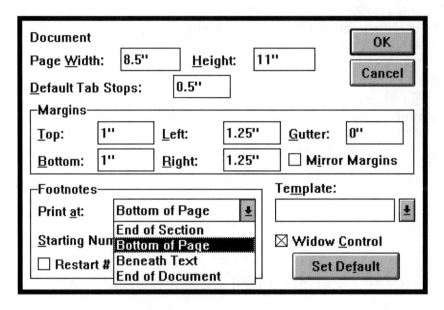

Figure 6.4   The Document dialog box.

The Quick Steps explain how to position footnotes so that they print at the end of a document.

Q Setting Footnotes to Print at the End of a Document

1. Choose the Format/Document command or press Alt,T,D.

   Word displays the Document dialog box.

2. Choose the Print at list box or press Alt-A.

   The Print at list box becomes active.

3. Click on the Arrow button or press Alt-Down Arrow.

   Word displays the list of footnote printing options.

4. Click or press the Down Arrow to highlight the End of Document option.

   Word highlights the End of Document option.

5. Choose the OK button or press Enter.

   Word is set up to print your footnotes at the end of your document.   □

The Footnotes box in the Document dialog box provides two additional options: the Starting Number text box and the Restart # Each Section check box. Choosing the Starting Number text box sets the starting number for your footnote markers (the default is 1). For example, if you enter 10, the footnote markers begin numbering at 10. Choosing the Restart # Each Section check box instructs Word to reset the footnote counter, beginning at each new section of your document. Section formatting is explained later in this chapter.

Changing Footnote Markers and Separators

In a small document with just a few footnotes, you may want to mark the footnote with an asterisk or some other symbol instead of using Word's default numbered markers. You can change footnote markers one at a time. Choose the Insert/Footnote command or press Alt,I,N. Word displays the Footnote dialog box. Type the symbol you want in the Footnote Reference Mark text box and then choose the OK button or press Enter. Word inserts the symbol you've entered as the footnote reference mark. Word returns to the default numbering format after you apply the new footnote marker. To insert additional special footnote markers, you must repeat this action for each footnote entry.

177

Word allows you to change the characters used to separate document text from footnote text. To change Word's default separators, choose the Insert/Footnotes command or press Alt,I,N. Word displays the Footnotes dialog box. Select the separator option you want to change by choosing either the Separator (Alt-S), the Cont. Separator (Alt-C), or the Cont. Notice (Alt-N) button. Word displays the pane with the default entry displayed. Make the appropriate change and then choose the Close button or press Alt-C.

Adding Hyphens to Your Document

By inserting an *optional hyphen* at the end of a line, you can clean up the ragged right edge of the text in your document. Recall that, because of Word's built-in wordwrap feature, a word wraps to the next line if it doesn't fit in the available line space. Adding hyphens creates a more visually balanced document and is particularly useful if you've created multiple columns of text in a document, as explained later in this chapter. To insert an optional hyphen, press Ctrl-Hyphen. Later, should you enter or edit text that causes both parts of the hyphenated word to be placed on the same line, Word will automatically remove the hyphen. An optional hyphen looks like the character " if the Show All feature is turned on.

> ▶ **Tip:** To move the Hyphenate window to a different position on your screen, move the mouse pointer to the window's title bar and drag the window to the new location; then release the mouse button.

178

Word provides a way to automatically insert optional hyphens throughout your entire document or a selected part of the document at one time. Using the Utilities/Hyphenate command, Word automatically inserts optional hyphens in your documents based on hyphenation breaks provided by Word's main dictionary. You can instruct Word to automatically hyphenate your document or to display a suggested hyphen position for confirmation or editing. Word inserts hyphens from the insertion point downward to the end of your document or selected text. Choose the Utilities/Hyphenate command or press Alt,U,H to display the Hyphenate window, as shown in Figure 6.5. Here are the options available in the Hyphenate window:

Hyphenate Window Options	Description
Hyphenate at text box	Displays the word to be hyphenated and Word's proposed hyphenation of the word when the Confirm check box is turned on (the default setting).
Hyphenate Caps check box	Instructs Word to hyphenate words that are in all capitals when this option is turned on (the default setting) or to exclude them when it is turned off.
Confirm check box	Instructs Word to display each proposed hyphenation

to allow you to accept, reject, or edit the proposed hyphenation when this option is turned on (the default setting). Turning this option off instructs Word to automatically hyphenate your document without asking for confirmation.

Hot Zone text box — Defines the distance between the right indent or margin and the end of the line where no hyphenation can occur. If the space available is greater than the Hot Zone space, Word tries to hyphenate the first word on the following line to bring it up to the previous line. Word's default setting is ¹/₄ inch (.25"). The smaller the Hot Zone measurement, the less ragged the right edge of text appears.

179

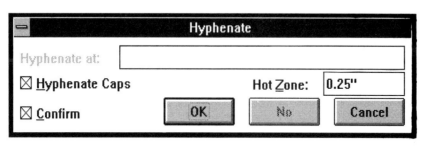

Figure 6.5   The Hyphenate window.

Adding and Confirming Hyphenation

In most cases, you'll want to keep the Confirm option turned on when using the Utilities/Hyphenate command. Having the Confirm option on allows you more control and flexibility when Word is inserting hyphens. As explained earlier, when Word finds a word to hyphenate and the Confirm check box is turned on, Word proposes a hyphenation for the word in the Hyphenate <u>a</u>t text box, as shown in Figure 6.6. The hyphenation is based on the syllable information provided by Word's dictionary. At that point, you have the option of accepting Word's suggested hyphenation break, rejecting it, or changing the hyphen location.

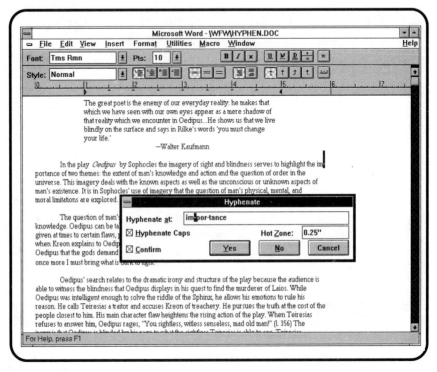

Figure 6.6   A word displayed in the Hyphenate <u>a</u>t text box.

You can hyphenate a word between any two letters; you don't have to break it between syllables. If you place the insertion point somewhere other than at a syllable break, Word displays the insertion point as a thin vertical line. The dimmed vertical line that appears in the word indicates the approximate number of characters that will fit on the current line. If you try to hyphenate the word to the right of the dotted line (i.e., the Hot <u>Z</u>one), there will not be enough room on the previous line to hold the first part of the hyphenated word. Word still inserts the optional hyphen in your document; however, the word break appears only if it is pushed to the end of the line.

Hyphenating a Document with Confirmations

1. Press Ctrl-Home.

   The insertion point moves to the beginning of your document.

2. Choose the Utilities/Hyphen-ate command or press Alt,U,H.

   Word displays the Hyphen-ate window.

3. Choose the OK button or press Enter.

   Word begins the hyphen-ation session and displays the first proposed hyphen-ation. Word's proposed hyphenation break appears as a highlighted rectangle, as shown in Figure 6.6.

4. Choose the Yes button or press Enter to confirm the suggested hyphenation.

   Choosing the No button skips the proposed hyphen-ation. To edit the sugges-tion, use the Left or Right Arrow key or the mouse to select a new hyphenation point. Then choose the Yes button or press Enter. Word continues to the next proposed hyphenation.

5. Repeat step 4 for each addi-tional suggested hyphenation.

   After Word finishes the hyphenation session, the Hyphenate window disap-pears. Pressing Esc cancels the hyphenation session. □

181

Nonbreaking Hyphens and Spaces

In addition to the commonly used optional hyphen, Word provides two other features for keeping word groups together: nonbreaking hyphens and nonbreaking spaces. For example, suppose you have a string of words connected by hyphens that you don't want Word to break up at the end of a line, such as *seventy-five*. You can use nonbreaking hyphens to keep words together on a line. To insert a nonbreaking hyphen, press Ctrl-Shift-Hyphen.

If you have two or more words you don't want Word to break up at the end of a line, such as *John Doe* or *New York,* you can use nonbreaking spaces instead of regular spaces to keep words together on a line. To insert a nonbreaking space, press Ctrl-Shift-Spacebar. A degree sign ( ) appears, indicating a nonbreaking space, if you've turned on the Show All button on the Ribbon.

Section Formatting

With Word, you can give part of your document a different page layout from the rest of the document. Simply separate that part into a different section and then apply the formats you want to the section. For example, you may want part of your document to be in two columns and part in single-column format. By default, Word treats your entire document as a section until you insert additional sections.

Creating and formatting a section is a two-step process. The first step involves defining the section, such as part of a page or an entire page, by using the Insert/Break command. The second step involves formatting the section by using the features in the Format/Section command.

Creating a Section Break

To create a section, simply place the insertion point where you want the previous section to end and the new section to begin. Then choose the Insert/Break command or press Alt,I,B. Word displays the Insert Break dialog box, as shown in Figure 6.7. The Section Break dialog box provides four section-break options. Each of these section-break options determines where the next section starts. Here are the options:

Section-Break Option	Description
Next Page	Starts a new section at the top of a new page (the default).
Continuous	Starts a new section on the same page.

Even Page

Starts the new section at the top of a new even-numbered page, leaving a blank odd-numbered page if necessary.

Odd Page

Starts the new section at the top of a new odd-numbered page, leaving a blank, even-numbered page if necessary.

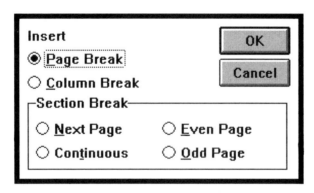

Figure 6.7   The Insert Break dialog box.

183

After selecting the section break you want, choose the OK button or press Enter. The Break dialog box closes, and the section break is inserted at the insertion point. The section break appears in your document as a double-dotted line extending across your document window in the Draft or Normal view modes. The section break marker contains all the formatting for the section that *precedes* it. To view the section break marker in the Page or Print Preview mode, choose the View/Preferences command and select the Text Boundaries option.

The section break marker is a character that you can select, copy, paste, and delete. When you copy or move a section break marker, you are copying or moving the section formatting. If you delete a section marker, all the text preceding the marker converts to the formatting of the following section. The status bar shows you the section number in which the insertion point is located, for example, Sec 1, Sec 2, Sec 3.

To create a continuous section break within a document, you must insert a section break to preserve the formatting above the section you want to insert. For example, if you want to create a double-column section on the same page as single-column text, first insert a continuous section break where you want the single-column text to end. Next, move the insertion point below the text you want to format as double column and insert another continuous section break. Remember, a section break marker contains the formatting for the section preceding it. The first continuous section marker you inserted is for the single-column text you want to preserve. The second section break is for the section you want to format as double-column text.

If you later want to change the starting point of the section, choose the Format/Section command (Alt,T,S) or double-click on the section break marker. Word displays the Format Section dialog box, as shown in Figure 6.8. To change a section starting point, choose the Section Start list box or press Alt-E. Click on the Down Arrow button or press Alt-Down Arrow to display the available Section Start options:

Section Start Option	Description
New Page	Starts on the next page.
Even Page	Starts on the next even-numbered page.
Odd Page	Starts on the next odd-numbered page.
New Column	Starts in the next column after a column break.
No Break	Starts immediately after the current section.

Creating Columns

Using the Format/Section command, you can create multiple equal-width columns within a section. Text in these columns flows from the bottom of one column to the top of the next. This type of column is called a *snaking column* and is frequently used in newsletters. Although you can set the number of columns before you type text in a section, generally it's easier to type all the text and then format it into columns. This technique makes it easier to see how the column width and the space between columns looks on a page. Word automatically figures out the width of the columns by subtracting the space between the columns (the default is ¹/₂ inch) from the width of the text area and dividing the remaining space by the number of columns you've selected.

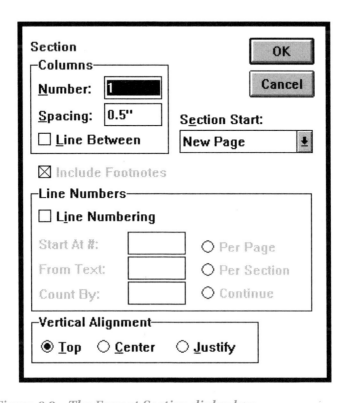

Figure 6.8   The Format Section dialog box.

You can't see multiple columns in the Normal or the Draft views, which display the multicolumn text as a single narrow column. You need to use the Page view or Print Preview to view multiple columns. The Page view allows you to view and edit the text in multiple columns. You can apply paragraph and character formatting to text in columns just as you do to a regular document.

 Creating Multiple Columns in a Section

1. Place the insertion point in the section where you want to create multiple columns of text.

185

2. Choose the Format/Section command (Alt,T,S) or double-click on the section marker.

The Format Section dialog box appears.

3. In the Number text box, type the number of columns you want.

The Number text box displays the number of columns you entered.

4. To change the default column spacing of ¹/₂ inch, choose the Spacing text box, or press Alt-S and enter the measurement you want.

5. To instruct Word to draw a line between your columns, choose the Line Between check box or press Alt-L.

Word draws a vertical line between your columns.

6. Choose the OK button or press Enter.

Word formats the section to reflect the number of columns you specified. Figure 6.9 shows two columns with a line between them in Page view mode. □

Changing Column Widths

While you can adjust your column widths and the spacing between columns by using the Format/Section command, an easier way to change column widths is to use the Ruler. As explained earlier, Word formats columns in equal widths. Any change you make to one column width adjusts all the columns. The Quick Steps explain how to use the Ruler to adjust column widths and spacing.

Q Changing Text Column Widths by Using the Ruler

1. Move the insertion point into the section where you want to change the column width.

2. Choose the View/Page command or press Alt,V,P.

Word displays your multicolumn text as it will print.

3. If the Ruler is not displayed, choose the <u>V</u>iew/<u>R</u>uler command or press Alt,V,R.

Word displays the Ruler.

4. Click on the View button located at the far right of the Ruler.

The Ruler display changes to show the margin markers for the columns, as shown in Figure 6.10.

5. Drag one of the inside column margin markers to a new location.

Word adjusts all the columns to the new width.

□

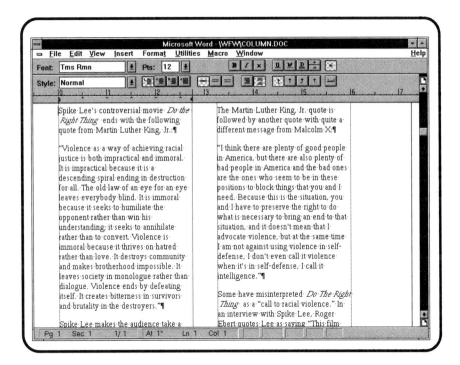

Figure 6.9   Two columns displayed in Page view mode.

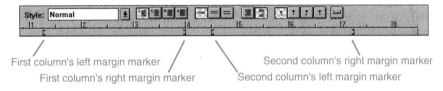

Figure 6.10   The Ruler in the View mode.

187

Creating Column Breaks

Column breaks are useful if you want to end a column and start a new one before Word automatically flows the text up to the next column. Word inserts a single dotted line as a column break marker. You can delete a column break by placing the insertion point on the column break marker and pressing the Del key.

Q **Inserting Column Breaks**

1. Place the insertion point where you want to insert a column break.

2. Choose the Insert/Break command or press Alt,I,B.

   Word displays the Break dialog box.

3. Choose the Column Break option button or press C.

4. Choose the OK button or press Enter.

   Word inserts a column break indicated by a single dotted line. □

> ► **Tip:** The shortcut method of adding a column break is to place the insertion point in the column where you want the column break and then press Ctrl-Shift-Enter.

Setting the Vertical Alignment

In Chapter 4, you learned how to align text horizontally within margins. Word can also align the contents of a page vertically. A common application of the vertical alignment feature is the creation of a title page. Use the Format/Section command to control the vertical position of text within a section. This feature works only when you've defined a section as a page. Three vertical alignment options are available:

Vertical Alignment Options	Description
Top	Aligns the first line of text flush with the top margin and is the default setting.
Center	Centers your text with blank space evenly distributed between the text and the top and bottom margins.
Justify	Justifies your text by adding space between paragraphs to fill the space between the top and bottom margins.

Vertically Centering a Section

1. Move the insertion point in the section you want to center.
2. Choose the Format/Section command (Alt,T,S) or double-click on the section marker.

   The Section dialog box appears.

3. Choose the Center option button or press Alt-C.
4. Choose the OK button or press Enter.

   Word centers the section's text.

5. To see how your centered text looks, choose the File/Print Preview command.

□

189

Numbering Lines

Numbering the lines of text in a document is helpful when you want to quickly reference text, and line numbering is commonly used in legal documents. The numbers Word assigns to each line of text are visible only when you choose the File/Print Preview command or when you print the document. You can choose how many lines you want to appear numbered. For example, you can add numbers to each line, every other line, or every line occurrence you specify, such as every tenth line. You can also turn off line numbering in selected paragraphs, such as headings.

Q Numbering Lines in a Document

1. Choose Format/Section or press Alt,T,S.

   The Section dialog box appears.

2. Choose the Line Numbering check box or press Alt-I.

   An X appears in the Line Numbering check box indicating it is turned on. The options in the Line Numbering box are activated, displaying Word's default settings.

3. To start the line numbering counter at a number other than 1 (the default), choose the Start At # text box or press Alt-A, and type a number to start the number counter.

4. If you want the distance between text and numbers to be greater or less than ¼ inch from the left edge of each line of text, in the From Text box, type the distance you want between text and numbers.

   Word defaults to the Auto setting, which is ¼ inch.

5. To change the frequency of the line numbers, in the Count By box type a number to specify the frequency of line numbers.

   For example, accept the default, 1, to number every line. To number every other line, type 2. To number every fifth line, type 5.

6. Choose the Continue option button or press Alt-U to number every line without starting the count from the last section or page.

   The default is Per Page, which restarts numbering on each page. Choose Per Section to restart numbering for each section and to begin numbering at the beginning of each section of your whole document.

190

7. Choose the OK button or press Enter.

Word adds the line numbers to your text. Remember, line numbers appear only when the document is printed or when you view the file in the Print Preview mode. ☐

To omit line numbers for selected paragraphs, select the paragraphs you don't want numbered. If you want to omit line numbering for the entire document, press Ctrl-5 (on the numeric keypad), and then choose the Format/Paragraph command or press Alt,T,P. Click on the Line Numbering check box (it should appear blank) and choose the OK button or press Enter. Word removes the numbering from the selected paragraphs.

Moving to a Numbered Line

191

Once you have added line numbers to a document, you can use the Edit/Go To command to jump to a specific line number. Type l (a lowercase *L*) followed by the line number you want to move to. You can also jump to a line relative to the line on which the insertion point is located by using the plus (+) or minus (−) signs. For example, to jump down 20 lines type l−20, or to move up 20 lines type l+20, in the Go To text box and then choose the OK button or press Enter. You can also move to a line number on a different page or in a different section by prefacing the line number with an *s* for section and then the section number, or *p* for page and then the page number. For example, typing p7l3 moves to page 7 line 3, and s3l40 moves to section 3 line 40.

Gutter and Mirror Margins

Whenever you bind printed pages together, such as for a business report, you lose some of each page's space to the binding. If your text falls too close to the binding, the reader is forced to pry the pages apart to read it. The kind of binding that you use dictates how much space should be left for the binding. There are two types of binding margin settings, depending on whether you're printing on one side of a page or on both sides of a page. Use the *Gutter* margin setting when you're binding on the left side of a page printed on a single side. Use the *Mirror* margin setting when you're printing on both sides of a page. To set these margins, use the Format/Document command and the Margins box.

If you're binding a document printed on one side of the page, choose the Format/Document command or press Alt,T,D. Choose the Gutter text box or press Alt-G. Enter the measurement to expand the left margin to allow for binding, such as an additional 1/4 inch. All your pages will have an additional 1/4-inch left margin to compensate for binding. If your printer is capable of printing on both sides of a page, the Quick Steps explain how to add mirror margins to your document.

 Adding Mirror Margins for a Double-Sided Document

1. Choose the Format/Document command or press Alt,T,D.	Word displays the Document dialog box.
2. Choose the Mirror Margins check box or press Alt-I.	Notice that the Left and Right margin text boxes change to Inside and Outside text boxes.
3. Choose the Inside text box or press Alt-N.	
4. Type a measurement.	This sets the right margin for even-numbered pages and the left margin for odd-numbered pages.
5. Choose the Outside text box or press Alt-O.	
6. Type a measurement.	This sets the left margin for even-numbered pages and the right margin for odd-numbered pages.
7. Choose the OK button or press Enter.	Word reformats your document to reflect the new margin settings. You can view the margin settings by using the View/Page command. □

What You Have Learned

▶ To add special characters to a document, hold down the Alt key, press 0 (zero), and enter the three-digit number for the character you want. These special characters include fractions, single or double quotation marks, bullets, and the copyright symbol.

▶ For a bulleted or numbered list, use the Format/Paragraph command (Alt,T,P) and enter measurement values in the From Left and First Line text boxes, or you can use the mouse by dragging the indent markers on the Ruler.

▶ Use the Insert/Footnote (Alt,I,N) to insert footnotes into your document. Word inserts a footnote marker in your document and displays a Footnote pane where you can enter your footnote text. To view and edit your footnotes at any time, choose the View/Footnotes command (Alt,V,F).

▶ Adding hyphens improves the appearance of your document. To automatically add hyphens to your entire document, use the Utilities/Hyphenate command (Alt,U,H).

▶ With the Insert/Break command (Alt,I,B), you can insert a section break in your document. This enables you to format parts of a document differently. To format a section, use the Format/Section command (Alt,T,S). By default, Word considers your entire document as one section until you create additional sections.

▶ To create multiple columns of text, choose the Format/Section command (Alt,T,S) and enter the number of columns you want to create in the Number text box.

▶ Gutter and Mirror margins create additional space at the margins for the binding of a document. The Gutter margin is for single-sided printing, and the Mirror margins are for double-sided printing. To set these special binding margins, use the Format/Document command (Alt,T,D).

193

Creating Tables and Outlines

In This Chapter

▶   *Creating, formatting, and sorting tables in a document*
▶   *Performing calculations*
▶   *Creating and using outlines*

Tables and outlines are two of Word's most powerful organizational features. Using tables in your document allows you to organize information in columns and rows for easy referencing. Creating an outline for a document lets you organize and later quickly rearrange the structure of your document. This chapter teaches you techniques to take advantage of Word's table and outline features.

Creating Tables

Tables are a useful way to present large amounts of information in a limited amount of space. One of Word's strongest features is that it allows you to easily add and edit tables of information in a document. In most other word processors, you set up tables using tabs. But editing tables set up with tabs can be a tedious experience. The Word for Windows table feature makes working with tables easier by dividing a portion of your document into a grid of dotted horizontal rows and vertical columns. The result is a series of boxes. These boxes, called *cells*, can contain words, numbers, graphics, or fields, and they can expand or contract to accommodate their contents. Because Word's tables expand to accommodate text, they are excellent for creating side-by-side paragraphs.

Inserting a Table in a Document

To insert a table in a document, use the Insert/Table command. When you insert a table, the space between the margins is divided into equal columns. If you are inserting a table into a document that's already divided into columns, the table divides the space in the column containing the insertion point. By default, the initial height of the columns is set to Auto, which means that the row height is set to the height of the tallest cell in the row. The column width setting is calculated by subtracting the space between columns from the total text width and then dividing the remaining space evenly among the columns. The default space between columns is .15 inch.

 Inserting a Table

1. Place the insertion point where you want to insert a table and choose the Insert/Table command or press Alt,I,T.

   The Insert Table dialog box appears.

2. Type the number of columns and rows you want, or accept the default (2 columns, 1 row).

   By default, the Initial Col Width is set to Auto.

3. If you want a table narrower or wider than the text column width, choose the Initial Col Width box or press Alt-W. Then type a measurement for the width of the columns.

4. Choose the OK button or press Enter.

Word inserts a blank table in your document.

5. Type the contents of the first cell in the table. Use the mouse or press the Tab key to move to the next column. Then type its contents. Continue to fill in the blank cells of the table.

Pressing the Tab key in the last cell of the last column creates a new column. If you want to use a tab in your text, press Ctrl-Tab.

6. Move the insertion point out of the table or press the Down Arrow in the last column to move out of the table.

□

> ▶ **Note:** The dotted lines that surround each cell do not print, and their display can be turned off. To prevent them from being displayed in your document, choose the View/ Preferences command and turn off the Table Gridlines check box in the View Preferences dialog box.

Navigating and Selecting Text in a Table

Navigating the cells of a table is easily done with a mouse; using the keyboard is a little trickier. The method for moving from cell to cell is similar to the way you move through an Excel spreadsheet. To quickly move around a table, use the following keys:

Press Key(s)	Insertion Point Moves to
Tab	Next cell
Shift-Tab	Previous cell
Alt-Home	First cell in a row
Alt-End	Last cell in a row
Alt-PgUp	Top cell in column
Alt-PgDn	Bottom cell in column

> **Note:** Because the Tab key is used for navigating tables, you must press Ctrl-Tab to insert a tab in a table.

Selecting text within cells is similar to selecting text elsewhere in a document. You select text in three ways: by using the mouse, by using the Shift and direction keys, or by using F8 (Extend mode) and the direction keys. Pressing Esc cancels the Extend Selection mode. To select text in a table, use the following keys:

Press Key(s)	To Select
Alt-5 (numeric keypad)	The whole table
F8-Up Arrow	The current cell and the cell above
F8-Down Arrow	The current cell and the cell below
F8-Left Arrow	The current cell one character at a time and then all of the adjacent cell
F8-Right Arrow	The current cell one character at a time and then all of the adjacent cell

At the left edge of each cell is a selection bar, similar to the document's selection bar. The mouse pointer changes to a right-pointing arrow when it is in a cell's selection bar. You can select a row, a column, or the whole table by using the mouse and the selection bar:

Selection	Action
Row	Point to any cell's selection bar in the row you want to select and double-click the left mouse button.
Column	Position the insertion point at the top of the column. When the pointer changes to a Down Arrow, click the left mouse button.
Whole table	Position the insertion point at the top of the first column. When the pointer changes to a Down Arrow, drag the pointer to the last column.

Inserting Rows or Columns in a Table

Frequently a table needs to be expanded to handle additional information. To insert a new row of cells at the bottom of a table, place the insertion point in the last cell of the bottom row of the table, and press the Tab key to start another row. The insertion point automatically moves to the first cell in the new row. You can also insert a row by choosing the Edit/Table command or pressing Alt,E,A. The Edit/Table command displays the Edit Table dialog box. This dialog box provides options for adding rows and columns to, or deleting rows and columns from, a table.

Normally, columns are inserted to the left of the current column. To add a column to the right of the table, place the insertion point in the area outside the edge of the table by moving to the last column and pressing the Right Arrow. If you have the Show All feature turned on, the insertion point appears between the edge of the table and the end-of-row mark (¤). If the Show All feature is turned off, the insertion point appears directly outside the right border of the table. Choose the Edit/Table command. The Edit Table dialog box appears, as shown in Figure 7.1. Choose the Column option button and then choose the Insert button. To delete a column, select the column and choose the Delete button in the Edit Table dialog box.

199

> ⊘ **Caution:** You must use the Edit/Table command to edit the rows and columns of a table. You cannot delete or insert rows by using normal text editing techniques. For example, using the Edit/Cut command to delete a column would delete only the text in the selected row or column.

 Inserting or Deleting a Column in a Table

1. Place the insertion point in the column to the right of the spot where you want to insert the new column.

   Word inserts columns to the left of the current column. To add a new column to the right of a column, place the insertion point in the area outside the right edge of the table. The insertion point appears between the edge of the table and the end-of-row mark.

2. Choose the Edit/Table command or press Alt,E,A.

   The Edit Table dialog box appears.

3. Choose the Column option button or press Alt-C.

4. Choose the Insert or Delete buttons, or press Alt-I to insert columns in a table or Alt-D to delete columns from a table.

   Word adds the selected column to the table, or deletes it.

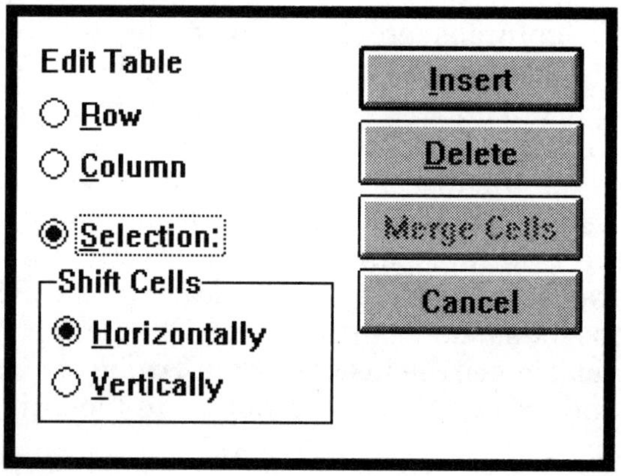

   □

Figure 7.1   The Edit Table dialog box.

Formatting Tables

The Format/Table command (Alt,T,A) displays the Format Table dialog box, as shown in Figure 7.2. The Format Table dialog box contains options for changing the indent and row alignments, column widths, space between columns, height of a row, and the addition of lines and borders inside or around a table. The Ribbon and the Ruler also can be used to format the contents of a cell or an entire table. Paragraphs in cells are indented and aligned relative to the cell margins, each cell being treated as a miniature document. For example, centering text in a cell aligns the text with the margins of the cell that contains it.

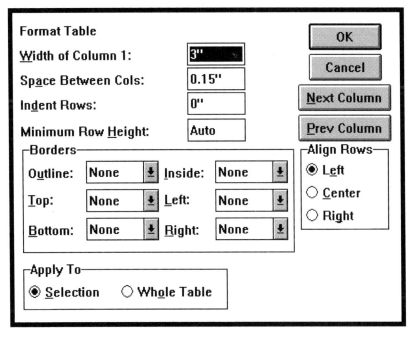

Figure 7.2   The Format Table dialog box.

201

Using the Ruler with Tables

Word provides three different views for using the Ruler when the insertion point is in a table: Indent view, Column view, and Margin view. When you choose the View/Ruler command or press Alt,V,R, the Ruler first displays indent markers for the current paragraph in the table, as shown at the top of Figure 7.3. You can use this Ruler view to format paragraphs as you do in a document.

If you click on the Ruler view button (the last button on the Ruler), the Ruler now displays column markers for the row containing the insertion point, as shown in the middle of Figure 7.3. In this view you can drag the left indent marker to indent selected rows in the table, or you can drag a column marker to make cells wider or narrower. If you click on the Ruler view button again, Word displays margin markers, as shown at the bottom of Figure 7.3. You can drag these markers to change the margins of the entire document, not just the table.

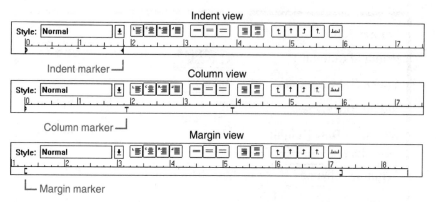

Figure 7.3 *Word's three Ruler views: Indent, Column, and Margin.*

Changing the Width of a Column

202

The easiest way to change the width of a column is to use the Ruler and the mouse. First make sure that the Ruler is displayed and select the column(s) whose width you want to change. Click on the Ruler view button to see the column markers on the Ruler and then drag the column markers to widen or narrow the columns. You can also change the width of existing columns by using the Format/Table command. The first option in the Format Table dialog box is the Width of Column setting, which automatically adjusts to reflect the number of columns selected.

Adjusting the Space Between Columns

Word automatically adds a .15-inch space between columns. You can change this setting in the Format Table dialog box. The space between columns determines the maximum space between the text area of a column. It doesn't change the boundary of the column. When you change the Space Between Cols setting, the width of your table's cells doesn't change. The space setting is divided in half and applied to the beginning and end of all cells in the selected row. Changing the setting of the Space Between Cols doesn't affect the horizontal alignment of text on a row, although text may wrap in a cell if you adjust the space between columns. You cannot specify a different space setting for different cells on the same row.

Changing the Height of a Row

Word automatically adjusts the height of individual rows to accommodate text. Both the font size and the number of lines affect the height of a row. You can adjust the row height by using the Format/ Table command. The Minimum Row Height text box in the Format Table dialog box is set to Auto. To change the height of a row, enter a measurement. If you enter a measurement less than the amount of space Word needs to separate text in adjacent rows, Word ignores your setting and uses the Auto setting so that the rows of your table don't overlap.

When Word increases the height of a row, it inserts the space only below the text. In order to add space above text, use the Open Space button on the Ruler or the Before setting in the Spacing box in the Format Paragraph dialog box. The Minimum Row Height setting affects all the cells in a row. You cannot have cells with different heights in the same row.

203

Indenting and Aligning Rows in a Table

You can enhance the appearance of a table's rows by indenting or aligning them. When you indent or align a row, the cell's contents and width remain the same; only the row is indented or aligned. To change the alignment of all the rows in a table, place the insertion point in the table and choose the Format/Table command or press Alt,T,A. In the Align Rows box, select either the Left, Center, or Right option button. In the Apply To box, select the Whole Table option button and choose the OK button or press Enter. Figure 7.4 shows the effects of applying the three different alignments to rows in a table.

 Aligning Selected Rows in a Table

1. Select the rows you want to align.

2. Choose the Format/Table command or press Alt,T,A.

   Word displays the Format Table dialog box.

3. In the Align Rows box, select the Left (Alt-E), Center (Alt-C), or Right (Alt-G) option button.

   Word selects the row alignment.

4. In the Apply To box, choose the Selection option button.

5. Choose the OK button or press Enter.

Word realigns the selected cells in your document to reflect the new alignment. ☐

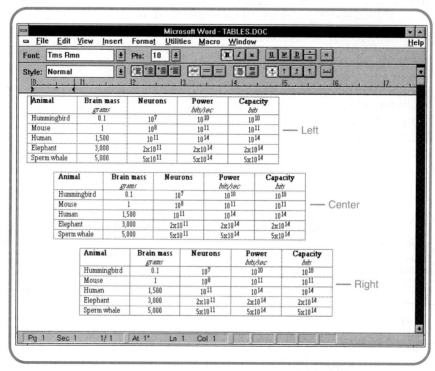

Figure 7.4   Different alignments of rows in a table.

Indenting a row means changing the amount of space between the document's margin and the edge of the row. Be careful that you don't indent the row beyond the document's margin, because Word doesn't print the part of the table that extends beyond the margin. To indent rows of a column, select the rows you want to indent and choose the Format/Table command. Enter a measurement in the Indent Rows text box and choose the OK button or press Enter. Figure 7.5 shows tables with different indent settings.

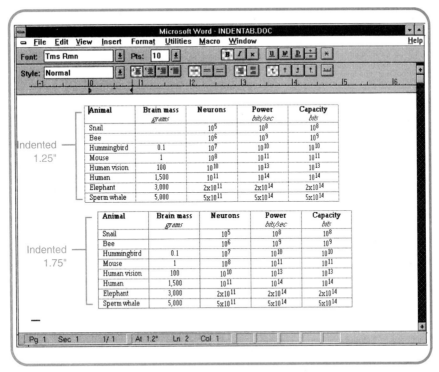

Animal	Brain mass grams	Neurons	Power bits/sec	Capacity bits
Snail		10^5	10^8	10^8
Bee		10^6	10^9	10^9
Hummingbird	0.1	10^7	10^{10}	10^{10}
Mouse	1	10^8	10^{11}	10^{11}
Human vision	100	10^{10}	10^{13}	10^{13}
Human	1,500	10^{11}	10^{14}	10^{14}
Elephant	3,000	2×10^{11}	2×10^{14}	2×10^{14}
Sperm whale	5,000	5×10^{11}	5×10^{14}	5×10^{14}

Animal	Brain mass grams	Neurons	Power bits/sec	Capacity bits
Snail		10^5	10^8	10^8
Bee		10^6	10^9	10^9
Hummingbird	0.1	10^7	10^{10}	10^{10}
Mouse	1	10^8	10^{11}	10^{11}
Human vision	100	10^{10}	10^{13}	10^{13}
Human	1,500	10^{11}	10^{14}	10^{14}
Elephant	3,000	2×10^{11}	2×10^{14}	2×10^{14}
Sperm whale	5,000	5×10^{11}	5×10^{14}	5×10^{14}

Figure 7.5   Tables with different indent settings.

205

Indenting Selected Rows in a Table

1. Select the rows you want to indent.

2. Choose the Format/Table command or press Alt,T,A.

   The Format Table dialog box appears.

3. Choose the Indent Rows list box or press Alt-D, and type a measurement.

   Indents are from the left margin. The default setting is 0". For example, type .25" to indent the selected rows ¼ inch.

4. Choose the Selection option button (Alt-S) in the Apply To box.

   You can also indent all the cells in a table by choosing the Whole Table option button in the Apply To box.

5. Choose the OK button or press Enter.	Word indents the selected cells in your document. □

Adding Borders to a Table

Adding borders to a table can make the table easier to reference. You can add borders of different thickness around individual cells, groups of cells, or whole tables. You can also insert lines between rows and columns, just between columns, or around the outside of a table. You can even outline just one cell to call attention to it.

If you're inserting a table, choose the Insert/Table command and type the number of columns and rows you want. Then choose the Format button to display the Format dialog box. The Borders box displays options to control the positions of borders. The options for these borders, shown in Figure 7.6, are the same as for paragraph borders: Single, Thick, Double, and Shadow. Here are the border options available:

206

Border Option	Applies a Border
Outline	Around the outside of selected cells.
Inside	Between all selected cells.
Top	Along the top edge of selected cells.
Left	Along the left edge of selected cells.
Right	Along the right edge of selected cells.

Q Adding an Outline to the Cells in a Table

1. Move the insertion point inside the table and choose the Format/Table command or press Alt,T,A.	The Format Table dialog box appears.
2. Choose the Outline option in the Borders box or press Alt-U.	The Outline list box is highlighted.
3. Choose the Shadow option in the Outline list box.	Word automatically fills in the other border options to create the shadow outline.
4. Choose the Whole Table option button in the Apply To box or press Alt-O.	

5. Choose the OK button or press Enter.

Your entire table appears with a shadow border. To remove borders, select the cells you want to affect, choose the appropriate position in the Borders box, and select the None option in the appropriate list box. □

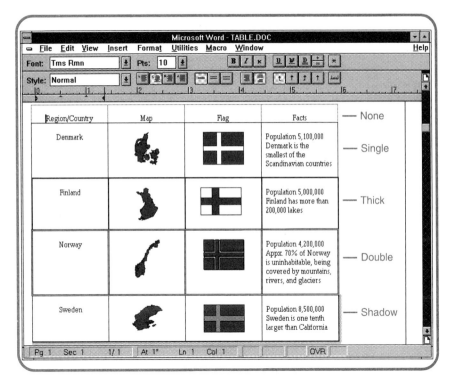

Figure 7.6   Table border positions.

Converting Text to Tables

Word provides options to convert text into a table or a table into text. If you select a text block and then choose the Insert/Table command, you can choose from three options: Paragraphs, which converts each paragraph of text into a separate cell; Tab Delimited, which converts each portion of text separated by a tab into a separate cell; and Comma Delimited, which converts each portion of text separated by a comma into a separate cell. In most cases you'll use the Paragraph option. The Tab Delimited and Comma Delimited options are generally used when importing data from other applications.

Q **Converting Text into a Table**

1. Select the text you want to convert into a table.
2. Choose the Insert/Table command or press Alt,I,T.

   The Insert Table dialog box appears.
3. In the Number of Columns text box, type a new number for the number of columns to create.
4. Make sure that the Convert From box is set to the Paragraphs setting. If it isn't, choose it or press Alt-P.
5. Choose the OK button or press Enter.

   Word converts the selected text into a table. □

When the insertion point is in a table, the Insert menu's Table command changes to the Table to Text command. Selecting this command displays a dialog box that provides three options for separating the text in different cells when it's converted to text in your document. You can choose to have the text converted to paragraphs or delimited (separated) by tabs or commas. Figure 7.7 shows the results of converting the text of a three-column table into text delimited by tabs.

Merging and Splitting Cells in a Table

Merging means taking the contents of multiple cells and combining them into one cell. *Splitting* does the opposite: it takes the contents of a cell and divides it into two different cells. You can only split cells that were previously merged.

To merge cells, select the cells you want to merge. Cells in a row can be merged; cells in a column *cannot* be merged. Choose the Edit/Table command or press Alt,E,A to display the Edit Table dialog box.

Choose the Merge Cells button or press Alt-M. The cells are merged into one cell. When selected cells contain only merged cells, the Merge button is replaced by the Split Cells button. To return the merged cells to their original state, select the merged cells and choose the Edit/Table command or press Alt,E,A. Choose the Split Cells button or press Alt-P.

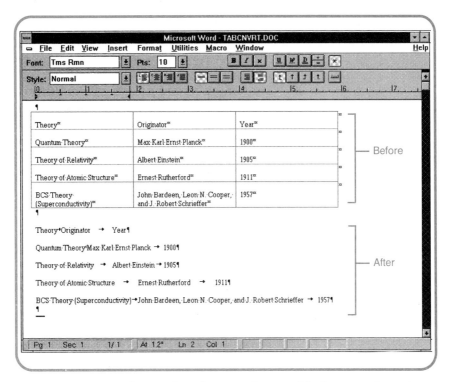

209

Figure 7.7   The results of converting a table into text by using the Tab Delimited option.

> ▶ **Tip:** To split an entire table and insert a paragraph mark between the two parts of the table, move to the row where you want to begin the next table and press Ctrl-Shift-Enter.

Sorting Tables

Many tables need to present information in alphabetical, numerical, or chronological (date) order. The Utilities/Sort command displays a dialog box, shown in Figure 7.8, that provides options to sort a table in any of these orders. When you sort a table, Word ignores indents, tabs, or blank spaces, and skips to the first alphanumeric character in the paragraph. Paragraph marks not preceded by text are placed before paragraphs with text in an ascending sort. By default, Word ignores the case of letters; for example, the letter *A* is treated as the letter *a*.

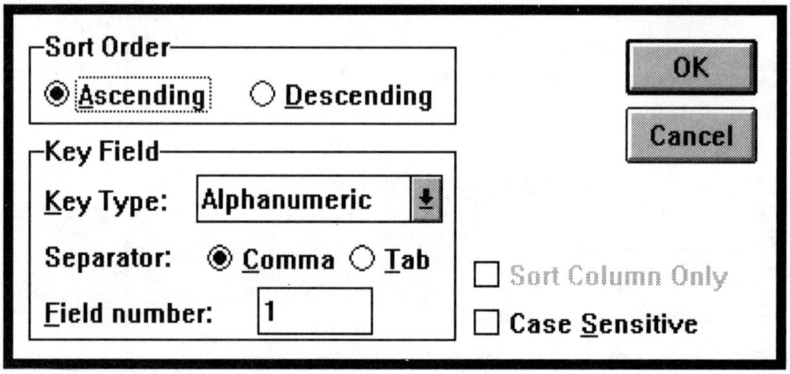

210

Figure 7.8   The Sort dialog box.

Two sort orders are available in the Sort dialog box: Ascending, which sorts alphabetically (A-Z), by date from the earliest date to the latest date, or numerically from the lowest number to the highest; or Descending, which sorts in the reverse order. You select the type of data to be sorted in the Key Type list box. Different sorting rules apply to the different types of data. The Alphanumeric option uses numbers, text, and all other characters to sort items.

You can activate case-sensitive sorting by using the Alphanumeric option; otherwise, this option isn't available. To activate case-sensitive sorting, choose the Case Sensitive check box or press Alt-S. This option sorts words so that text beginning with a capital letter precedes words beginning with a lowercase letter.

Dates are treated as three numbers, not as dates. The Date option sorts only text in a date format. All other characters not in recognizable date format are ignored. The dates must be the first characters of the paragraphs to be sorted. You can sort by date using the following date formats:

Date Format	Example
MMM-YY	JAN-91
M/D/YY	1/01/91
M-D-YY	1-01-91
D-MMM-YY	01-JAN-91
MMM D, YYYY	JAN 01, 1991
M/D/YY H:MM AM/PM	01/01/91 12:00 AM

The Numeric option sorts only by number; all other characters are ignored. The numbers may be anywhere in the paragraphs to be sorted. You can sort only a column by choosing the Sort Column Only option or pressing Alt-O. This option sorts only the selected column and needs to be turned off to sort entire rows of a table.

211

 Sorting a Table

1. Select the paragraphs or rows for sorting.

2. Choose Utilities/Sort or press Alt,U,O.

   The Sort dialog box appears.

3. In the Key Type list box, select the type of sort you want.

   In a numeric sort, only numbers are used to sort items. All other characters are ignored. In a date sort, the dates must be at the beginning of the cell's paragraph.

4. Choose the OK button or press Enter.

   Word sorts the selected columns in ascending order. ☐

Performing Calculations

Because tables are frequently used to list numerical information, you may need to perform some math in one or more columns. This discussion explains how to perform calculations by using the Utilities/Calculate command. However, fields offer even more power for performing calculations in a document and are covered in Chapter 10.

To calculate a selection, type the numbers and the appropriate math symbols needed for the calculation. Word adds the numbers if you do not include a math symbol. Table 7.1 lists the various operations that can be performed and shows the corresponding symbol and an example.

Table 7.1   Math Symbols with Examples

Operation	Symbol	Example
Addition	+	33 + 12
Subtraction	–	9–5
Multiplication	*	7*70
Division	/	12/144
Percentage	%	50%
Power	^	5^2

To calculate a selection, select the calculation and choose the Utilities/Calculate command or press Alt,U,C. Word pastes the result onto the Clipboard and temporarily displays it in the status bar. Place the insertion point at the spot where you want to insert the result and press Shift-Ins.

Using Outlines in Word

An outline helps you organize your thoughts before and during the writing of a document. It is a helpful tool for arranging ideas and concepts in a hierarchical order to show their relative importance. Using Word's Outline view mode, you can create an outline for your document by organizing your topics into different heading levels. Your outline can include up to nine levels of headings. These headings, which are specially formatted paragraphs, provide the structure of your document. You can then flesh out the outline by adding the appropriate body text to the headings.

In Word, an outline isn't a separate document. Rather it is a document view mode showing headings and body text arranged in an indented outline format. Using Word's Outline view mode, you can collapse your document to view just the outline headings and rearrange your document's structure by manipulating the headings. Another important use of headings is to create entries for a table of contents, as explained in Chapter 12, "Creating Form Letters, Labels, Tables of Contents, and Indexes."

To switch to the Outline view mode, choose the View/Outline command or press Alt,V,O. The View/Outline command is a toggle switch between your normal editing view (Normal and Draft view modes) and the Outline view mode. Figure 7.9 shows the Outline view mode with a sample document outline. Word indents each sequential subheading level by $1/2$ inch, and the body text is always indented $1/4$ inch to the right under the heading. The Outline bar appears where the Ruler is usually displayed.

The arrow buttons let you move a selected heading up or down in the document's outline or promote or demote a heading level. The Expand button lets you expand a collapsed heading, and the Collapse button lets you collapse an expanded heading. The View Level buttons allow you to display specified outline headings.

Notice the special heading icons that appear before each heading paragraph in the outline, as shown in Figure 7.9. The plus icons next to a heading indicate that the heading has subheadings or body text. A rectangle icon next to a heading indicates that the heading has no subheadings or body text. The small square icon appears next to any visible body text. These icons can be used to perform various outline editing tasks, as explained later in this chapter.

213

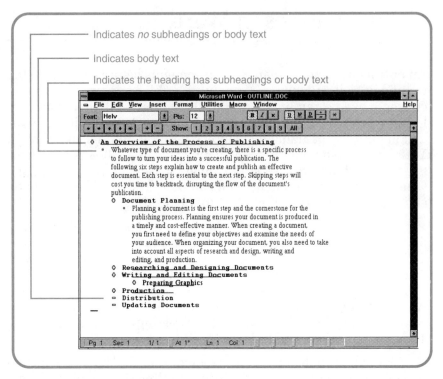

Figure 7.9   *The Outline view mode.*

Understanding Outline Headings

To understand how the Outline View mode works, you must understand Word's heading styles. *Heading styles* are a collection of premade character and paragraph formats that are applied to paragraphs you designate as headings. Each heading level is assigned its own style name indicating the heading level it creates, such as heading 1, heading 2, heading 3, and so on down to heading 9. When you apply a heading style, Word applies the formatting to the heading text. For example, heading 1 uses boldfaced and underlined characters in the 12-point Helv (Helvetica) font.

> **Note:** How to change heading styles and work with Word's styles feature is explained in Chapter 9, "Saving Time Using Glossaries, Macros, Styles, and Templates."

By default, Word applies the Normal style to every paragraph in a document. The Normal style provides the basic formatting for Word's paragraphs, such as 10-point Times Roman font and flush left alignment. The Style list box on the Ruler always shows the style applied to the paragraph containing the insertion point. For example, if the paragraph has been formatted as a level-1 outline heading, Word displays `heading 1` in the Style list box. If the paragraph is formatted as a Normal paragraph, Word displays `Normal` in the Style list box.

Creating a Document Outline

The easiest way to use Word's outlining feature is to create an outline before you type the text for your document. Building your document from an outline allows you to organize your concepts before adding the body text. Word also allows you to create an outline in an existing document, as explained later in this chapter. Creating an outline using the Outline view mode involves typing the text for each heading and then assigning an outline heading level from 1 to 9.

215

 Creating an Outline for a New Document in the Outline View Mode

1. With a new document displayed, choose the View/Outline command or press Alt,V,O.

   Word changes to the Outline view mode.

2. Type the text for the first level-1 heading and press Enter.

   The heading text appears in underlined boldfaced characters, preceded by a rectangle icon.

3. Type the text for the next heading. If you want it to be a level-1 heading, press Enter. If you want the text to be a level-2 heading, choose the Demote (Right Arrow) button or press Alt-Shift-Right Arrow.

   If you made the heading a level-2 heading, it's indented to the right $1/2$ inch and a plus sign appears to the right of the previous heading.

4. Type the text for the next heading. If you want it to be a level-2 heading, press Enter. For a level-3 heading, choose the Demote (Right Arrow) button or press Alt-Shift-Right Arrow. For a level-1 heading, choose the Promote (Left Arrow) button or press Alt-Shift-Left Arrow twice from the level-3 heading.

If you made the heading a level-3 heading, it's indented to the right ½ inch relative to the level-2 heading, and a plus sign appears to the right of the level-2 heading.

5. Type the text for each additional heading. Choose the Demote or Promote buttons or press Alt-Shift-Right Arrow or Alt-Shift-Left Arrow to move the heading paragraph to the level you want.

Each time you click the appropriate button or key combination, Word promotes or demotes the heading by one level.

6. After entering all your outline headings, choose the View/Outline command or press Alt,V,O.

Word displays the headings in the text editing view you have selected (Draft, Normal, or Page). □

You can delete an outline heading in the Outline view mode by selecting it and then choosing the Del key. To quickly select a heading, click on the heading icon located to the left of the heading you want. You can also change the character formats of a heading paragraph by using the Ribbon while you are in the Outline view mode.

Adding Body Text to Outline Headings

You can enter and edit body text by using the Outline view mode, but it's easier to enter and edit body text by using the Normal or Draft view modes. After completing your outline using the Outline view mode, choose the View/Outline command or press Alt,V,O to return to the view mode you normally work in. Word displays the heading level assigned to the paragraph containing the insertion point in the Style list box on the Ruler. To add body text under a heading, simply move the insertion point to the end of the heading text and press

Enter. The new paragraph you create after a heading is automatically formatted as a Normal paragraph for level-1 and level-2 headings and is formatted as an indented paragraph for level-3 and lower headings. You can then enter and edit text as you normally do. Heading paragraphs can also be edited and formatted as you would other text in a document.

Viewing Different Heading Levels in Your Outline

In the Outline view mode, Word initially displays all the document's headings and body text paragraphs, as shown earlier in Figure 7.9. Using the View Level buttons (the numbered buttons at the far right of the Outline bar), you can collapse the entire document to display just specified headings. Collapsing an outline to headings is useful for viewing the structure of your document and for rearranging your document by manipulating the outline headings. When you choose a View Level button, only the headings at and above the level you choose are displayed, as shown in Figure 7.10. Notice in the figure that the level-3 button is pressed; thus only heading levels 1 through 3 are displayed. Any lower-level headings and body text are collapsed under the headings above them. Word adds a thick dotted bar beneath a heading to show that the heading has subheadings or body text beneath it.

217

To choose a View Level button, click on the appropriate heading-level number button, or press Alt-Shift with the number key for the heading level you want to choose. For example, to view headings at level 3 and above, press Alt-Shift-3. You can quickly expand an outline to include all its headings and body text by choosing the All button or pressing Alt-Shift-A.

You can also expand and collapse a specific heading within an outline. To collapse a specific heading's body text and subheadings, make sure that the Num Lock key is off, place the insertion point in the heading or click on the heading icon, and then click on the Minus button or press Alt-Shift-Minus (–). To expand a collapsed heading to display any subheadings and body text, move the insertion point into the heading or click on the heading icon, and then click on the Plus button. From the keyboard, press Alt-Shift-Plus (+). To quickly expand or collapse a heading's body text and subheadings, double-click on the heading's icon.

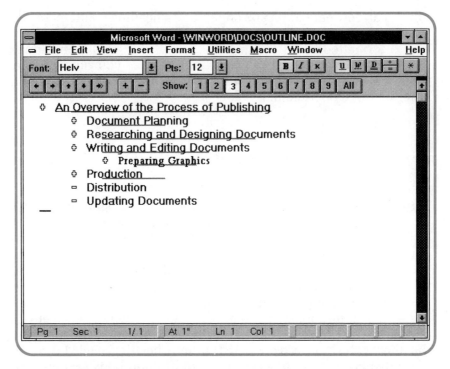

Figure 7.10   A collapsed document showing outline headings.

> ▶ **Note:** To print an outline, first expand or collapse headings to display the heading levels and body text you want to print. Then choose the File/Print command (Alt,F,P) or press Ctrl-Shift-F12.

Promoting and Demoting Headings

Because an outline uses a hierarchical structure, when you change the order of your outline you either promote or demote heading levels. Promoting a heading assigns it to a higher-level status, such as changing a level-3 heading to a level-2 heading. Demoting a heading assigns it to a lower-level status. It's easier to change heading levels if you are displaying just the document's headings in the Outline view mode.

To change a heading to a different level, first collapse or expand the outline to include the headings you want to work with. Next place the insertion point in the heading you want to promote or demote or click on the heading's icon. Choosing the Promote (Left Arrow) button or pressing Alt-Shift-Left Arrow promotes a heading one level. Choosing the Demote (Right Arrow) button or pressing Alt-Shift-Right Arrow demotes a heading one level. You can also promote or demote a heading by dragging the heading icon to either the left or the right. When you move the mouse pointer to the heading icon, the pointer changes to a four-headed arrow. Press and hold down the left mouse button, drag the heading to the left to promote it or to the right to demote it, and then release the mouse button.

Word allows you to change a heading into body text by first placing the insertion point in the header you want to affect and then choosing the Demote to Text button (the last arrow button on the Outline bar) or pressing Alt-Shift-5 (the 5 key on the numeric keypad with the Num Lock turned off). You can also change body text to a heading by selecting the text and then choosing the Demote (Alt-Shift-Right Arrow) or the Promote (Alt-Shift-Left Arrow) button.

219

Moving Headings

You can rearrange your document by moving its outline headings while in the Outline view mode. When you move an outline heading, any body text under the heading is also moved. When you move a heading that has collapsed subheadings, the subheadings are also moved. It's easier to move heading levels if you're displaying just headings in the Outline view mode.

To move any subheadings with a heading, you must collapse or select all the subheadings before moving the heading. Otherwise, only the selected heading is moved while its subheadings remain in their original location. For example, if you want to move a level-2 heading with level-3 subheadings, display only level-2 headings or select the level-2 and level-3 headings.

To move headings up or down in the outline, collapse the document to display the heading levels you want to move. Place the insertion point within the heading you want to move, or click on the heading icon. Then click on the Up Arrow button or press Alt-Shift-Up Arrow to move the heading upward in your outline, or click on the Down Arrow button or press Alt-Shift-Down Arrow to move the heading down. The body text moves with the heading. You can also move a heading by dragging the heading icon. When you move the mouse pointer to the heading icon, the mouse pointer changes to a four-headed arrow. Press and hold down the left mouse button and then drag the heading up or down. Release the mouse button when you've positioned the heading where you want it.

Applying Outline Heading Styles in a Document

As explained earlier, the easiest way to create an outline using the Outline view mode is to create the outline first and then add the body text to the outline in the editing view that you normally work in. If you have an existing document without an outline, you can apply heading styles to create an outline for the document.

To apply outline header styles to an existing document, it's easier to use the Style list box on the Ruler in the Normal or Draft view editing modes, rather than the Outline view mode. You can apply a heading-level style to any selected Normal paragraph in your document. Once you've assigned the outline headings to your existing document, you can then switch to the Outline view mode to do any document rearrangement tasks. The Quick Steps explain how to apply a heading style by using the Style list box on the Ruler in the view mode that you normally edit your documents in.

 Applying a Heading Style to a Paragraph by Using the Style List Box

1. In editing view mode (Draft, Normal, or Page), place the insertion point in the paragraph that you want to change into an outline heading. Make sure the Ruler is activated by choosing the View/Ruler command or pressing Alt,V,R.

   The paragraph can be either a normal paragraph or a heading paragraph for which you want to change the level.

2. Press Ctrl-S and then press Alt-Down Arrow or click on the Down Arrow button next to the Style list box on the Ruler.

Word displays the list of available styles. By default, Word displays only heading levels 1, 2, and 3 in the Style list box. If you've added levels beyond the first three by using the Outline view mode, those additional heading styles are also displayed.

3. Choose the heading level you want or use the Down or Up Arrow key to select a heading level, and then press Enter. If the heading level you want isn't displayed, type the heading level name, such as heading 6.

Word applies the heading style to the paragraph you specified. The heading level appears in the Style list box on the Ruler.

□

221

If you don't have the Ruler displayed, pressing Ctrl-S displays the message prompt Which style? in the status bar. Type the style name of the heading you want to apply, and then press Enter. Word applies the heading style you've specified to the selected paragraph. By pressing the F4 key or choosing the Edit/Repeat command (Alt,E,R), you can format several headings with the last heading level style you applied without having to reselect or retype the style name each time.

Displaying the Heading Style Names

You can view all heading levels for paragraphs in both the editing and the Outline view modes by using Word's style name area feature. Activating the style name area displays the name of the paragraph style (Heading or Normal) at the immediate left of each paragraph, as shown in Figure 7.11.

To display the style name area, choose the View/Preferences command or press Alt,V,E. In the View Preferences dialog box, choose the Style Area Width or press Alt-W. Type a width for displaying style names in the left margin area, such as .80". You can easily adjust this width later by using the mouse. Choosing the OK button or pressing Enter displays the style area with each paragraph's style name.

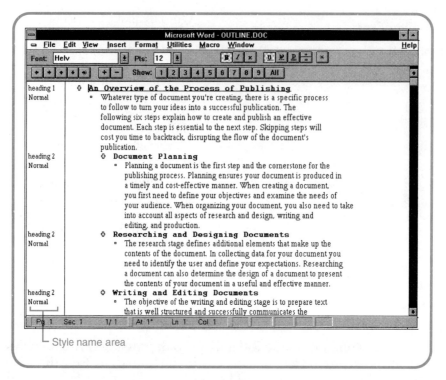

Figure 7.11   The style name area.

To quickly adjust the width of the style area, move the mouse pointer to the vertical line separating the style area from the document. The mouse pointer changes to two vertical lines with arrows on the outside of each line. Drag the style area line to expand or reduce the style area width. Dragging the line to the far left removes the style area.

Numbering Outline Headings

With the Utilities/Renumber command, you can number headings in the Outline view mode. This command inserts a field called AUTONUMOUT into the Word document. A *field* is an embedded command that instructs Word to perform a specific task. Using a field for numbering outline headings allows Word to automatically renumber headings when you make any changes to your document's outline.

Word provides three different outline numbering schemes: Outline, Sequence, and Legal. Figure 7.12 shows the three numbering schemes. The Quick Steps explain how to number your outline headings.

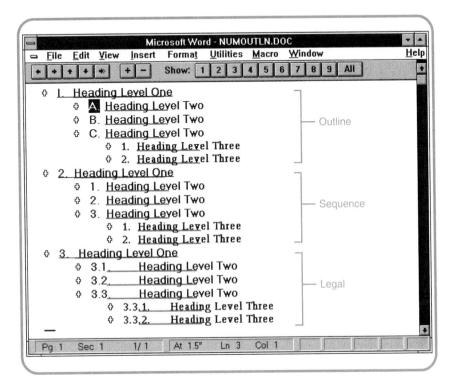

Figure 7.12 *Word's three options for outline heading numbering.*

 Numbering Headings in an Outline

1. Choose the View/Outline command or press Alt,V,O.

   Word displays your document in the Outline view mode.

2. Collapse your outline to display all your headings by choosing the appropriate View Level button (don't use the All button) or pressing Shift-Alt and the number key for the View Level you want.

   The outline collapses to display all your headings without body text.

3. Choose the Utilities/Renumber command or press Alt,U,R.

   Word displays the Utilities Renumber dialog box, as shown in Figure 7.13.

4. Choose the outline numbering scheme you want to use from the Format list box, or using the keyboard press Alt-F to activate the Format list box and use the Up or Down Arrow to select a numbering scheme. Choose the OK button or press Enter.

   Word inserts the number fields and tab characters in front of the headings, as shown in Figure 7.14. You can see the numbers by turning off the Show All feature.

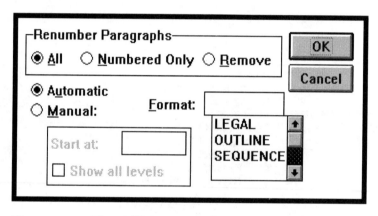

Figure 7.13   The Utilities Renumber dialog box.

To remove numbers from headings, collapse the outline to display only the headings in the Outline view mode. Choose the Utilities/Renumber command or press Alt,U,R. Word displays the Utilities Renumber dialog box. Choose the Remove option button or press Alt-R, and then choose the OK button or press Enter. Word removes the numbering from the outline headings.

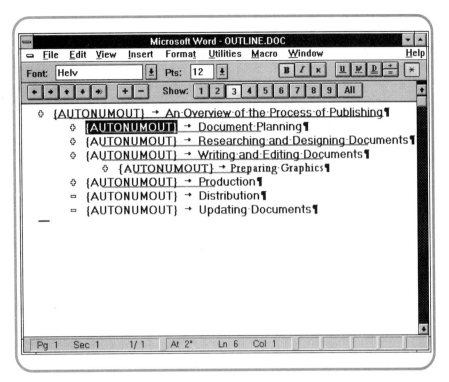

Figure 7.14   Outline headings with number fields.

Navigating a Document by Using the Outline View Mode

If you're working on a long document, the Outline view mode is handy for navigating your document by using headings. To use an outline to travel quickly through a long document, first choose the View/Outline command or press Alt,V,O. Collapse the outline to display just the headings by choosing the appropriate View Level button or pressing Alt-Shift and the heading level number you want. Scroll through the outline until the heading you want to move to is displayed at the top of the screen in the Outline view mode. Choose the View/Outline command or press Alt,V,O to return to the editing view mode. The heading you choose in the Outline view mode appears at the top of your screen.

What You Have Learned

▶ Tables are good ways to organize information and present large amounts of information in a limited space. To insert a table into a document, use the Insert/Table command or press Alt,I,T.

▶ To edit tables, use the Edit/Table command or press Alt,E,A. To format tables, use the Format/Table command or press Alt,T,A.

▶ You can perform selected calculations in your table by using the Utilities/Calculate command or pressing Alt,U,C.

▶ Outlines help you organize your thoughts and provide a hierarchical structure for a document. In Word, an outline is a view mode rather than a separate document.

▶ To create an outline for a new document, use the View/Outline command or press Alt,V,O.

▶ Word has nine different heading levels. To view one or more levels, click on the appropriate View Level button or press Alt-Shift and the number key for the heading level you want.

▶ With the Outline view mode, you can promote, demote, or move heading levels.

▶ To apply a heading style, use the Style list box on the Ruler or press Ctrl-S to display the Style list box. Select the heading style you want and then press Enter.

▶ Display heading style names in the style name area by entering a measurement in the Style Area Width text box found in the View Preferences dialog box.

▶ Number outline headings by using the Utilities/Renumber command or pressing Alt,U,R and choosing one of the three outline numbering schemes: Legal, Outline, and Sequence.

Enhancing Documents with Pictures and Spreadsheets

In This Chapter

▶ *Inserting and working with graphics and spreadsheets*
▶ *Positioning objects on a page*
▶ *Linking other Windows-based applications with documents*

Inserting graphics, spreadsheets, and charts into your documents adds a visual dimension that can increase the effectiveness of your document. This chapter teaches you the techniques to take advantage of Word's powerful graphics, layout, and linking features.

Working with Graphics in Documents

Word provides an impressive collection of tools for inserting and manipulating graphics in your documents. You can easily insert a wide variety of graphics, including pictures created with popular graphics and drawing programs, digitized images from scanners, and spreadsheets and charts from spreadsheet programs. Word doesn't actually insert the picture into your document. Rather it inserts an *import field* that establishes a link between the Word document and the file containing the image. Chapter 10 explains in more detail how to work with fields.

There are two methods for inserting pictures into documents. The first imports a graphic file using the Insert/Picture command. The second uses the Windows Clipboard to copy a picture from another Windows-based application, such as Microsoft Paint or Excel, and then paste it into Word.

Word provides a number of tools for enhancing an inserted picture, such as resizing, cropping, and adding borders. However, Word doesn't provide tools for drawing or editing the actual graphic image; this must be done with the appropriate software package.

Viewing Pictures

Word displays pictures three ways, depending on the view features you're using. Pictures can be displayed as a field code, an empty frame, or the actual graphic image, as shown in Figure 8.1. Displaying pictures on your screen slows down Word because the program has to redraw the picture when the screen changes. By not displaying pictures, you can speed up Word when you are working only on text. If you're displaying pictures, the pictures disappear from your screen as you enter text. When you stop typing or editing, Word redisplays the pictures. Here are the settings needed to display the different picture views:

Picture View	View Feature Settings
Field Code	Use Normal, Draft, or Page view mode with the Show All feature turned on.
Picture Frame	Use Normal or Draft view mode with the Show All feature turned off.
Graphic Image	Use Normal or Page view mode with the Show All feature turned off and the Picture option turned on in the View Preferences dialog box. The Page view mode displays the picture in the size it will print and displays its actual position in your document. The Print Preview mode also displays the picture as it will print on the page.

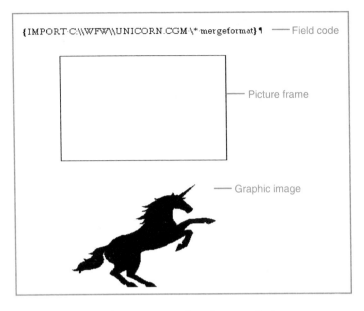

Figure 8.1   *The three views of an inserted picture.*

229

How a picture is displayed on the screen is determined, in part, by your printer and its resolution. Generally, if you insert a picture, and the Display As Printed option in the View Preferences dialog box is turned on, the size of the picture on your screen matches its printed size. Changing the display resolution, such as changing from EGA to VGA, can affect the display of the picture.

Inserting Graphic Files in a Document

Graphic images produced in drawing programs or scanners are saved in files having unique file formats. Many of these files can be read by Word if the appropriate graphics filter (which translates the file formats) has been installed. With the exception of Tagged Image File Format (TIFF) files, you must install the appropriate graphics filter in Word, by using the Setup program (see Appendix A), before you can insert the picture file in Word. For example, if you create a graph chart using Lotus 1-2-3, the graphic image is saved in a Lotus .PIC file format. Before you can display the image in Word, the .PIC graphics filter must be installed. Table 8.1 lists the different file formats that Word supports. The TIFF file format is a standard file format supported by many graphics programs as well as scanned images. TIFF files are identified by a .TIF filename extension.

Table 8.1   File Formats Supported by Word

File Type	Description
CGM (Computer Graphics Metafile)	A standard file format generated by such programs as Harvard Graphics, Ventura Publisher, and PageMaker.
ADI	Files generated using AutoCAD.
HPGL	Plotter files generated by programs such as AutoCAD. HPGL files use the filename extension .PLT.
PCX	Files created using PC Paintbrush. This format is supported by a wide range of programs.
PIC	Lotus 1-2-3 graphic files. This is a widely supported but less sophisticated graphic file format.
IMA	Zenographics Mirage file format.
NAPLPS	Video Show file format. Uses the extension .PIC.
Micrografx Draw	Micrografx Draw and Micrografx Designer file format. Uses the filename extension .DRW.
Windows Metafile	A file format supported by a number of Windows applications, including Arts and Letters, Page-Maker, and others. Most Windows programs cannot accept a Windows Metafile larger than 64K.
TIFF	Tagged Image File Format files are generated by many programs and scanners. This is the graphic file format for Word.

230

To insert a picture file into a document, choose the Insert/ Picture command. The Insert Picture dialog box appears, as shown in Figure 8.2. The Quick Steps explain how to insert a picture file in the TIFF format into your document. You can follow these steps for any file format supported by Word if you've installed the appropriate graphics filter.

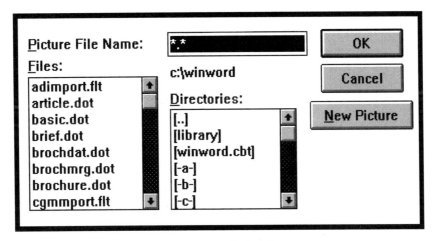

Figure 8.2   The Insert Picture dialog box.

Inserting a TIFF Format Picture in Your Document

231

1. Make sure you're in Normal view mode, the Show All feature is turned off, and the Picture check box in the View Preferences dialog box is turned on.

    This enables the picture to be displayed on your screen.

2. Place the insertion point at the spot where you want to place the picture.

    Word displays the Insert Picture dialog box.

3. Choose Insert/Picture command or press Alt,I,P.

4. Type *.TIF in the Picture File Name text box.

    This command instructs Word to display only files with the .TIF filename extension in the Files list box. If you want to use another installed file format, enter the appropriate filename extension, such as *.PIC or *.PCX.

5. Choose the Directories list box or press Alt-D.

    Word displays in the Files list box any files having the .TIF extension.

6. Choose the LIBRARY subdirectory from the directory in which you have installed the Word program.

For example, if you used Word's default directories, the directory is WINWORD\LIBRARY. The file MONIQUE.TIF is displayed in the Files list box.

7. Choose the Files list box or press Alt-F.

8. Double-click on the MONIQUE.TIF file, or press the Down Arrow key to highlight MONIQUE.TIF. Then choose the OK button or press Enter.

Word imports and displays the MONIQUE.TIF picture file into your document, as shown in Figure 8.3.

□

232

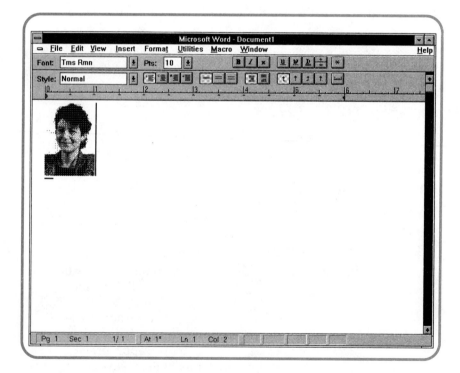

Figure 8.3   The MONIQUE.TIF picture displayed in your document.

Pasting Pictures from a Windows-Based Graphics Program

If you use a Windows-based graphics program, such as Microsoft Paint (bundled with Windows), to draw a picture, you can use the Windows Clipboard feature to copy all or part of a picture into your Word document. This copying and pasting between applications within the Windows environment is one of the most useful features of working with Windows-based applications. Because features such as copying and pasting with the Clipboard are standardized across Windows applications, you can use the same procedures to quickly copy and paste pictures from any Windows-based drawing program. The Quick Steps explain how to paste a graphic from Microsoft Paintbrush into your document.

 Pasting a Graphic from Microsoft Paint into Your Word Document

233

1. Using the Microsoft Paint-brush program (found in the Accessories program of the Windows Program Manager), create a graphic to paste into a Word for Windows document.

2. With your graphic displayed, select the entire graphic or the part you want by using the Pick tool (the scissors box at the top right corner of the tool box).

   Select only what you want: you don't need to include any white space around the picture. You can add white space around a picture in Word, but you can't edit the picture once it's in your document.

3. Choose the Edit/Copy command or press Alt,E,C.

   The picture is copied onto the Windows Clipboard.

4. Switch to the Word program window and open the document file into which you want to paste the picture.

5. Place the insertion point at the spot where you want to insert the picture.

   Most of the time you'll want to insert a picture into a blank paragraph to make it easier to change the size of the picture and position it.

6. Choose the Edit/Paste command or press Alt,E,P.

Word pastes the picture into your document. The shape and size of the picture may appear different from the original dimensions in the graphics program. You can change the size of the graphic, as explained later in this chapter. □

> **Note:** Word treats tables, pictures, spreadsheets, and charts just like paragraphs. As such, you can copy, move, and delete them as you would paragraphs.

234

Pasting in Spreadsheets and Charts from Microsoft Excel

If you're using Excel with Windows, you can add a new dimension to your business document by copying into it a spreadsheet or chart as if it were a picture. To copy a spreadsheet or chart from Excel, use the Windows Clipboard. Once the spreadsheet and/or chart images are in your Word document, you can resize and enhance them in the same way you would any inserted picture. The Quick Steps explain how to copy and paste a spreadsheet or chart as a picture into your Word document.

 Copying a Spreadsheet or Chart into a Word Document

1. After starting the Excel program, display the spread-sheet or chart you want to incorporate into your Word document.

2. If you're copying a spread-sheet, select the portion of a spreadsheet you want by dragging the mouse.

Word highlights the se-lected portion of the spread-sheet. If you don't want the column and row headings or grid lines to appear in a spreadsheet, choose the

3. If you're copying a chart, choose the Chart/Select Chart command or press Alt,C,C.

Options/Display command and turn the appropriate check boxes off.

Word displays handle boxes on the sides and corners of the chart. You can drag these handles to select just a portion of the chart.

4. Hold down the Shift key and choose the Edit/Copy Picture command or press Alt,E,C.

Holding down the Shift key changes the usual Copy command to the Copy Picture command. If you're copying a spreadsheet, Excel displays a dialog box, as shown in Figure 8.4(A). If you're copying a chart, Excel displays an expanded dialog box, as shown in Figure 8.4(B).

235

5. If you're copying a spread-sheet, choose the As Shown on the Screen option button (Alt-S), and choose the OK button or press Enter.

The selected spreadsheet is copied into the Windows Clipboard.

6. If you're copying a chart, choose the As Shown on Screen option button (Alt-S) in the Appearance box and the As Shown on Screen (Alt-C) option in the Size box. Then choose the OK button or press Enter.

Word copies the selected chart into the Windows Clipboard.

7. Switch to the Word program window, open the document file into which you want to paste the spreadsheet or chart, and then place the insertion point where you want the spreadsheet or chart to appear.

It's a good idea to insert the spreadsheet or chart into a blank paragraph. This avoids any formatting conflicts.

8. Choose the Edit/Paste command or press Alt,E,P.

Word pastes the spreadsheet or chart into your Word document, which is displayed on your screen according to the view mode you're using. The text or chart may appear larger than you want. You can change the size of the spreadsheet or chart in Word, as explained later in this chapter. □

236

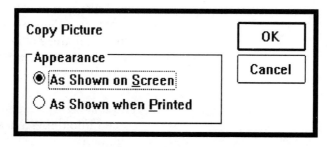

(A)   The Spreadsheet Copy Picture Dialog Box

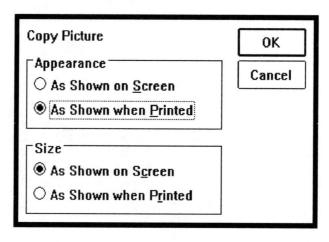

(B)   The Chart copy Picture Dialogue Box

Figure 8.4.   The Spreadsheet and Chart Copy Picture dialog boxes.

Inserting Blank Picture Frames

You can reserve a blank space in your document by inserting an empty picture frame. This enables you to manually paste a graphic at that location *after* printing the document. To insert a picture frame into your document, first place the insertion point where you want to insert the picture frame. Choose the Insert/Picture command or press Alt,I,P. Word displays the Insert Picture dialog box. Choose the New Picture button or press Alt-N. Word inserts a 1-inch by 1-inch picture frame. You can resize this frame as you would any picture.

Resizing Pictures

Pictures vary in size, depending on the source of the graphic image and other factors. Once you've inserted any graphic image into your document, you can resize it by using Word's scaling feature. *Scaling* shrinks or expands a graphic image by changing the height and/or width relative to the initial 100% measurement. For example, if you change the height and width to 150%, you're expanding the picture size by one-half its original size, or if you change the height and width to 50%, the picture is shrunk to one-half its original size. You can set the height and width settings differently, which you may need to do for rectangular-shaped pictures.

237

The mouse provides the quickest way to perform scaling functions and enables you to see your changes as you work. To scale a graphic image with the mouse, drag the handles that are displayed when you select the graphic. You can also use the Format/Picture command to scale a picture.

 Scaling a Picture with the Mouse

1. With the graphic image displayed in your document, move the mouse pointer anywhere within the picture or frame, and then click the left mouse button.

Small black square handles appear at the edges of the picture or frame, as shown in Figure 8.5. The corner handles affect the two sides that intersect at the corner. The side handles, located at the middle of each of the four sides, affect only the side on which the handle is located.

2. Move the mouse pointer to the handle you want to use, hold down the Shift key, and drag the handle to the new position you want.

An outline of the picture moves with the mouse pointer as you drag it. The percentage of the original size of the picture appears in the status bar and changes as you move the mouse.

3. Release the Shift key and mouse button.

Word redraws the picture.

Figure 8.5   A selected graphic image.

Using the Format/Picture command allows you to pinpoint a more exact scaling percentage measurement than when using the mouse. However, fine tuning using this method requires you to switch between the picture display and the Format Picture dialog box, as shown in Figure 8.6.

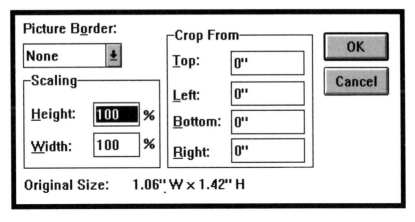

Figure 8.6   The Format Picture dialog box .

 Scaling a Picture with the Format/Picture Command

1. Select the picture you want to scale.

2. Choose the Format/Picture command or press Alt,T,R.

   Word displays the Format Picture dialog box. If a picture isn't selected, the Picture command is dimmed in the Format menu.

3. Type a scaling percentage in the Height text box.

   Any value less than 100% shrinks the picture, and any value greater than 100% expands the picture. The original measurement size of the picture is displayed at the bottom of the dialog box.

4. Choose the Width text box or press Alt-W.

   The Width text box is highlighted.

5. Type a scaling value in the Width text box.

   If you want to keep the width of the picture the same proportion as the height of the picture, type the same percentage you entered in step 3.

6. Choose the OK button or press Enter.	Word redraws the picture based on the new scaling values. □

> **Note:** To quickly restore any picture to its original size, enter 100% in the Height and Width text boxes found in the Format Picture dialog box.

Cropping Pictures

Cropping a picture means to trim a picture's size. The process is similar to trimming a photograph with a pair of scissors. Word provides two ways to crop a picture: with the mouse or with the Format/Picture command. To crop a picture using the mouse, first click on the picture to display its handles. Move the mouse pointer to the handle for the part of the picture you want to affect. Using the side handles generally allows you more accuracy than using the corner handles, which pull the two sides that intersect at the corner. Drag the handle until only the portion of the picture you want is displayed, and then release the mouse button.

Cropping a Picture by Using the Format/Picture Command

1. Select the picture you want to crop.	The picture frame is displayed with handles.
2. Choose the Format/Picture command or press Alt,T,P.	Word displays the Format Picture dialog box.
3. Choose the Top text box in the Crop From box or press Alt-T.	The Top text box is highlighted.
4. Enter the measurement for the amount of picture space you want to crop, such as .15".	If you want to use the same measurement in the other Crop From text boxes, select the measurement and then press Ctrl-Ins to copy the measurement onto the Clipboard.
5. Press Tab.	The Left text box is highlighted.

6. Enter a measurement.

If you're using the same measurement for all the Crop From text boxes and you copied the first entry onto the Clipboard, press Shift-Ins to insert the copied measurement.

7. Repeat steps 5 and 6 for the Bottom and Right text boxes.

8. Choose the OK button or press Enter.

Word redraws your picture to reflect your cropping measurements. □

Adding Borders to Pictures

Adding a border to a picture can enhance it or help distinguish the picture from the surrounding text. The process is similar to adding a border to a paragraph or table. However, you can't draw a line on just one side of a picture as you can for paragraphs and tables. The border style options for pictures are the same as those for tables:

241

Border Option	Result
None	No border is placed around a picture.
Single	A single thin-line border is placed around a picture.
Thick	A single thick-line border is placed around a picture.
Double	A double thin-line border is placed around a picture.
Shadow	A shadowed line is placed around a picture.

To add a picture border, first select the picture around which you want to place a border. Then choose the Format/Picture command or press Alt,T,R. In the Format Picture dialog box, choose the Picture Border list box or press Alt-O. Click on the Down Arrow button or press Alt-Down Arrow to display the list of border options. Click on the border option you want or press the Down or Up Arrow keys to select the option. Then choose the OK button or press Enter. Word displays a border around your picture.

Adding Captions to Pictures

A *caption* is a short sentence or phrase used to describe a picture. You can add a caption directly to the same paragraph that contains the picture. Adding text directly into the paragraph containing the picture ensures that the caption text always stays with the picture should you later reposition it. You can also add text in a paragraph that is separate from the picture paragraph. If you reposition the picture, as explained later in this chapter, you need to select both the picture and the caption paragraphs. Figure 8.7 shows a caption added to a picture paragraph.

Figure 8.7 A captioned picture paragraph.

To caption a picture, first place the insertion point immediately after the picture and press Shift-Enter. This inserts a newline character to begin a new line but keeps the picture and the text in the same paragraph. Then type your caption text. If you want your caption text to be more than a single line, press Shift-Enter for each additional line. You can format the caption text as you would format any characters. You can apply paragraph formats, but keep in mind that if you use any paragraph formatting options, you will change the format of the picture as well as the caption because they're in the same paragraph.

Adding White Space Around a Picture

Adding white space to a picture creates a white mat effect around the picture. If you've added a border around your picture, the white space is added between the picture and the border line. Adding white space around a picture is similar to cropping a picture, except that the movement is in the opposite direction.

To add white space around your picture, use the Crop From text boxes in the Format Picture dialog box or use the mouse. In most cases, using the Format/Picture command provides the easiest way to add white space because you can quickly add all spacing measurements at one time. The Quick Steps explain how to add an equal amount of white space around a picture by using the Format/Picture command. Of course, you can specify unequal measurements for white spaces as well.

243

 Adding White Space Around a Picture by Using the Format/ Picture Command

1. Select the picture you want to add space around.	Word displays the picture frame with handles around the picture.
2. Choose the Format/Picture command or press Alt,T,R.	The Format Picture dialog box appears.
3. Choose the Top text box or press Alt-T.	The Top text box is highlighted in the Crop From box.
4. Type a negative decimal measurement, such as –.15.	The negative measurement indicates you're adding space around a picture, the opposite of the cropping direction. The new measurement is displayed in the text box.

5. Select the measurement and then press Ctrl-Ins.	Word copies the measurement onto the Clipboard.
6. Press Tab.	Word highlights the <u>L</u>eft text box.
7. Press Shift-Ins.	The measurement entered in the <u>T</u>op text box is displayed in the <u>L</u>eft text box.
8. Repeat steps 6 and 7 for the <u>B</u>ottom and <u>R</u>ight text boxes.	The same measurement that is in the <u>T</u>op and <u>L</u>eft text boxes appears in the <u>B</u>ottom and <u>R</u>ight text boxes.
9. Choose the OK button or press Enter.	Word redraws the picture according to your specifications. □

244

To add white space using the mouse, first select the picture you want to add white space around. Word displays the handles at the edges of the picture. Drag each side handle to expand the picture beyond its size for each of the four sides. An outline of the picture frame moves as you move the mouse pointer, and the measurement coordinates are displayed in the status bar. We recommend that you use the side handles because it is difficult to achieve an even spacing with the corner handles.

Positioning Objects on a Page

You can use the Forma<u>t</u>/P<u>o</u>sition command to achieve exact positioning of an object on a page. An object can be anything contained in a paragraph, such as a picture, spreadsheet, chart, table, or sidebar. Positioning an object is a two-step process for each horizontal and vertical position coordinate. The first step is setting the relative reference point, such as margins or page edges, on which you want to base your object positioning. The second step involves selecting a positioning option, such as center, left, or right, relative to the margin or page edge.

You can also specify exact locations by using your own measurements relative to the margins or page edges. Choosing the Forma<u>t</u>/P<u>o</u>sition command or pressing Alt,T,O displays the Format Position dialog box, as shown in Figure 8.8.

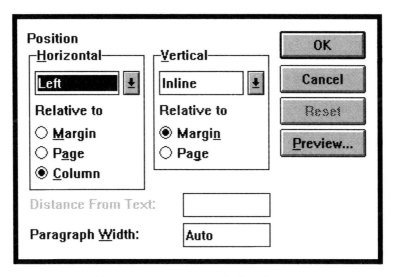

Figure 8.8   The Format Position dialog box.

245

Once you position an object, the surrounding text automatically wraps around it. You don't see this effect in Normal or Draft view modes. You do see the objects in their assigned positions with the text wrapped around them in Page view or Print Preview modes.

Any object you've positioned with the Format/Position command can be repositioned by using the Boundaries feature in the Print Preview mode, as explained in Chapter 5. Choosing the Preview button in the Format Position dialog box displays the object in Print Preview mode. You can always return a positioned object to its original location by selecting the positioned object, choosing the Format/Position command, and then choosing the Reset button.

> ▶ **Note:** You must first position an object using the Format/
> Position command before you can reposition it using the
> Boundaries command in the Print Preview mode.

Position Options

The Format Position dialog box contains two clusters of options in the Horizontal and Vertical boxes. When you position an object, you must choose its horizontal and vertical coordinates from these two

boxes. The Horizontal and Vertical list boxes provide several predefined position options for each coordinate. Alternatively, you can
enter your own measurement in each text box to specify an exact
location. All the position options in these list boxes are set relative
to reference points, which are specified in the Relative to boxes.

The Horizontal box in the Format Position dialog box allows
you to choose the horizontal coordinate for an object. There are three
options for setting the relative reference points. The Margin option
anchors an object horizontally relative to the left and right margins.
The Page option anchors an object relative to the left and right page
edges. The Column option anchors an object relative to the column
width and is the default setting. After selecting a Relative to option
button, you can choose a position option from the Horizontal list
box, or you can enter your own measurement into the text box, such
as 3". Here are the available horizontal position options:

Horizontal Option	Result
Left	Anchors the object to the left side of the margin, page, or column.
Center	Anchors the object midway between the left and right margins, page edge, or column.
Right	Anchors the object to the right side of the margin, page edge, or column.
Inside	Used when the Mirror margins feature is turned on. Anchors the object to the inside edge of the margin, page edge, or column. The inside position is the left side of odd-numbered pages, and the right side of even-numbered pages.
Outside	Used when the Mirror margins feature is turned on. Anchors objects to the outside edge of the margin, page edge, or column. The outside position is the right side of odd-numbered pages and the left side of even-numbered pages.

The <u>V</u>ertical box provides the options for establishing the vertical coordinate of an object. There are two options for setting the vertical relative reference points. The <u>M</u>argin option anchors an object vertically relative to the top and bottom margins. The Page option anchors an object relative to the top and bottom page edges. After selecting the Relative to option, you can choose a position option from the <u>V</u>ertical list box, or you can enter your own measurement into the text box, such as 6". Here are the available vertical position options:

Vertical Option	**Result**
Inline	Anchors the object to wherever it falls in the text.
Top	Anchors the object flush with the top margin or page edge.
Center	Centers the object between the top and bottom margins or page edges.
Bottom	Places object flush with the bottom margin or page edge.

247

Enhancing a Positioned Object

In addition to the setting position coordinates, the Format Position dialog box has two other features: the <u>D</u>istance From Text and the Paragraph <u>W</u>idth text boxes. If you change the default horizontal and vertical coordinates to position an object, the <u>D</u>istance From Text text box is activated, displaying a .13-inch measurement. This default measurement is the white space that Word places around the object to separate it from any surrounding text. You can change this default measurement by simply entering your own measurement.

The Paragraph <u>W</u>idth text box allows you to adjust the width of a paragraph from Word's default (Auto) column width setting. For example, if you position an object in a single-column page, the width of the paragraph takes on the width of the entire column. By entering a measurement value in the Paragraph <u>W</u>idth text box, you can shrink the width of a paragraph to allow surrounding text to wrap around it, as shown in Figure 8.9.

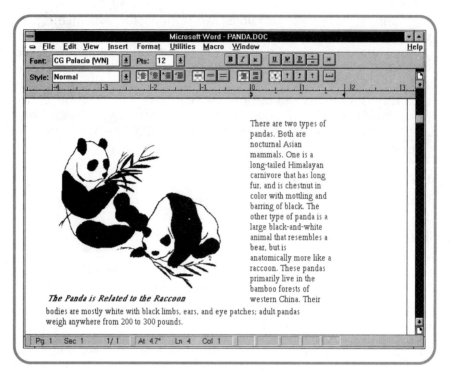

Figure 8.9   A shortened paragraph width.

248

A Positioning Example

In most cases, you'll want to position an object, such as a picture, spreadsheet, or chart, within your document. The Quick Steps explain how to position a picture in the center of a page, using the Format/Position command.

 Centering a Picture by Using the Format/Position Command

1. Select the picture that you want to position on the page.	The picture frame and handles are displayed.
2. Choose the Format/Position command or press Alt,T,O.	Word displays the Format Position dialog box.
3. In the Horizontal box, choose the Center option from the list box.	

4. Choose the <u>M</u>argin option button in the <u>H</u>orizontal box or press Alt-M.

5. Choose the <u>V</u>ertical box or press Alt-V.

Word highlights the Vertical List box.

6. Choose the Center option from the Vertical list box.

7. Choose the Margi<u>n</u> option button in the <u>V</u>ertical list box or press Alt-N.

8. To change the white space between the graphic and the surrounding text, choose the <u>D</u>istance From Text text box or press Alt-D and enter a measurement.

For example, enter .25" for $\frac{1}{4}$ inch of white space around the picture.

9. If you want the object to have a different width than the surrounding column width, choose the Paragraph <u>W</u>idth text box or press Alt-W and enter a measurement.

For example, using Word's single-column default measurement, enter a measurement less than 6 inches to narrow the paragraph width. This causes any surrounding text to wrap around the object.

249

10. Choose the <u>P</u>review button or press Alt-P.

Word displays the positioned picture in the Print Preview mode, showing its new position. You can now reposition the graphic, using the <u>B</u>oundaries command in the Print Preview window. Choose <u>C</u>ancel or press Alt-C to exit the Print Preview mode. □

Creating Links with Other Windows Applications

An important feature of Windows is its ability to easily share information between files and programs. Many Windows-based applications support a feature called Dynamic Data Exchange (DDE), which allows you to link Windows application files to one another. For example, you can set up a link between your business report composed in Word for Windows and a spreadsheet or chart file created in Microsoft Excel.

You can set up the link so that the Word document is automatically updated if any changes are made to the linked spreadsheet or chart file. Whenever you open a document that contains an auto update link, Word displays a message asking if you want to establish the link to update the information. You can unlink a linked object by first selecting it and then pressing Ctrl-Shift-F9.

The Quick Steps explain how to link a spreadsheet file from Microsoft Excel to your Word document. When the spreadsheet text is inserted into your document, it is converted to a table format. You can then edit the information by using Word's table editing and formatting commands.

 Linking an Excel Spreadsheet to a Word Document

1. After starting the Excel program, open the Excel spreadsheet file that you want to link to a Word document.

2. Select the entire spreadsheet or any portion and then choose the Edit/Copy command or press Alt,E,C.

   The selected cells are highlighted and then copied onto the Windows Clipboard.

3. Switch to the Word program and open the document file into which you want to insert the Excel information.

4. Position the insertion point where you want to insert the linked data.

5. Choose the Edit/Paste Link command or press Alt,E,L.

Word displays the Paste Link dialog box, as shown in Figure 8.10.

6. Choose the Auto Update check box or press Alt-A.

Word sets up a link that inserts new data automatically. If you leave the Auto Update check box turned off, you must press F9 to update the linked information.

7. Choose OK or press Enter.

Word inserts selected information into your document in a table format. □

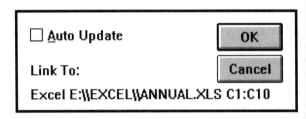

Figure 8.10   The Paste Link dialog box.

251

What You Have Learned

▶   There are two methods for inserting pictures into documents: importing a graphics file with the Insert/Picture command or using the Windows Clipboard.

▶   Word displays pictures in three ways, depending on the view features you are using: as a field code, an empty frame, or the actual graphic image.

▶   To insert picture files from other applications, use the Insert/Picture command or press Alt,I,P.

▶   With the Windows Clipboard, you can copy pictures, spreadsheets, and charts from other Windows-based applications and paste them into documents.

▶ To scale and crop pictures, use the mouse or choose the Format/Picture command (Alt,T,R).

▶ To add borders, white space, and captions to pictures, choose the Format/Picture command or press Alt,T,R.

▶ Position objects, such as tables, pictures, and spreadsheets, anywhere on a page by using the Format/Position command (Alt,T,O).

252

Saving Time: Using Glossaries, Macros, Styles, and Templates

In This Chapter
253

- ▶ *Saving and inserting glossary entries*
- ▶ *Recording and running macros*
- ▶ *Defining and applying styles*
- ▶ *Working with templates*

Word for Windows provides powerful time-saving features to improve your word processing productivity. These features allow you to store and retrieve text, graphics, keystrokes, and paragraph and document formats. By utilizing these stored components, you can quickly assemble documents without having to start from scratch.

Glossaries, Macros, Styles, and the Template Connection

Every document provides you with three time-saving elements: *glossaries,* for storing frequently used text and/or graphics that can then be easily inserted in your document; *macros*, a recorded series of actions; and *styles*, a group of predefined paragraph-formatting instructions.

Generally these elements are stored in a template. A *template* is a document-formatting stencil, which provides a pattern or foundation for creating a particular type of document, such as a memo or a report. Every document is based on a template. Word's default template (NORMAL) provides default settings, such as margins, page dimensions, and character and paragraph formats.

Word makes features available to you in three contexts: document, template, and global. The *global* context is Word's default template, NORMAL. Saving glossaries, macros, and styles using the global context (NORMAL) makes them available to all documents. Saving glossaries, macros, and styles to a template other than NORMAL makes them available only to documents based on that template. Glossaries and macros cannot be saved by using the document context; however, styles can be.

Using Glossaries to Save Time

Glossary entries save you time by storing frequently used blocks of text and/or graphics and allowing you to insert them later in a document. You are saved the work of having to retype the text or import the picture each time. Glossary entries work similarly to the Clipboard. Unlike the Clipboard, however, you can permanently save up to 150 glossary entries until you are ready to delete them. Keep in mind that the more glossary entries stored, the slower Word runs.

Saving and inserting glossary entries is performed by using the Edit/Glossary command. Word displays the Edit Glossary dialog box, as shown in Figure 9.1. Initially, the Glossary command in the Edit menu is dimmed, indicating it's unavailable. To activate the Glossary command, you need to select something in your document, such as text or a picture, and then choose the Edit/Glossary command or press Alt,E,O. The Quick Steps explain how to save a selected item in your document as a glossary entry.

Saving Text or Graphics as a Glossary Entry

1. Select the text and/or graphics you want to save.

2. Choose the Edit/Glossary command or press Alt,E,O.

   Word displays the Edit Glossary dialog box.

3. In the Glossary Name text box, type a name for the new glossary entry.

   A glossary name can be up to 31 characters long, and can include spaces. Word displays the first 38 characters of the selected text at the bottom of the dialog box. If there is more text in the glossary entry, Word displays an ellipsis (...).

4. In the Context box, choose the Global (Alt-G) or Template (Alt-T) option button.

   The Global option saves the glossary entry in the NORMAL template, making the glossary entry available to all Word documents. The Template option saves the glossary entry to the current document's template.

255

5. Choose the Define button or press Enter.

   Word automatically saves glossary entries when you save the document and its template. ☐

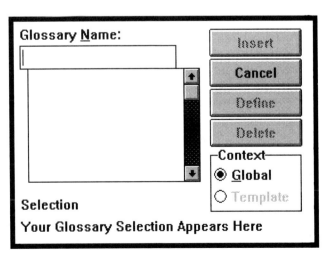

Figure 9.1   The Edit Glossary dialog box.

Q **Inserting a Glossary Entry into Your Document**

1. Place the insertion point where you want to insert the glossary entry.

2. Choose the Edit/Glossary command or press Alt,E,O. — Word displays the Edit Glossary dialog box.

3. Double-click on the glossary entry's name or press the Down Arrow to highlight the glossary entry name you want and then choose the Insert button (Alt-I) or press Enter. — Word inserts the glossary entry's contents into your document, starting at the insertion point.

□

256

After saving a glossary entry, you can insert that entry into your document. To quickly repeat the insertion, place the insertion point at a new location and then press F4 or choose the Edit/Repeat command.

> ▶ **Tip:** If you know the name of the glossary you want to insert, type the name of the glossary entry and then press F3.

Changing, Deleting, and Printing Glossary Entries

To change an existing glossary entry, first insert the glossary entry and make your changes. Next, select the text or graphic and then choose the Edit/Glossary command or press Alt,E,O. Select the name of the glossary entry you want to replace from the Glossary Name List box, and then choose the Define button or press Alt-D. Word displays a confirmation dialog box asking if you want to redefine the glossary entry. Choose the Yes button or press Y. Word replaces the entry's contents.

To delete a glossary entry, select the glossary entry name from the Glossary Name List box in the Edit Glossary dialog box, and then choose the Delete button or press Alt-L. Choose the Close button or press Enter to delete the glossary entry and close the Edit Glossary dialog box.

Word allows you to print a list of those glossary entries and their contents that are attached to the current document's template. Choose the File/Print command (Alt,F,P) or press Ctrl-Shift-F12. Word displays the Print dialog box. Choose the Glossary option from the Print list box, and then choose the OK button or press Enter. Word prints each glossary entry name (alphabetically), followed by its contents.

Using Macros

Macros are a powerful tool for increasing your productivity because they automate a sequence of commands and keystrokes. You can create a macro to do almost anything in Word. And after you've created the macro, you can quickly execute it by selecting a single command or pressing a key combination.

257

There are two ways to create macros in Word: using Word's macro recorder to record your actions or using Word's macro language. This book focuses on the easiest way to create macros—using Word's macro recorder. Before you record a macro, think about what you want the macro to do. Keep in mind that every action you perform is recorded when recording a macro. In general, you should plan to select text before running a macro that affects it.

Recording a Macro

Recording a macro records keystrokes or commands as you enter or choose them. After you've recorded the macro, you can replay it to reproduce the recorded actions. Word responds just as if you were performing the actions again. To record a macro, select the Macro/Record command. Word displays the Macro Record dialog box, shown in Figure 9.2.

When you are recording a macro, the mouse pointer appears as a transparent arrow, rather than the usual I-beam, when it's in the text area. The arrow indicates that you cannot use the mouse to perform such actions as moving the insertion point or selecting text.

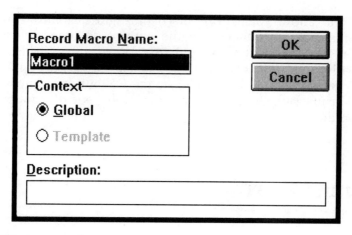

Figure 9.2   The Macro Record dialog box.

Q Recording a Macro

258

1. Choose the Macro/Record command or press Alt,M,C.

   Word displays the Macro Record dialog box.

2. In the Record Macro Name text box, type a name for the macro.

   Word proposes the name Macro1 for the first macro you record, Macro2 for the second, and so on. We recommend that you enter a more descriptive name. The name can be up to 33 characters long but cannot contain spaces. For example, if the macro loads a file named REPORT, you might enter the name LoadReport.

3. In the Context box, choose the Global (Alt-G) or Template (Alt-T) option button.

   The Global option saves the macro to the NORMAL template, making it available to all documents. The Template option saves the macro only to the template that the current document is based on.

4. Choose the Description text box or press Alt-D, and type a short description of the macro.

   This description is displayed in the Macro Run dialog box when you select the macro.

5. Choose the OK button or press Enter.

Word starts your macro recording session and displays REC in the status bar, indicating that the macro recorder is turned on.

6. Perform the actions you want to record.

The recorder records only when you press the keys or use the mouse.

7. After you have performed all the steps, choose the Macro/ Stop Recorder command or press Alt,M,C.

The Macro/Stop Recorder command appears only after the Macro/Record command.

□

Running a Macro

To run a macro, choose the Macro/Run command or press Alt,M,R. Word displays the Macro Run dialog box, as shown in Figure 9.3. Select the macro you want to run from the Run Macro Name list box. As each macro is highlighted, Word displays the description (if any) of the selected macro within the Description box. For example, selecting the macro Delete To End Of Line runs a macro that deletes text from the insertion point to the end of the current line. After selecting the macro you want to run, choose the OK button or press Enter. Double-clicking on the macro name selects it, executes it, and closes the Macro Run dialog box.

259

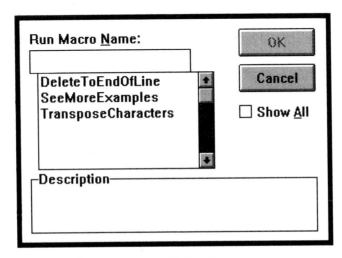

Figure 9.3   The Macro Run dialog box.

Choosing the Show <u>A</u>ll button or pressing Alt-A displays all the Word program commands used in the menus (which are macros), in addition to any macros you've created. Word's command macros can be chosen and executed by using the <u>M</u>acro/<u>R</u>un command. To interrupt a macro after you've started it, press Esc.

Deleting, Renaming, and Changing a Macro

When you no longer need a macro that you created, you can delete it to free up memory and disk space. First choose the <u>M</u>acro/<u>E</u>dit command or press Alt,M,E. Word displays the Edit Macro dialog box, as shown in Figure 9.4. From the Edit Macro <u>N</u>ame list box, choose the name of the macro you want to delete and then choose the <u>D</u>elete button or press Alt-D.

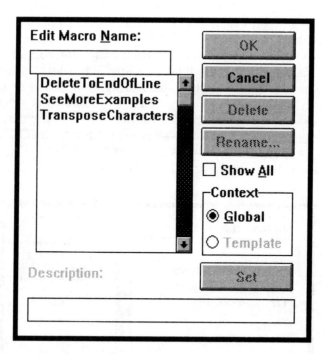

Figure 9.4   The Macro Edit dialog box.

To rename your macro without changing the macro's instructions, first choose the macro name from the Edit Macro <u>N</u>ame list box and then choose the <u>R</u>ename button or press Alt-R. Word displays the New Macro Name dialog box. Type the new name for the selected macro, and then choose the OK button or press Enter. To change the description of your macro, first select the macro name in the Edit Macro <u>N</u>ame list box and then choose the Descri<u>p</u>tion text box or press Alt-I. Enter your new description text.

Assigning Macros to Keys

To use a keyboard shortcut to run macros, simply assign a macro to a key combination, such as a Ctrl and another key you specify. By assigning a macro to a unique key combination, you can quickly execute a macro by pressing the key combination. Because each macro's key combination must be unique, you must choose a combination of keys that is currently unassigned. Assigning a key combination is performed in a trial-and-error manner by first choosing the key combination and then having Word tell you if that key combination is already assigned to another macro (or command). To improve your chances of picking a unique combination, try using Ctrl-Shift and another key or Ctrl and a number key from the top keyboard row.

261

 Assigning a Macro to a Key Combination

1. Choose the <u>M</u>acro/Assign to <u>K</u>ey command or press Alt,M,K.

   Word displays the Macro Assign to Key dialog box, as shown in Figure 9.5.

2. From the Assign Macro <u>N</u>ame list box, select the macro name you want to assign to a key combination.

   In the Current <u>K</u>eys box, Word displays any current key combinations assigned to the macro.

3. Press the key combination you want to assign to the selected macro.

   The keys you press appear in the Key box. If the key combination is currently assigned, Word lists the macro it's assigned to. If the key combination isn't currently in use, Word displays the message `currently unassigned`.

4. If the key combination you entered is assigned, repeat step 3 until you see the message `currently unassigned` in the Key box.

5. Choose the <u>A</u>ssign button or press Alt-A.

Word assigns the key combination to the macro you've selected.

6. Choose the OK button or press Enter.

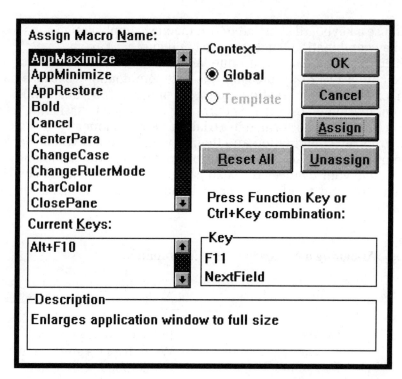

Figure 9.5   The Macro Assign to Key dialog box.

You can check macro key assignments at any time by selecting the macro name in the Macro Assign to Key dialog box. To unassign a macro's key assignment, select the macro in the Assign Macro <u>N</u>ame list box and then choose the <u>U</u>nassign button or press Alt-U.

Occasionally you may find that key assignment becomes so confusing you'd like to return to using Word's default assignments. You can quickly restore macro key combinations to the default Word settings by choosing the <u>R</u>eset All button or pressing Alt-R, and then choosing the OK button or pressing Enter.

Assigning Macros to Menus

When you assign a macro to a menu, Word displays it in the menu. The macro works just like any other command in the menu because, as you'll recall, all of Word's commands are themselves macros. Every command on a Word menu has an underlined letter that you can press to choose the command from the keyboard. Likewise, when you assign a macro to a menu, you need to designate a letter in the macro name. When you are assigning a macro to a command menu, Word suggests a letter from your macro name. Word's suggestion is based on which other letters are already used in the menu.

 Assigning a Macro to a Command Menu

1. Choose the Macro/Assign to Menu command or press Alt,M,M.

   Word displays the Macro Assign to Menu dialog box, as shown in Figure 9.6.

2. Select the macro name from the Assign Macro Name list box.

3. Choose the Menu list box or press Alt-M, and then select the name of the command menu into which the macro will go.

4. Choose the Menu Text box and then type a different macro name if you want.

   Word initially suggests a letter to be underlined by placing an ampersand (&) in front of the letter in the name. You can change the underlined letter by placing the ampersand in front of any other letter in your macro name. Make sure the letter you select doesn't conflict with the underlined letter in any other command in that menu, as listed in the Menu Text list box.

263

5. Choose the Global (Alt-G) or Template (Alt-E) option button in the Context box.

The Global option saves the assignment to the NORMAL template, which makes it available to all documents. The Template option saves the assignment to the template on which the current document is based.

6. Choose the Assign button or press Alt-A.

Word adds the selected macro to the menu.

7. Choose the OK button or press Enter.

Word closes the Macro Assign to Menu dialog box and then displays the macro as a command in the menu you selected. □

264

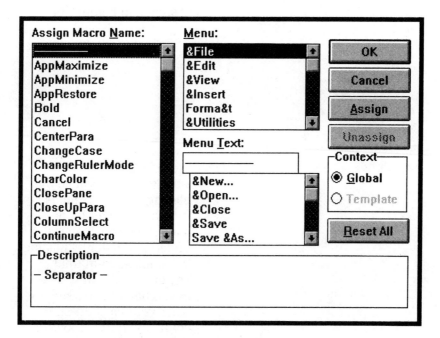

Figure 9.6   The Macro Assign to Menu dialog box.

To remove a macro from a menu, choose the macro name in the Assign Macro Name list box. In the Menu list box, select the name of the menu to which the macro is assigned. Next, choose the Unassign button or press Alt-U to remove the selected macro from the menu.

Using Word's Auto Macros

You can create five automatic macros that Word will run at specific times. By using these special macros, you can automate certain tasks: starting Word, creating a document, opening a document, closing a document, and exiting Word. You create each automatic macro as you would create any other macro by using the Macro/Record command. However, in the Record Macro Name box, you must specify one of the five special macro names that Word recognizes as an automatic macro. Table 9.1 describes these five macros.

Table 9.1 Automatic Macros from the Macro/Record Command

Macro Name	Description
AutoNew	Runs when you create a new document. It does not run when you open an existing document. Available in both the global (NORMAL) and the template context.
AutoOpen	Runs when you open an existing document. Available in both the global (NORMAL) and the template context.
AutoExec	Runs when you start Word. You can prevent AutoExec from running by typing the /m switch when you start Word, for example, WINWORD /M. Available only in the global context (NORMAL).
AutoClose	Runs when you close a document. Exiting Word before closing the document also triggers this macro. Available in both the global (NORMAL) and the template context.
AutoExit	Runs when you exit Word. Available only in the global context (NORMAL).

265

Working with Styles

A *style* is a collection of character and paragraph formats that are recorded, saved, and identified by name. Once these formatting instructions have been saved, you can reapply them to paragraphs requiring the same formats. Using styles instead of formatting each paragraph individually saves time and preserves consistency in your documents. A style can encompass a wide variety of formats, including character formatting, paragraph formatting, tab settings, and paragraph positioning.

In Word, every paragraph is based on a style. By default, Word automatically applies the Normal style to every paragraph in a document. The Normal style formats each new paragraph to include left-aligned text with no indents or spacing before or after, single spacing, and 10-point Times Roman font. The active style name is displayed in the Style list box on the Ruler. Word provides an initial collection of 39 different styles for performing such formatting features as headers and footers, footnotes, headings, indexes, and tables of contents. Most of these styles are not normally displayed in the Style list box on the Ruler because they are integrated into the appropriate command from Word's menu. The only four styles initially displayed in the Style list box are `Normal`, `heading 1`, `heading 2`, and `heading 3`.

266

Defining a Style by Recording a Paragraph's Formats

The easiest way to define a new style is to create and format a paragraph and then save the formats to a style. There are two ways to save a paragraph's formats as a style: using the Style list box on the Ruler or using the Format/Define Styles command. Remember, a style can include character formatting, paragraph formatting, tab settings, and paragraph positioning. However, all characters in the paragraph must have the same character format.

By default, Word saves any new styles to the document. However, as explained later, you can add your styles to the document's template. Style changes are not saved to disk until you save or close your document or exit Word. At that point, Word displays a dialog box asking if you want to save your style changes. Choosing the Yes button or pressing Y saves your changes.

 Recording and Defining a New Style by Using the Ruler

1. Format a paragraph the way you want it and then select it by placing the insertion point anywhere within it.

2. If necessary, choose the View/ Ruler command or press Alt,V,R to display the Ruler.

3. Choose the Style list box or press Ctrl-S.

Word activates the Style text box.

4. Type the name for your new style.

A style name can contain up to 20 characters and can include spaces.

5. Press Enter.

Word displays a message box asking for confirmation to create the style you've specified.

6. Choose the Yes Button or press Y.

Word saves the new style to your current document, and you can view it as an option in the Style list box on the Ruler. □

267

The second way to record and save a style is to use the Format/ Define Styles command. After formatting and selecting the paragraph you want to save as a style, choose the Format/Define Styles command or press Alt,T,F. Word displays the Format Define Styles dialog box, as shown in Figure 9.7. In the Define Style Name text box, type a name for the style. The name can be up to 20 characters long and can include spaces. Choose the OK button or press Enter.

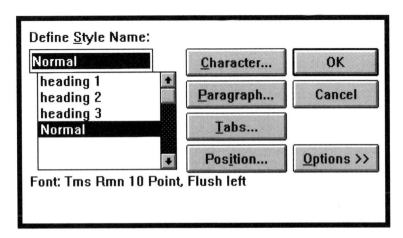

Figure 9.7   The Format Define Styles dialog box.

Defining a Style by Using the Define Styles Command

By using the Define Styles dialog box, you can define a style without actually formatting an existing paragraph. Using this method involves naming the new style and then defining its various formatting characteristics one by one. Choosing the Format/Define Styles command or pressing Alt,T,F displays the Define Styles dialog box, as shown in Figure 9.7. The Define Style Name text box displays the highlighted style from the list box directly below it. The Character, Paragraph, Tabs, and Position buttons access the appropriate Format command dialog box. At the bottom of the Format Define Styles dialog box is a description of the formats included in the selected style. The Options >> button displays an expanded Define Style box with additional features for defining and managing styles, as explained later.

268

 Defining a New Style by Using the Format/Define Styles Command

1. Choose the Format/Define Styles command or press Alt,T,F.

   Word displays the Format Define Styles dialog box.

2. In the Define Style Name text box, type a name for your new style.

   A style name can be up to 20 characters long and can include spaces.

3. Choose one of the formatting option buttons.

   The Character button (Alt-C) displays the Format Character dialog box. The Paragraph button (Alt-P) displays the Format Paragraph dialog box. The Tabs button (Alt-T) displays the Format Tabs dialog box. The Position button (Alt-I) displays the Format Position dialog box.

4. Choose the options you want in the dialog box you selected and then choose the OK button or press Enter.

   Word closes the dialog box, and the Format Define Styles dialog box becomes visible again.

5. Repeat steps 3 and 4 for each additional formatting level you want to incorporate into the style.

6. Choose the OK button or press Enter.

Word closes the Format Define Styles dialog box, defines your style, and displays the style in the Style list box on the Ruler. □

Basing a New Style on an Existing Style

You can save time defining styles by using one style as the basis for defining another. For example, you can use the Normal style as a basis for another style having additional formats. The new style is linked to the Normal style. The benefit (and drawback) of basing a new style on an existing style is that if you change the base style, all the styles based on that style are affected.

269

 Basing a New Style on an Existing Style

1. Choose the Format/Define Styles command or press Alt,T,F.

Word displays the Format Define Styles dialog box.

2. Type a name for the new style in the Define Style Name text box.

3. Choose the Options >> button or press Alt-O.

Word displays the expanded Format Define Styles dialog box.

4. From the drop-down list in the Based On list box, choose the existing style on which the new style will be based.

5. Choose the appropriate format buttons for making additional format entries into your new style.

The style description displayed in the dialog box shows any format additions.

6. Choose the OK button or press Enter.

□

Specifying the Next Style

Whenever you apply a style you've created to a paragraph and then press Enter, Word by default applies the previous style to the new paragraph. In many instances, you may want a particular style to always follow the previously applied style. For example, Word's heading 1 style is set up so that it creates a Normal style paragraph as the next style after a heading 1 style. By using the Next Style list box in the expanded Format Define Styles dialog box, you can specify the next style to be applied after you press Enter, as explained in the Quick Steps.

Q Specifying the Next Style

1. Choose the Format/Define Styles command or press Alt,T,F.

   Word displays the Format Define Styles dialog box.

2. In the Define Style Name list box, choose the style that you want.

3. Choose the Options >> button or press Alt-O.

   Word displays the expanded Format Define Styles dialog box.

4. Choose the Next Style list box or press Alt-N. Then press Alt-Down Arrow or click on the Down Arrow button.

   Word displays the list of available styles.

5. Choose the style that should follow the style specified in the Define Style Name list box.

   If the Next Style text box is left empty, the selected style in the Define Style Name list box is applied as the next style.

6. Choose the OK button or press Enter.

   The next style is specified for the selected style, and Word closes the Format Define Styles dialog box. □

Applying Styles

Once you've saved a paragraph format as a style, you can apply that style to a paragraph you've already typed, or you can apply it to a paragraph mark before you type the text. Before applying a style to a paragraph, you must place the insertion point in or before the paragraph mark. To apply a style to multiple paragraphs, you must select them. You can then apply a style by using the Style list box on the Ruler or the Format/Styles command (Alt,T,Y).

The easiest way to apply a style to the selected paragraph(s) is to select the style from the Style list box on the Ruler. Choose the Style list box or press Ctrl-S, and then click on the Down Arrow button or press Alt-Down Arrow to display the list of available styles. Click on the scroll buttons or press the Up or Down Arrow key to move through the list of styles. Choose the style you want to apply by clicking on the style name or pressing Enter after highlighting the style you want. Word applies the style to the selected paragraph(s).

Another way to apply a style is to choose the Format/Styles command or press Alt,T,Y. Word displays the Format Styles dialog box, as shown in Figure 9.8. Notice that at the bottom of the dialog box are the formats included in the highlighted style. Select the style name from the Style Name list box, and then choose the OK button or press Enter. Double-clicking on the style name automatically applies the style to the selected paragraph(s). The Define button displays the Format Define Styles dialog box, allowing you to create or modify styles.

271

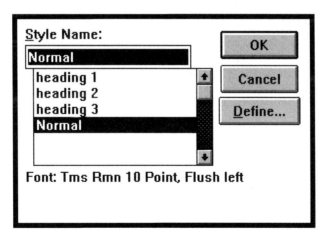

Figure 9.8   The Format Styles dialog box.

You can add formatting to a paragraph after you've applied a style to the paragraph. Formatting added with a Format command overrides the style's formatting. Selecting the paragraph(s) and then pressing Ctrl-X removes all formats after the style was applied. To return the paragraph(s) to the Normal style, apply the Normal style by using the Styles list box on the Ruler. The last style applied can be repeated by selecting the next paragraph(s) and then pressing F4 or choosing the Edit/Repeat Styles command (Alt,E,R).

Viewing Style Names in the Document Window

Word provides two ways for you to view which styles have been applied to your document's paragraphs. In the first way, as you move the insertion point through paragraphs, the style applied to each paragraph is displayed in the Style list box in the Ruler. In the second way, Word displays the style names in a style name area located at the left side of your document.

To display the style name area, choose the View/Preferences command or press Alt,V,E. In the View Preferences dialog box, choose the Style Area Width or press Alt-W. Type a width for displaying style names in the left margin area, such as .80". This width can be adjusted later by using the mouse. Choosing the OK button or pressing Enter displays the style area with applied style names, as shown in Figure 9.9. The style name applied to each paragraph is displayed to the left of the paragraph's first line.

To quickly adjust the width of the style area, move the mouse pointer to the style area split line. The mouse pointer changes to two parallel lines with back-to-back arrows. Next, drag the split line to expand or reduce the style area width. Dragging the split line to the far left removes the style area.

Changing a Style

You can change any style. When you change a style, Word automatically updates every paragraph having that style in your document. If you change a style on which other styles are based, all the other styles reflect the change. There are two ways to change a style: creating a new formatted paragraph and saving it as a style or using the Format/Define Styles command. The Format/Define Styles command allows you to make fine-tuning changes to an existing style, rather than recreating the style. Changing a style by either method is similar to defining a new style, except that you select an existing style name to work with.

You can also change any of Word's default styles. Highlight the Define <u>S</u>tyle Name text box and then press Ctrl-A to display the additional 35 default styles. These styles cover such formatting features as headers and footers, footnotes, headings, and entries for indexes and tables of contents. Because Word applies the Normal style to every paragraph by default, changing the formatting options can save considerable time in formatting your paragraphs. For example, you can specify a different font and/or font size than the default Times Roman, 10-point font. The Quick Steps explain how to change Word's default Normal style to affect the current document, and you can adapt these steps for modifying any style.

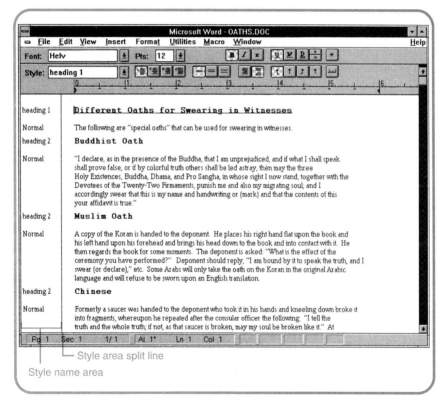

Figure 9.9   The style name area.

Changing the Normal Style

1. Display a document based on the default Normal template. Choose the Forma<u>t</u>/<u>D</u>efine Styles or press Alt,T,F.

Word displays the Define Styles dialog box.

2. With the Normal style displayed in the Define Style Name text box, choose the button for the formatting you want to affect.

The **Character** button (Alt-C) displays the Format Character dialog box. The **Paragraph** button (Alt-P) displays the Format Paragraph dialog box. The **Tabs** button (Alt-T) displays the Format Tabs dialog box. The **Position** button (Alt-I) displays the Format Position dialog box.

3. Choose the options in the Format dialog box that you want, and then choose the OK button or press Enter.

Word returns to the Define Styles dialog box.

4. Repeat step 3 for each additional type of formatting you want to incorporate into the Normal style.

274

5. After selecting all your formatting, choose the OK button or press Enter.

Word saves your changes to the Normal style for the current document. ☐

Deleting and Renaming Styles

You can rename or delete any styles you've defined, However, you can't rename or delete any of Word's default styles. When you delete a style, all paragraphs formatted with that style revert to the Normal style. When you rename a style, the paragraphs formatted with the previous name are changed to the new name.

To rename or delete a style, choose the Format/Define Styles command or press Alt,T,F. In the Format Define Styles dialog box, choose the style name you want to rename or to delete from the Define Style Name list box. Choose the Options >> button or press Alt-O. To rename the selected style, choose the Rename button or press Alt-R. Word displays the Rename dialog box. Type the new name for the style, and choose the OK button or press Enter. To delete the selected style, choose the Delete button or press Alt-L. Word displays a confirmation dialog box. Choose the Yes button or press Y to delete the selected style. If the selected style is one of Word's default styles, the Delete or Rename button is dimmed, indicating the style can't be deleted.

Adding Styles to a Template

By default, Word saves styles to the current document. You can instruct Word to save styles in the current template. This makes the styles available to all documents based on that template. If your document is based on the default NORMAL template, the styles become *global*—available to all Word documents.

You can add styles to a template one at a time, or you can add all styles associated with the document to a template at once. It's easiest to add a style to the current template by choosing the Options >> button (Alt-O) to display the expanded Format Define Style dialog box. Next, choose the Add to Template check box or press Alt-A.

To add an existing style to the current template, choose the Format/Define Styles command and select a style from the Define Style Name list box. Then choose the Options >> button or press Alt-O in the Format Define Styles dialog box. In the expanded Format Define Styles dialog box, choose the Add to Template check box or press Alt-A. You can quickly add all the styles you've created in a document to the current template by using the Merge button in the expanded Format Define Styles dialog box.

275

⊘ **Caution:** Be careful when you are merging styles. The incoming styles always take precedence over any existing styles of the same name.

Q **Adding Styles from a Document into its Current Template**

1. With the document displayed, choose the Format/Define Styles command or press Alt,T,F.

   The Define Styles dialog box appears.

2. Choose the Options >> button or press Alt-O.

   The expanded Define Styles dialog box appears.

3. Choose the Merge button or press Alt-M.

   Word displays the Merge Template Styles dialog box, as shown in Figure 9.10.

4. Choose the To Template button or press Alt-T.

   Word displays a confirmation dialog box.

5. Choose the Yes button or press Y.

Word adds all the styles from your document to the template on which your document is based and then returns to the expanded Format Define Styles dialog box.

6. Choose the OK button or press Enter.

Word closes the Format Define Styles dialog box. Your merged styles are not actually saved until you close, save your document, or exit Word. At that time, Word displays a dialog box asking if you want to save your style changes.

276

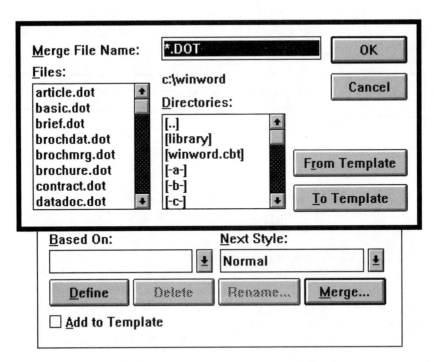

Figure 9.10   The Merge Template Styles dialog box.

Printing a List of Styles

You can print an alphabetical list of the styles attached to a document. The list includes their contents. Such a list provides a useful reference of available styles for a template. Display the document containing the styles you want to print. Choose the File/Print command (Alt,F,P) or press Ctrl-Shift-F12. The Print dialog box appears. In the Print list box, click on the Down Arrow button or press Alt-Down Arrow. The list of print options appears. Choose the Styles options, and then choose the OK button or press Enter. Word prints the styles list with descriptions.

Document Templates

Templates are the foundation of all Word's documents. A template provides the pattern on which your document is based. For example, the default template (NORMAL) contains the styles, glossary entries, macros, and menus used to create a basic Word document. Word comes with several other predefined templates that can save you the time of creating different formats for documents. These include templates for tasks ranging from memos to brochures. In addition to these predefined templates, you can create your own templates from commonly used documents, either from scratch or based on an existing template.

277

Besides being timesavers, templates can ensure uniformity for standardized documents. Whenever you create a new document using the File/New command, Word displays the New File dialog box, as shown in Figure 9.11. Word provides all available templates in the Use Template list box; by default the NORMAL template is automatically selected.

Creating a Template from a Document

The easiest way to create a template is to save an existing document with its text, formats, styles, glossary entries, and macros as a template. Remember, documents based on your new template initially appear exactly like the document from which you're creating the template. With the document displayed, choose the File/Save As command or press Alt,F,A. Choose the Options >> button or press Alt-O. Choose Document Template option from the File Format list box. Then choose the OK button or press Enter.

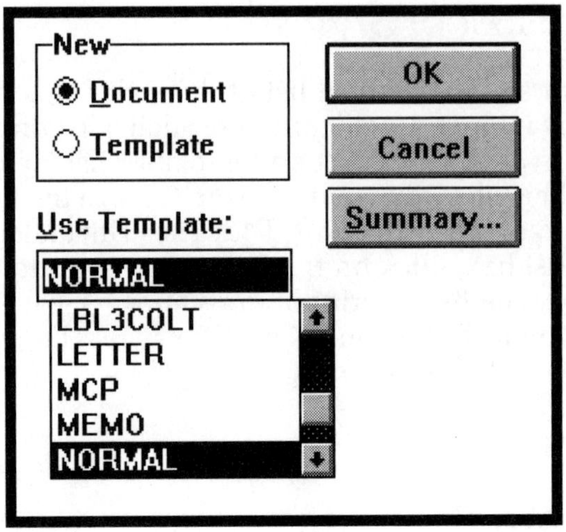

Figure 9.11   The New File dialog box.

278

If a dialog box appears that prompts you for summary information, fill in the information you want and then choose the OK button or press Enter. Word automatically adds the extension .DOT to the filename, indicating that the file is a template.

Creating a Template from Scratch

To create a template from scratch, choose the File/New command or press Alt,F,N. The New File dialog box appears. Choose the Template option button, and then choose the OK button or press Enter. Notice that the window title bar displays Template1, indicating that you are creating a template, not a document.

You can now add text and formats; create styles, glossary entries, macros, and key and menu assignments; and save them as part of the template. Choose the File/Save command or press Alt,F,S. Type an eight-character name for the new template. Then choose the OK button or press Enter.

If a dialog box appears that prompts you for summary information, fill in the information you want and then choose the OK button or press Enter. Word automatically adds the extension .DOT to the filename, indicating that the file is a template.

Word's Predefined Templates

To open a new document based on a template other than NORMAL, choose the File/New command or press Alt,F,N. In the Use Template list box, choose one of Word's predefined templates. Choose the OK button or press Enter. Word opens a new document, based on the selected template. Table 9.2 lists Word's commonly used predefined templates.

Table 9.2 *Word's Predefined Templates*

Template Name	Description
ARTICLE	Magazine-article format with multiple-column text. Automatically wraps text around positioned paragraphs and graphics.
BASIC	Simplified word processor commands.
BRIEF	Legal-brief format with paragraphs numbered in legal style. Customized Insert command and customized glossary listing allow you to insert specific licensing paragraphs.
BROCHURE	Links text from other files to a frequently changing document with graphics. Uses the template files BROCHMRG.DOT and BROCH.DOT.
CONTRACT	Legal contract and license agreement format.
ENVELOPE	Prints envelopes.
FRMLTR	Form-letter format that merges addresses from the ADDRESS.DOT template. Automatically changes the greeting, depending on whether a first name is available, and uses a glossary to insert a closing and signature block. The template file DATADOC.DOT contains data for this template.
LETTER	Letter format that contains the AutoNew macro, which automatically updates information such as the date.
LBL#COL(T)	Different label formats. The # represents the number of label columns. The *T* indicates continuous-feed labels. Label templates without a *T* specify a single-sheet printer, such as a laser printer. The LBL#COL(T) templates use the addresses in the ADDRESS.DOT template. LBL15COLT creates continuous 1.5" wide labels.

279

(continued)

Table 9.2   *(continued)*

Template Name	Description
MEMO	Memorandum format that displays a graphic letterhead and prompts the user to fill in information such as whom the memo is for.
PAPER	Academic or scientific research papers. This template also supports equations.
PCWORD	Converts Word 5 (Word for DOS) glossaries to Word for Windows glossaries.
REPORT	Business-report format with heading styles for title and headings. Supports easy insertion of graphs, charts, and tables.
TERM	Term-paper format.

280 *Creating a Template Based on an Existing Template*

Basing a new template on an existing template saves time in creating templates. When you base one template on another, Word makes a copy of the first template as a foundation for the new template. The new template has all the same information and formatting as the original. Basing one template on another allows you to take advantage of previously created formats.

To create a template based on an existing template, choose the File/New command or press Alt,F,N. Choose the Template option button. In the Use Template list box, type or select the name of the template on which you want to base the new template. Choose the OK button or press Enter. Change the template as desired. Choose the File/Save command or press Alt,F,S, and type a name for the new template. Then choose the OK button or press Enter. If a dialog box appears that prompts you for summary information, fill in the information you want and then choose the OK button or press Enter.

Editing a Template

Editing templates is like editing regular documents: you open the template, make your changes, and save the template. However, templates aren't linked to documents in the same way styles are linked to paragraphs. You can create a document by using a template and then change the template, but the changes won't affect the documents previously created with the template. Remember, changes made to the default template NORMAL.DOT change Word's defaults.

 Editing a Template

1. Choose the File/Open command or press Alt,F,O.

   The Open File dialog box appears.

2. Type or select the name of the template you want to edit.

   To display a list of document templates, enter `*.dot` in the Open File Name text box and press Enter. Use the Directories list box to move to another directory.

   as you would a document.

3. Edit and format the template

   Remember that any text in the template will be inserted into every new document based on that template.

   command or press Alt,F,S.

4. Choose the File/Save

   Word displays the Save File Name list box and the template's filename.

   press Enter.

5. Choose the OK button or

   Word saves the changes to the template. □

281

Changing the Template for a Document

Because Word automatically defaults to the NORMAL template, you may want to change to another template after you've entered text. Changing to another template gives you access to the macros, glossary entries, key assignments, and menus assigned to that template. Be aware, however, when you change templates, the text, graphics, and styles from the old template are not available. You can merge the styles with the styles that you have been using in your document by using the Format/Define Styles command, as explained in the upcoming Quick Steps.

To change the document template of a document, display the document and choose the Format/Document command or press Alt,T,D. In the Format Document dialog box, choose the Template list box or press Alt-M. Select the new template and choose the OK button or press Enter.

Merging Template Styles

Word allows you to merge styles from another template into the current template. Styles you merge into a template take precedence over the existing styles with the same names. To merge styles, choose the **Merge** button in the expanded Format Define Styles dialog box. Word then displays the Merge Template Styles dialog box. The Quick Steps explain how to merge the styles of the current template.

Q **Merging Template Styles**

1. Choose the Format/Define Styles command or press Alt,T,F.	The Define Styles dialog box appears.
2. Choose the Options button or press Alt-O.	The expanded Define Styles dialog box appears.
3. Select the **Merge** button or press Alt-M.	Word displays the Merge Template Styles dialog box.
4. Type a template filename or select a template filename from the Files list box.	
5. Choose the From Template button.	Word merges the styles from the selected template to the document. If styles exist with the same names, Word prompts you to confirm replacing them. Word then closes the Merge Template Styles dialog box.
6. Choose the OK button or press Enter.	Word closes the Format Define Styles dialog box. □

What You Have Learned

▶ Every document provides you with three time-saving elements: a *glossary*, *macros*, and *styles*. These elements are stored in a *template*, the foundation on which your document is based.

▶ You can save text or a picture from your document as a glossary entry. These items can then be inserted again at any time. To save and insert glossary entries, use the Edit/Glossary command (Alt,E,O).

▶ *Macros* automate the execution of a sequence of commands for performing tasks. The easiest way to create a macro is to record your keystrokes by using the Macro/Record command (Alt,M,C). Once a macro has been created, you can run it again by choosing the Macro/Run command (Alt,M,R).

▶ You can save as a style a collection of character and paragraph formats. Later you can quickly apply the style to paragraphs by using the Style list box on the Ruler. To define styles, use the Format/Define Styles command (Alt,T,F).

▶ A *template* provides the pattern on which your document is based, similar to the way a style forms the pattern for a paragraph's formatting. You can create and apply templates by using the File/New command (Alt,F,N).

283

Managing Documents and Windows

In This Chapter

▶ *Sorting and searching document files*
▶ *Copying, renaming, deleting, and converting document files*
▶ *Working with multiple document windows*
▶ *Manipulating the Word for Windows program window*

Inevitably, as you work with Word, the number of document files that you have grows. Word provides sophisticated methods for managing your many documents. Besides these file management features, Word also provides features that streamline the process of working with multiple documents simultaneously. This chapter explains how to work with Word's file management system and how to work with multiple document windows.

Organizing Files

The File/Find command provides document retrieval features that enable you to sort and locate document files easily. Much of the information used for document retrieval depends on the information you fill in using the Summary Info dialog box. Filling out the summary information makes searching for documents a breeze. For example, you can easily locate specific documents, or you can quickly list a series of documents that deal with the same subject, have the same author, were created on the same day, or share other common elements. Remember, you can easily add or change information in the Summary Info dialog box by using the Edit/Summary Info command. The first time you use the File/Find command, Word sorts (by name) and lists all files with .DOC extensions in all directories on the active drive, as shown in Figure 10.1.

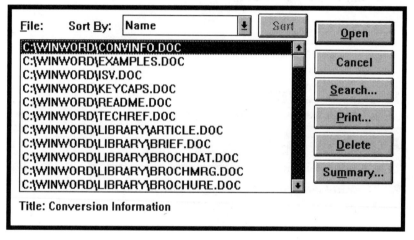

Figure 10.1   The File Find dialog box.

Selecting and Opening Multiple Files

The File list box, displayed in the File Find dialog box, allows you to select one or more files by pressing the Shift key and clicking the left mouse button. Pressing Shift and clicking again on a selected file unselects it. To select files using the keyboard, hold down the Ctrl key and press an Arrow key until a dotted box encloses the file you want to select. While continuing to hold down the Ctrl key, you can then press the Spacebar to select or unselect files.

You already know how to open a new document file or how to open one of the last four document files you've worked on by using the File menu. To open multiple files at one time, choose the File/Find command or press Alt,F,F. The File Find dialog box appears, as shown in Figure 10.1. Select the files you want to open, and then choose the Open button to open the selected files.

 Opening Multiple Document Files

1. Choose the File/Find command or press Alt,F,F.

   Word sorts your files and displays a Cancel button enabling you to cancel the File/Find command. Word then displays the File Find dialog box.

2. To select the files to open by using the mouse, hold down the Shift key and click on the filenames.

   From the keyboard, use the Up or Down Arrow key to highlight the first file you want to select. To select additional files, press and hold down the Ctrl key; then press the Up or Down Arrow key to move to the next file that you want to select. While continuing to hold down the Ctrl key, press the Spacebar to select the file. Repeat this action to select additional files. If you selected a document that you do not want opened, press the Shift key and click on the selected filename, or hold down Ctrl and use the Arrow keys to move to the selected file and press the Spacebar.

3. Choose the Open button or press Alt-O.

   Word opens the files in separate windows in the order you selected them. Managing windows is explained later in this chapter. □

Copying, Renaming, and Deleting Files

Copying and renaming files are both accomplished by using the File/ Save As command. To copy a file, choose the File/Save As command or press Alt,F,A. In front of the filename, type the path name for the new directory to which the file will be copied. To rename a file, choose the File/Save As command (Alt,F,A) and type the new name for the document. Word creates a new file with the new name; you then can delete the file having the old filename.

The more files you create, rename, and copy, the more cluttered your directories become. Eventually you'll want to delete old and unused files to make locating your files easier. Storing unwanted files forces Word to waste time searching through them when it is locating files. To delete one or more files, choose the File/Find command or press Alt,F,F, and then select the file(s) you want to delete in the File list box. Keep in mind that you cannot delete open documents, even though they are listed in the File list box. Choose the Delete button; Word erases from your hard disk all the files selected in the File list box. Once Word erases a file, the file can be recovered only by using a third-party utility program, like the Unerase program available in Norton Utilities.

Protecting Document and Template Files

In some cases, you'll want to protect a document or template file from being written to. You can lock or unlock a document or a template. When you lock a document or template, you or others can insert annotations by using the Insert/Annotations command, but the locked document or template cannot be changed. *Annotations* are special notes or comments that relate to a document and that normally aren't displayed or printed with the document. Only a person who knows the name of the document's author can lock or unlock the document.

To lock a document, first open the document you want to lock. Choose the File/Save As command or press Alt F,A. Choose the Options button or press Alt-O, and then click on the Lock For Annotations check box. Choose the OK button or press Enter. This locks and saves the open document.

> **Caution:** Don't rely on the Lock For Annotations check box in the expanded File Save As dialog box to protect your documents and templates. Because the lock feature is dependent on the name of the author, anyone who knows the document's original author can break the lock and alter the document.

Besides protecting your document by using the Lock For Annotations check box in the expanded File Save As dialog box, you can protect any document or template file by using the DOS ATTRIB command. For example, to protect a template file named STANDARD.DOT so that it cannot be altered but can be used to create documents, enter the following command at the DOS prompt:

```
attrib +r standard.dot
```

To change the file so that it can be read and written to, at the DOS prompt enter the ATTRIB command and replace the plus sign with a subtraction symbol (the hyphen). For more information on the DOS ATTRIB command, see any book on DOS.

If you open a document with the Read Only check box turned on in the File Open dialog box, Word allows you to edit and format that document but will not allow you to save the changed document under its original name. To save the document file, use the File/Save As command to save the document under a new name.

289

Sorting Documents

The File Find dialog box displays a Sort By list box. This list box allows you to specify different sorting criteria for displaying the filenames in the File list box. By selecting a sort option and choosing the Sort button or pressing Alt-R, you can sort the documents listed in the File list box according to their names, authors, dates created, dates saved, name of the person who last saved the file, or the file's size. After the list has been sorted, a status message appears at the bottom of the dialog box. This message displays information for the selected file relating to the option in the Sort By list box. For example, sorting by author displays the selected file's author below the File list box, as shown in Figure 10.2. Table 10.1 describes the options for sorting documents in the File list box.

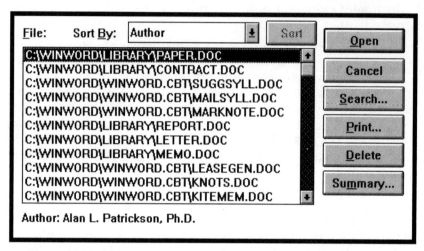

Figure 10.2   Files sorted by author in the File list box.

Table 10.1   Sorting Options in the File List Box

Option	Sorts
Name	Alphabetically A to Z by document name.
Author	Alphabetically A to Z by author.
Creation Date	Chronologically, listing the most recently created files last.
Last Saved Date	Chronologically, listing the most recently saved files last.
Last Saved By	Alphabetically A to Z by name of the user saving the document.
Size	By size from smallest to largest.

Searching for Files

Summary sheets are an integral part of Word's file management system. They act like an index, allowing you to search your documents for particular words, phrases, or other information, such as the document's title, subject, or any keywords related to the document.

Sooner or later you'll find that you want to open a document file but you can't remember where you stored it or what you named it. The Search button in the File Find dialog box can help you locate lost files. Choosing the Search button or pressing Alt-S displays the Search dialog box, as shown in Figure 10.3. The Search List text box allows you to specify the directories in which you want Word to search for documents. The other text boxes are directly tied to the document summary sheets. You can enter the search criteria you want Word to use, and Word will search and list any matching files in the File list box.

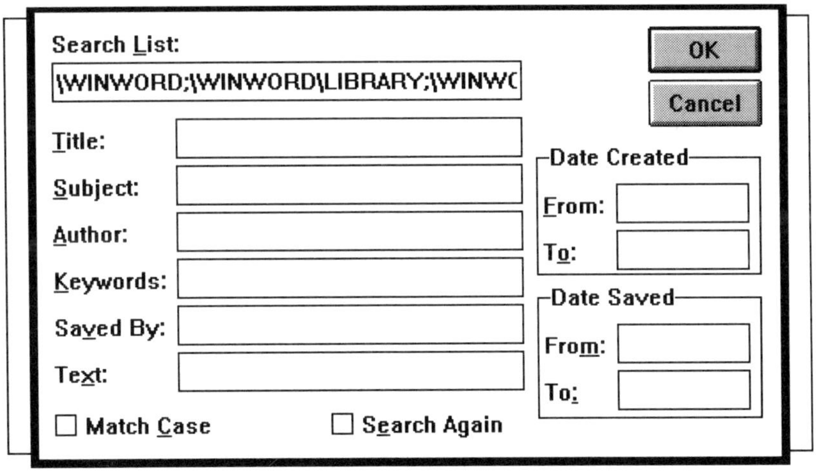

291

Search List:

\WINWORD;\WINWORD\LIBRARY;\WINW(

OK

Cancel

Title:

Subject:

Author:

Keywords:

Saved By:

Text:

Date Created
From:
To:

Date Saved
From:
To:

☐ Match Case   ☐ Search Again

Figure 10.3   The Search dialog box.

Except for the Comments text box in the Summary Info dialog box, the text boxes in the Search dialog box match the text boxes in the Summary Info dialog box. The Search dialog box provides you with the Date Created To and From text boxes and the Date Saved To: and From text boxes. You can use these text boxes to narrow or broaden searches for documents created and saved between a certain time period. The Search dialog box also provides two check boxes: the Match Case, which matches the capitalization of a text box entry, and the Search Again check box, which repeats the search.

> ▶ **Tip:** You can list filenames for several directories by separating each path name in the Search List text box with a semicolon (;). For example, C:\WINWORD;C:\DOCS searches both the WINWORD and the DOCS directories on the C: drive.

Using the Search dialog box, you can search through specified directories to find documents that meet your search criteria. For example, you can look for documents created by a certain author on a specific date. You can also use Word's wildcard characters and logical operators to broaden or limit a search.

The *?* (question mark) wildcard matches any single character; for example, *f?x* matches *fax, fix,* and *fox.* The * (asterisk) wildcard matches any group of characters; for example, *f** matches any word beginning with the letter *f.* The ^ (caret) instructs Word to treat the following special character as a regular character; for example, ^? matches a question mark and ^ ^ matches a caret.

Besides the three characters just mentioned, Word has logical operators that can be used to limit or broaden a search:

Logical Operator	Description
, (comma)	The logical OR operator locates text matching any or all items in the text box. For example, entering `memo, report` locates documents containing the words *memo* or *report.*
& (ampersand)	The logical AND operator retrieves documents that match all criteria in a list of items in the text box. For example, entering `memo&report` locates documents containing the words *memo* and *report.*

~ (tilde)

The logical NOT operator retrieves documents that do not meet the criteria following the tilde. For example, `memo~report` locates documents containing the word *memo* but excludes files also containing the word *report*.

Q Searching for Documents with Specific Text

1. Choose the File/Find command or press Alt,F,F.

   The first time that Word sorts your files, it displays a Cancel button enabling you to cancel the File/Find command. After sorting your files, Word displays the File Find dialog box.

2. Choose the Search button or press Alt-S.

   Word displays the Search dialog box.

3. Enter the directories that you want to search in the Search List list box.

   Be sure to separate each path name with a semicolon.

4. Choose the Text text box or press Alt-X.

   Word moves the insertion point to the Text text box.

5. Fill in the Text text box with the words you want to match your document files.

   You are instructing Word to match the words in your documents with the specified words in the Text text box. You can use any of Word's wildcard characters or logical operators in the search.

6. Choose the OK button or press Enter.

   Word compiles a list of documents with words that match the words entered in the documents and in the Text text box, located in the Search dialog box. Word displays the matching document files in the File list box of the File Find dialog box. ☐

Until you exit Word, the File list box displays the documents found during the previous search. An asterisk before a document name means that the document was last saved with the Fast Save check box turned on in the File Save As dialog box.

⊘ **Caution:** Word may not find specific text in files that were saved by using the Fast Save option in the File Save dialog box.

Printing Multiple Files

To print multiple documents, choose the File/Find command or press Alt,F,F, select the filename of each document you want to print, and then choose the Print button. The Print dialog box appears. The settings in the Print dialog box apply to every selected file. For example, if you enter *2* in the Copies text box, Word prints two copies of every selected document.

 Printing Multiple Files

1. Choose the File/Find command or press Alt,F,F.

   The first time that Word sorts your files, it displays a Cancel button enabling you to cancel the File/Find command. Word then displays the File Find dialog box.

2. To select the files to print using the mouse, hold down the Shift key and click on the filenames.

   Using the keyboard, use the Up or Down Arrow key to highlight the first file you want to select. To select additional files, hold down the Ctrl key and then press the Up or Down Arrow key to move to the next file you want to select. Still holding down the Ctrl key, press the Spacebar to select the file. Repeat this action to select additional files. If you have selected a document you do not want printed, press the Shift key and click on the selected filename, or hold down Ctrl and use the Arrow keys to move to the selected file and press the Spacebar.

3. Choose the Print button or press Alt-P.

Word displays the File Print dialog box.

4. Select the printing options you want in the File Print dialog box.

If you specify a range of pages, that range will be printed for each of the documents selected in the File Find dialog box.

5. Choose the OK button or press Enter.

Word prints your files in the order you selected them, using the options you've chosen in the File Print dialog box. □

295

Saving Documents in Different File Formats

Word allows you to save files in several different formats so that you can easily transfer a document file to another program, such as another word processor. To save a file in a different file format, choose the File/Save As command or press Alt,F,A. Type a new filename and choose the Options >> button or press Alt-O. In the File Format list box (Alt-F), choose the file format you want to convert your file to. The choices you have depend on the conversion file formats you chose to include when you installed Word. After selecting a file format, choose the OK button or press Enter. Table 10.2 describes the program formats that Word supports.

Table 10.2. **Program Formats Supported by Word**

Format	Description
DCA	IBM's Document Content Architecture format, which includes DisplayWrite and Display Writer.
Document Template	A Word for Windows template format.
Microsoft Works	Microsoft Works word processing files.
Multimate	Multimate 3.3, 3.6, Advantage, and Advantage II file formats.
Normal	Word for Windows format.
RTF	Rich Text Format—a Microsoft word processing format that embeds special formatting with ASCII codes so that they can be interpreted by other programs that support this format, including Microsoft Word for the Macintosh and Microsoft Works for DOS.
Text Only	Text file format that retains tab characters and paragraph marks but strips all other formatting codes from your document.
Text Only (PC-8)	The same as the Text Only file format, but instead uses the IBM character set.
Text+breaks	Text file format that adds a carriage return character at the end of each line and replaces tab characters with spaces in your document.
Text+breaks (PC-8)	The same as the Text+breaks format, but instead uses the IBM character set.
Windows Write	Microsoft Windows Write format (Write is bundled with Windows).
Word for DOS	Microsoft Word 5.0 and 5.5 formats.
WordPerfect	WordPerfect 4.1, 4.2, and 5.0 formats.
Wordstar	WordStar 3.3, 3.45, and 4.0 formats.

Working with Word's Windows

Using Windows, you can display multiple Windows-based applications on your screen, as shown in Figure 10.4. Each program is displayed within its own program window, including Word for Windows.

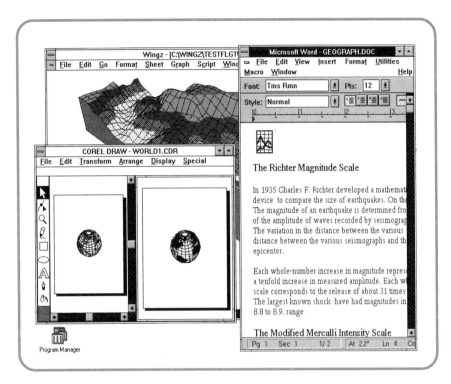

Figure 10.4   Multiple Windows-based applications.

Within the Word program window, you can display up to nine document windows, each containing a different document file, as shown in Figure 10.5. This is a helpful feature when you want to have more than one Word document file open at a time. For example, you might want to refer to another document to reference information, copy or move text between documents, or simply view the same document in a different view mode or location. You can resize and move each document window, as well as move information between document windows. Regardless of the number of open document windows displayed, only one can be the active window. The procedures for manipulating windows in Windows or in Word for Windows are similar.

Figure 10.5   Two document windows displayed in the Word window.

298

Restoring and Maximizing Word's Document Windows

When you begin a Word for Windows session, both the Microsoft Word window and your document window are *maximized*, or expanded to full-screen size, as shown in Figure 10.6. In the maximized mode, the Word program window and the document window appear as one window, but they are in fact two distinct windows. *Restoring a document window* means shrinking the window from the maximized (full-screen) size to a smaller size. Once a window is restored, you can manipulate the window to make room for displaying other document windows at the same time.

Restoring a maximized document window separates the document window from the Word program window. Notice that the document window is displayed with its own window border, win-

dow title bar, and control menu. You can then resize and move the
document window to allow additional document windows to be
displayed. To restore a maximized document window in the Word
program window, press Ctrl-F5 or choose the Document Control/
Restore command (Alt,Hyphen,R).

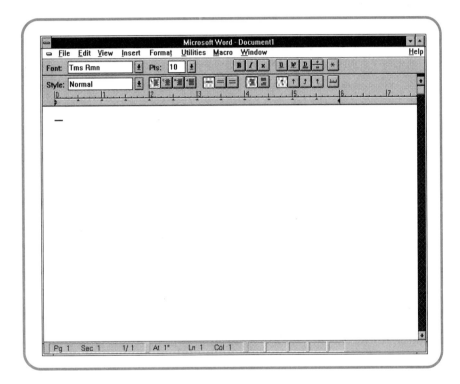

Figure 10.6   The initial Word session screen.

Figure 10.7 shows a restored document window within a
maximized Word program window. Notice that the document
filename and path have moved from the Word program window's
title bar to the document's window title bar. In addition, the
Document Control menu box has moved from the menu bar to the far
left side of the document window title bar. The Ruler is displayed at
the top of the document window. Each document window has its
own Ruler. However, the Ribbon always remains part of the Word
program window, and its settings reflect the active document window.

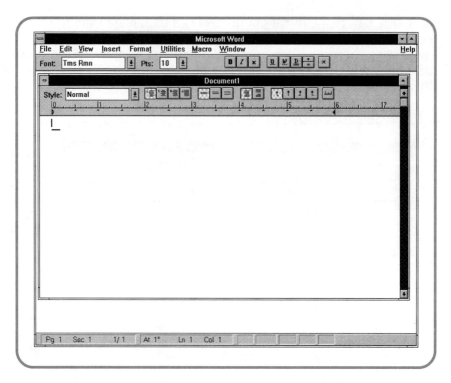

Figure 10.7   The restored document window.

To quickly return a restored document window to its maximized size, double-click anywhere on the document window's title bar or click on the Maximize button (the Up Arrow button located at the far right of the window's title bar). To maximize a document using the keyboard, press Ctrl-F10 or choose the Document Control/Maximize command (Alt,Hyphen,X).

Resizing a Document Window

Once a document window is restored, you can resize it to make room for displaying other document windows. You can't resize a document window to be larger than the Word program window, however.

Resizing a Document Window by Using the Mouse

1. Move the mouse pointer anywhere on the document window border.

   The mouse pointer changes to a double-headed sizing pointer. Positioning the mouse pointer on a corner moves the two sides that connect at that corner. Positioning anywhere on a side moves just that side.

2. Press and hold down the left mouse button.

3. Drag the mouse in the direction you want to expand or contract the window.

   The border(s) moves as you drag the mouse.

4. When you've moved the border to the desired position, release the mouse button.

   Word displays the resized document window.

   □ **301**

To resize a document window by using the keyboard, first press Ctrl-F8 or choose the Document Control/<u>S</u>ize command (Alt,Hyphen,S). A four-headed pointer appears in the document window. Then press one of the Arrow keys to move the pointer to the border you want. The four-headed pointer changes to a double-headed sizing pointer.

If you want to resize a window from a corner instead of a side, press an Arrow key to move the sizing pointer to one of the corners of the side that the pointer is on. For example, after pressing the Up Arrow to move the sizing pointer to the top border, press the Right Arrow key to move the sizing pointer to the top right corner, or press the Left Arrow key to move the sizing pointer to the top left corner. When the sizing pointer is in the corner, it cannot be repositioned.

After positioning the pointer, press the Arrow keys to move the border in the direction you want to resize the window. Pressing Enter completes the resize operation. Pressing Esc exits the sizing session without making any changes.

Moving a Document Window

When you resize document windows to shrink their size, you can then move them within the Word program window. As with resizing a window, the mouse provides the easiest way to move a window. To move a window with the mouse, first move the mouse pointer anywhere on the window's title bar and then press and hold the left mouse button. Drag the window to the desired location and then release the mouse button.

To move a document window by using the keyboard, first press Ctrl-F7 or choose the Document Control/Move command (Alt,Hyphen,M). Word displays a four-headed direction pointer. Use the Arrow keys to move the window in the direction you want. After repositioning the document window where you want it, press Enter. Pressing Esc cancels the window moving session.

302   Navigating Multiple Document Windows

While Word for Windows allows you to have up to nine document windows open at one time, only one document window can be active at a time. If you're displaying multiple document windows in the restored mode, the window on the top of the layered stack is the active window; any other visible parts of other document windows are dimmed. If you have multiple resized document windows displayed side-by-side, all but the active window appear dimmed.

Word for Windows provides a number of options for navigating through multiple document windows. You can quickly move between document windows in sequential order by pressing Ctrl-F6. Pressing Ctrl-Shift-F6 displays the previous document window.

If you're displaying multiple document windows as maximized (full-screen) windows or multiple-layered document windows, you can switch between document windows by using the Window menu. Choosing the Window menu or pressing Alt-W displays the Window command menu, as shown in Figure 10.8. Any opened document files are listed in the bottom of the menu with a number assigned to each one. The active window is noted with a check mark to the left of the document window's number.

To switch between your document windows, simply click on the document filename you want, or simultaneously press Alt and the underlined number next to the filename you want, such as Alt-3 to choose the third document in the list. The chosen document filename becomes the active document window. If you're displaying multiple document windows, you can click on any dimmed part of a visible document window to activate the window. When you click on a dimmed window, it becomes active and is displayed on the top of the previous active window.

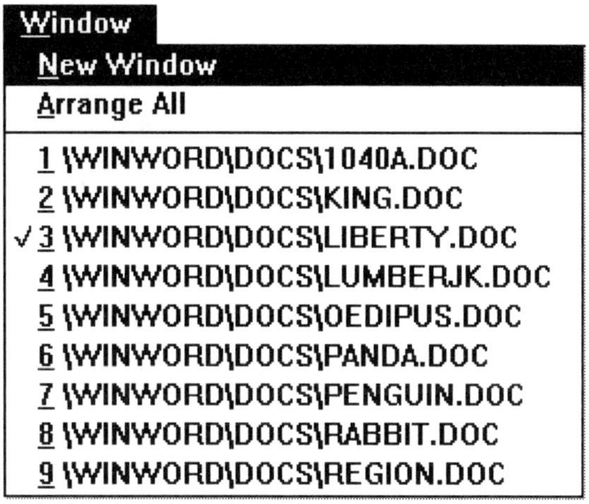

```
Window
  New Window
  Arrange All

  1 \WINWORD\DOCS\1040A.DOC
  2 \WINWORD\DOCS\KING.DOC
√ 3 \WINWORD\DOCS\LIBERTY.DOC
  4 \WINWORD\DOCS\LUMBERJK.DOC
  5 \WINWORD\DOCS\OEDIPUS.DOC
  6 \WINWORD\DOCS\PANDA.DOC
  7 \WINWORD\DOCS\PENGUIN.DOC
  8 \WINWORD\DOCS\RABBIT.DOC
  9 \WINWORD\DOCS\REGION.DOC
```

Figure 10.8   The Window menu.

▶ **Note:** You can copy and move text between document windows by using Word's Edit/Cut, Edit/Copy, and Edit/Paste commands.

Arranging Multiple Document Windows

If you're displaying multiple document windows in restored mode, your screen can get cluttered, and some document windows become hidden from view. Choosing the Window/Arrange All command or pressing Alt,W,A arranges all your open windows so that they are all visible at one time. The document windows are resized and arranged so that you can view each window's title bar and part of the contents of each window. The window sizes vary, depending on the number of opened document windows. Figure 10.9 shows how the Window/Arrange All command arranges opened document windows.

303

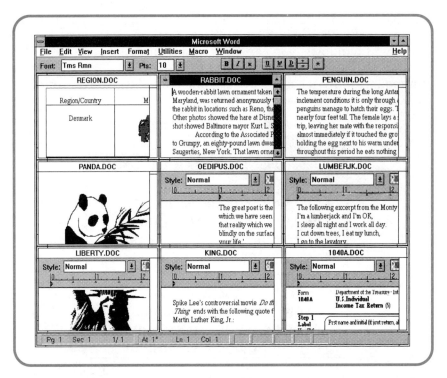

Figure 10.9   Document windows arranged by using the Window Arrange All command.

Closing a Document Window

After you're finished using a document window, you can close it to remove it from the screen. The easiest way to close a document window is to double-click on its Document Control menu box or press Ctrl-F4. You can also close the document window by choosing the Document Control/Close command or pressing Alt,Hyphen,C. If there are any changes in the document window you're closing, Word displays a message box asking if you want to save your changes before closing the document window. Choose the Yes button or press Y to save the changes and close the document window. You can also close the active document window by choosing the File/Close command or by pressing Alt,F,C.

Opening Duplicate Document Windows

The Window/New Window command opens a special window that displays a duplicate of the active document window. Document windows created using the Window/New Window allow you to view different parts of a long document or display the same document in different view modes.

To open a duplicate window, choose the Window/New Window command or press Alt,W,N. Word displays the same document that is in the active document window. Word adds DOC:1 in the title bar of the original document window and DOC:2 to the duplicate window, as shown in Figure 10.10. Each additional duplicate window based on the same original document window is numbered sequentially. For example, DOC:3, DOC:4, and so on up to a total of nine. Because these windows are duplicates of the original, any changes you make in one window are immediately reflected in all the windows. You can close each of these duplicate document windows individually, or you can use the File/Close command to close all the windows at one time.

305

Splitting a Document Window

To view two different sections or to view modes of the same document without opening an entire duplicate window, you can split a document window horizontally into two panes, as shown in Figure 10.11. A horizontal bar splits the document into two panes. You can adjust the panes to make one pane larger or smaller than the other. Each pane has its own scroll bar so that you can navigate the documents separately. You can quickly move between panes by clicking the mouse in the pane you want or pressing F6.

The easiest way to split a document window is to first move the mouse pointer to the split box (the tiny black box at the top of the vertical scroll bar). The mouse pointer changes to a split window pointer. Then press and hold down the left mouse button and drag the pointer to the spot where you want to split the window; release the mouse button.

To split a document window from the keyboard, choose the Document Control/Split command or press Alt,Hyphen,T. A horizontal dotted line appears, which you can move by using the Up or Down Arrow keys. When you reach the split position you want, press Enter.

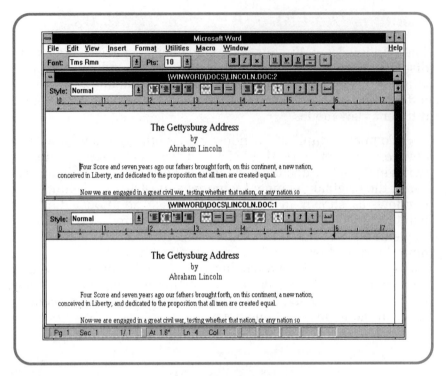

Figure 10.10   A duplicated document window.

To reposition the split bar, either drag the split box using the mouse or choose the Document Control/Split command from the keyboard. To return your document to a single pane window using the mouse, drag the split bar to the top or bottom of the document window or double-click on the split box. You can also choose the Document Control/Split command or press Alt,Hyphen,T. Next, use the Up or Down Arrow key to move the split bar to the top or bottom of the document window, and then press Enter.

Manipulating the Word Program Window

Like Word document windows, the Word program window, after you have restored it, can be resized and moved to make room for additional application windows on the Windows Desktop. You can also restore and resize the Word program window to allow you to quickly view and access other icons displayed at the bottom of the

Windows desktop, as shown in Figure 10.12. Remember, icons are small symbols that typically represent other programs not currently open.

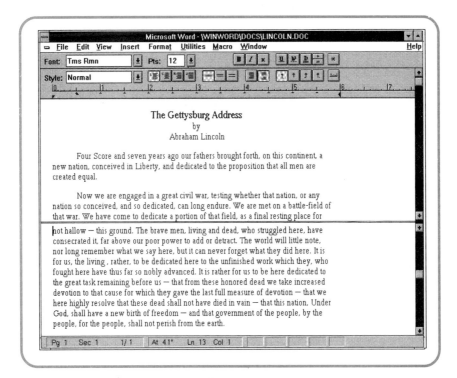

Figure 10.11   A split window.

The procedures for manipulating the Word program window are similar to working with document windows. The easiest methods to restore the Word program window are by double-clicking on the Word program window title bar, clicking on the Restore button (the double-headed arrow button located at the far right of the title bar), or pressing Ctrl-F5. You can also restore the maximized Word program window by choosing the Word Control/Restore command or pressing Alt,Spacebar,R.

The quickest methods for maximizing the restored Word program window are by clicking on the Maximize button (the Up arrow symbol on the right side of the title bar), double-clicking the mouse pointer on the window title bar, or pressing Alt-F10. You can also maximize a Word program window by choosing the Word Control/Maximize command or pressing Alt,Spacebar,X.

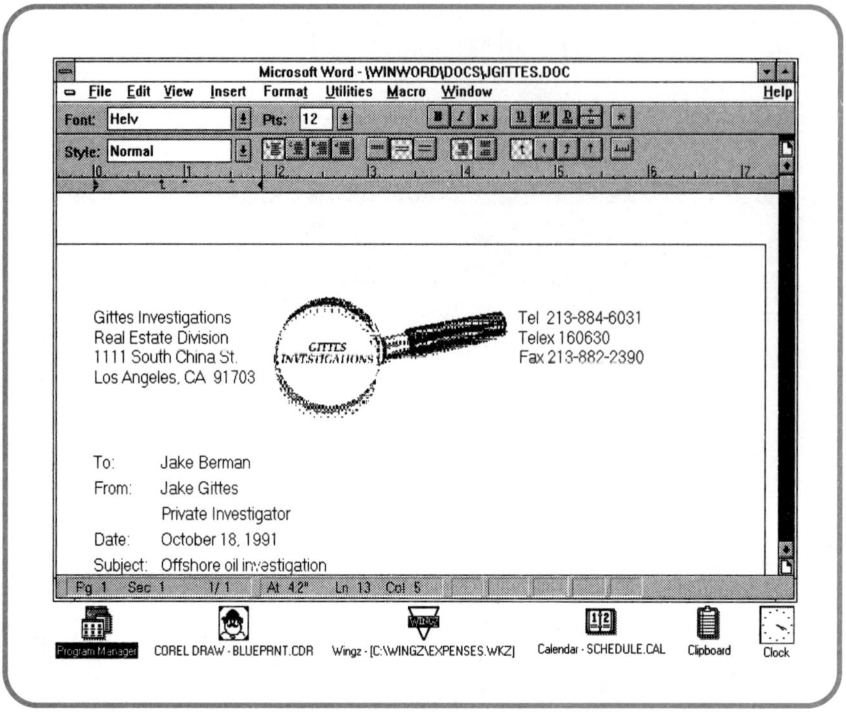

Figure 10.12   The Word program window on the Windows desktop.

308

Except for the command to activate the Word Control menu (Alt-Spacebar), the Word Control menu and the Document Control menu options are virtually the same. You manipulate Word's program window in the same manner as you manipulate document windows. For example, to resize the Word program window, you press Alt,Spacebar,S (the Document Control menu equivalent is Alt,Hyphen,S). You can then resize the program window in the same way that you resized the document windows.

Minimizing the Word Program Window

Minimizing the Word program window closes it to an icon on the Windows desktop without exiting the program. With the Word program window minimized, you can easily switch between other applications. The minimized Microsoft Word icon appears on the Windows desktop, as shown in Figure 10.13.

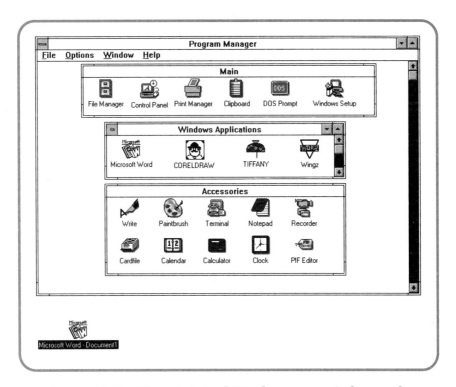

309

Figure 10.13   The minimized Word program window on the Windows desktop.

To quickly minimize the Word program window, click on the Minimize button (the Down Arrow symbol on the right side of the window's title bar), or press Alt-F9. Choosing the Word Control/Minimize command or pressing Alt,Spacebar,N also minimizes the Word program window. To restore the minimized Word program window, double-click on the Word icon. From the keyboard, select the Word icon by pressing Alt-Esc and then press Alt-F5. Alternatively, you can click once on the Word icon or press Alt-Spacebar to bring up the Control menu; then choose the Restore or Maximize command.

Switching to Other Windows Applications from Word

You can easily switch to other program windows from Word by choosing the Word Control/Switch To (Alt,Spacebar,W) or pressing

Ctrl-Esc. The S<u>w</u>itch To command is available in every program window's Control menu. After choosing the S<u>w</u>itch To command, Word displays the Task List window, as shown in Figure 10.14. You can select the name of the program you want to switch to by double-clicking on the name or using the Down or Up Arrow keys to highlight the name, and then choosing the <u>S</u>witch To button (Alt-S). The Application you've chosen is activated. Here are the additional command buttons available in the Task List window and their effects:

Command Button	Effect
<u>E</u>nd Task	Word closes the highlighted program window.
<u>C</u>ascade	All the open windows are sized and staggered in such a way that the title bar and edge or corner of every window is visible.
<u>T</u>ile	All the open windows are sized and lined up like tiles on a wall.
<u>A</u>rrange Icons	Word lines up all the icons on the Windows desktop.

310

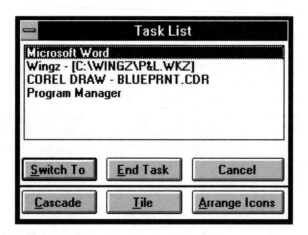

Figure 10.14   The Task List window.

What You Have Learned

▶ Besides storing information about your documents, the Summary Info dialog box allows you to use the File/Find command (Alt,F,F) to organize, sort, and locate files.

▶ Using the File/Save As command (Alt,F,S), you can rename files. Using the File/Find command (Alt,F,F), you can copy and delete document files.

▶ The Sort By list box in the File Find dialog box lets you sort documents by creation date, last saved date, author's name, or the size of your document files.

▶ The Search button (Alt-S) in the File Find dialog box enables you to search for documents by title, subject, author, keywords, or who last saved the file. The Search button also lets you locate documents containing specific text.

▶ By pressing Ctrl-F5, you can *restore* a document window (separate it from the program window). To return a restored window to its maximized state, click on the maximize button (the Up Arrow) in the top-right corner of the window or press Ctrl-F10.

311

▶ To resize a document window, position the mouse pointer on the restored document window's border and drag the side or corner till it matches the size you want. Press Ctrl-F8 and use the Arrow keys to resize the window by using the keyboard. To move a window, position the mouse pointer in the window's title bar and drag the window to its new location, or press Ctrl-F7 and use the Arrow keys to relocate the window.

▶ Click the mouse in any window to which you want to move, or press Ctrl-F6 to move from one window to another. You can also change windows by using the Windows menu (Alt-W) options.

▶ Quickly arranging multiple windows is a snap using the Window/Arrange All command (Alt,W,A). You can open duplicate windows by using the Window/New command (Alt,W,N).

▶ The split box above the scroll bar allows you to split a window by dragging the split box to where you want to split the window. The keyboard equivalent is the Document Control/Split command (Alt-Hyphen-T).

► Using the Word Control menu, you can manipulate the Word program window in a manner similar to the way you manipulate the document windows. To access the Word Control menu, click on the rectangle in the upper-left corner of the title bar, or press Alt-Spacebar.

Using Bookmarks, Fields, and Document Revision Features

In This Chapter

▶ *Inserting bookmarks into a document*
▶ *Using fields in your documents*
▶ *Adding annotations to a document*
▶ *Applying revision marks to a document*

Word's bookmark and field features are building blocks that you can use to create sophisticated documents. *Bookmarks* allow you to reference portions of a document by using a simple unique name. You can then quickly incorporate this name into any document having fields. *Fields* are embedded instructions that allow you to automate a wide variety of tasks, from inserting a date stamp to creating form letters. In this chapter, you'll learn the fundamentals of working with bookmarks and fields. This information will be a foundation for Chapter 12, where you'll use bookmarks and fields to create a table of contents, an index, and form letters. In addition, this chapter explains Word's annotation and revision features. These features allow others to edit your documents and to mark their revisions so that you can review and accept or reject them.

Bookmarks

Word's bookmarks work similarly to bookmarks used to mark a place in a book. Using Word's bookmark feature, you can identify any selected portion or location in your document by assigning it a unique name. You use this name to reference the bookmark. Word does not display any special mark in your document to show where the bookmark is. A document can have up to 150 bookmarks, and the selected portion of a document can be any length.

Once you mark a location or portion of a document with a bookmark, you can use the bookmark in a number of ways. You can quickly move to the bookmark by using the Edit/Go To command. However, the most important use of a bookmark is to reference a selected portion of a document for use with Word's fields, as explained later in this chapter.

314

Inserting Bookmarks in Your Document

Inserting a bookmark into your document is easy. First, select the portion of your document that you want the bookmark to reference, or place the insertion point at the location you want to reference. Next, choose the Insert/Bookmark command or press Alt,I,M. Word displays the Insert Bookmark dialog box, as shown in Figure 11.1. The Bookmark Name list box lists any bookmarks that have been inserted in the current document in alphabetical order.

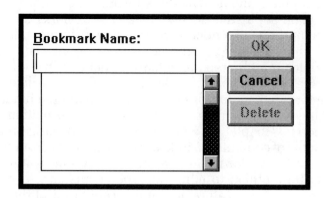

Figure 11.1   The Insert Bookmark dialog box.

A bookmark name cannot exceed 20 characters in length and must begin with a letter. In addition, bookmark names can contain only letters, numbers, and the underline character (_). You cannot include any spaces in a bookmark name. However, you can use the underline character to denote a space, such as *Sales_1991*.

Inserting a Bookmark in a Document

1. Select the part of your document that you want to name as a bookmark, or place the insertion point at a location you want to mark.

2. Choose the Insert/Bookmark command (Alt,I,M).

   Word displays the Insert Bookmark dialog box.

3. In the Bookmark Name text box, type the name of your bookmark.

4. Choose the OK button or press Enter.

   Word closes the Insert Book mark dialog box and marks the selected portion of your document. Nothing is displayed in your document window. ☐

315

If you're sure that a bookmark name hasn't been used before in your document, select the portion of your document to which you want to attach the bookmark name and then press Ctrl-Shift-F5. Word displays the prompt `Insert bookmark:` in the status bar. Type the name for your bookmark and then press Enter.

Caution: Be careful when you use the keyboard shortcut for inserting a bookmark (Ctrl-Shift-F5). If you accidentally use a bookmark name that already exists, Word replaces the contents of that bookmark without asking for confirmation.

Redefining and Deleting a Bookmark

You can redefine the contents or location of an existing bookmark to refer to a different portion or location in your document. To do this, first move to the new location or select the portion of your document you want to redefine. Next, choose the Insert/Bookmark command (Alt,I,M) to display the Insert Bookmark dialog box. From the Bookmark Name list box, select the bookmark name you want to redefine, and then choose the OK button or press Enter. Word closes the Insert Bookmark dialog box and redefines the bookmark.

To delete an existing bookmark, choose the Insert/Bookmark command (Alt,I,M) to display the Insert Bookmark dialog box. Select the bookmark name from the Bookmark Name list box, and then choose the Delete button or press Alt-D. Word deletes the bookmark and removes the name from the list. Choose the Close button or press Enter to close the Insert Bookmark dialog box.

Navigating and Viewing Bookmark Contents

Choosing the Edit/Go To command or pressing Alt,E,G lets you jump to specific bookmarks in your document. If the bookmark you specified marks a location in your document, Word moves to that location. If the bookmark you specified marks a selected portion of your document, Word moves to the bookmark location and selects the bookmark's contents.

To jump to a bookmark, first choose the Edit/Go To command (Alt,E,G). Word displays the Edit Go To dialog box, as shown in Figure 11.2. The Go To list box lists all the bookmarks in your document. Choose the bookmark name you want to move to by double-clicking on the bookmark name or highlighting it, and then choose the OK button or press Enter. Word moves to the bookmark location in your document and selects the bookmark's text—if any text is contained in the bookmark.

If you know the name of the bookmark you want to jump to, you can use the Go To keyboard shortcut. Pressing F5 displays `Go To:` in the status bar, prompting you to enter the bookmark name. Type the bookmark name and press Enter. Word moves to the bookmark.

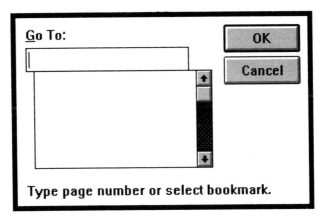

Figure 11.2   The Edit Go To dialog box.

Working with Fields

Fields are instructions that tell Word to retrieve and insert information or perform some kind of action. Using fields to insert information into your document links that information to its original source. In previous chapters, you worked with fields when you inserted page numbers into headers, inserted pictures, and linked spreadsheets into your documents.

Fields allow information in a document to be updated to reflect any changes made to the original source. For example, inserting a DATE field into a document causes Word to retrieve the date from your computer's clock/calendar. Word updates the field whenever it prints or repaginates the document containing the field.

Fields are used to perform a wide range of actions. Using fields, you can insert simple entries, such as date and time stamps, bookmarks from other documents, or cross-references. Using more sophisticated fields, you can create a table of contents or an index, or you can merge names and addresses into a form letter (Chapter 12 explains these). Word provides an extensive collection of predefined fields that you can modify to meet your needs.

Viewing Field Codes and Results

Fields are displayed in two forms in your document: a field code or a field code result, depending on which view options are activated. A *field code* is the embedded instructions, and a *field result* is the effect of the field's instructions. Figure 11.3 shows an example of a field code and its result.

{date·\@·"MMMM·d,·yyyy"} — Field code

October 19, 1991 — Field result

Figure 11.3   A field code and a field result.

318

To switch between viewing the field code and its results, choose the View/Field Codes command (Alt,V,C). Turning on the View/Field Codes command displays the field codes. Turning off the View/Field Codes command displays the field code results (if the Show All feature is turned off). A check mark next to the View/Field Codes command indicates it is turned on. If the Show All feature is turned on, the View/Field Codes command is disabled. You can quickly turn off the Show All feature by clicking on the Show All button at the far right of the Ribbon or by choosing the Show All *** check box in the View Preferences dialog box.

You can display field codes and their results in the Normal, Draft, or Page view modes. Choosing the File/Print Preview command or pressing Alt,F,V always displays the field results. To view the results for a specific field or group of fields in a document, select the field code(s) and then press Shift-F9.

 Tip: You can split a document window to view the field codes in one pane and the results in the other pane.

Understanding the Parts of a Field Code

Depending on the field's function, each field code can include as many as four different parts: field characters, field types, field instructions, and field switches. Figure 11.4 shows a field code containing each of these parts. Note that every field includes field characters and a field type. Field instructions and switches are optional but are included in many fields.

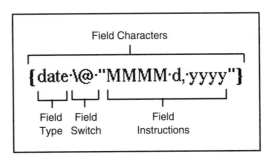

Figure 11.4   The parts of a field code.

319

Field characters designate the beginning and ending of a field. Each field must be enclosed within field characters (‹ ›). To insert field characters, you must either choose the Insert/Field command, which displays a list box with fields from which to choose, or press Ctrl-F9, which inserts the field characters only in your text. When you select one field character, the entire field is selected.

Field type identifies the action or effect the field has in the document. For example, DATE inserts the current date in your document. Each field contains a field type.

Field instructions add specific information and directions to the field type, allowing you to tailor the action of the field. Instructions can consist of a string of characters, mathematical expressions, bookmarks, document filenames, and switches.

Field switches change a field's default actions or set the field's formatting. Switches always have a backslash (\) as their first character. For example, the switch * UPPER converts all characters in the field's result to uppercase, and the switch \@ "MMMM d, yyyy" after the DATE field formats a date as *Month Date, Year.*

When an argument in a field's instruction consists of several words, you need to surround them with quotation marks ("). For example, {QUOTE "Quoth the raven nevermore"}. The quotation marks do not appear in the result. If an argument contains quotation marks that you want to appear in the result, precede each quotation mark with a backslash, such as {QUOTE "Ask the question \"Why?"\"}. The result will appear as: Ask the question "Why?" If an argument contains a backslash that you want to appear in the result, type another backslash in front of the argument's backslash (\\), such as {QUOTE "Change to the Root Directory by typing (\\)"}. The result will appear as: Change to the Root directory by typing \.

Inserting Fields

Fields are inserted into your document at the insertion point location. However, as we'll explain later, you can copy or move the fields after they have been inserted. There are two ways to insert a field into your document. The easiest way is to choose the Insert/Field command or press Alt,I,D. Word displays the Insert Field dialog box, as shown in Figure 11.5. This dialog box prompts you as you create your field codes.

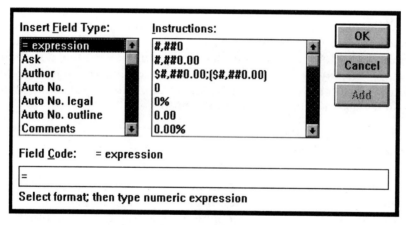

Figure 11.5   The Insert Field dialog box.

The Insert Field Type list box shows all of Word's predefined fields. When you select a field type from the list, its name is displayed in the Field Code text box. Above the Field Code text box, Word displays the field type in uppercase letters. Following it in lowercase letters are the instructions and switches that you can use with the field type. Below the Field Code text box, Word prompts you for any information needed to complete the field.

To add instructions or switches to your selected field type, enter them directly into the Field Code text box following the field type. You can also choose Word's predefined instructions or switches from the Instructions list box, if available. To include an instruction from the Instructions list box, select an option from the list and choose the Add button or press Alt-A. The instruction or switch is added to the Field Code text box after the field type. You can add multiple instructions into the Field Code text box. After you enter the field type and any instructions or switches you want, choose the OK button or press Enter to close the dialog box and insert the field at the insertion point.

Once you're familiar with how fields are created using the Insert/Field command, you can bypass the Insert Field dialog box and insert fields directly into your document. To insert a field without using the Insert Field dialog box, move the insertion point where you want to insert the field code and press Ctrl-F9. Word inserts the field characters, { }, and moves the insertion point between the field characters. You can then add each part of the field's code as needed.

The Quick Steps explain how to use the Insert/Field command to create and insert the INCLUDE field. This field adds the contents of another document or a bookmark from another document into the current document.

321

 Inserting the INCLUDE Field

1. Position the insertion point where you want to insert the field and its results.

2. Choose the Insert/Field command or press Alt,I,D.

   Word displays the Insert Field dialog box.

3. Select the `Include` field from the Insert Field Type list box.

   Word displays the field type name `Include` in the Field Code text box.

4. Choose the Field Code text box or press Alt-C, and then press the Right Arrow key once.

   The insertion point appears in the text box after the field type name.

5. To include a document, type the path and the document filename, for example, `c:\\winword\\memos\\fired.doc`. To include a bookmark, type the path name and the document name followed by the bookmark name, for example, `c:\\winword\\animals\\dogs.doc mean.`

   When entering the path for including a document file, you must use a double backslash (\\)to separate the drive, directory, and document names.

6. Choose the OK button or press Enter.

Word closes the Insert Field dialog box and inserts the field into your document. ☐

The following Quick Steps explain how to create a cross-reference to a bookmark by using the PAGEREF field. This field allows you to cross-reference the page number on which a bookmark is located. For example, if you use the PAGEREF field to reference a table on page 10 of a document, and the table is later moved to page 20, the PAGEREF field reflects the changed location of the table.

 Creating a Cross-Reference to a Bookmark

1. Place the insertion point where you want to insert the cross-reference.

2. Type any text that you want to precede the cross-reference page number in your document.

For example, you might enter:
`For more information on Sales Forecasting, see page 7.`

3. Choose the Insert/Field command or press Alt,I,D.

Word displays the Insert Field dialog box.

4. Select the `Page ref.` field from the Insert Field Type list box.

Word displays a list of the bookmarks for the current document in the Instructions list box.

5. Choose the Instructions list box or press Alt-I, and select the bookmark name you want to cross-reference.

6. Choose the Add button or press Alt-A.

Word displays the complete field code in the Field Code text box.

7. Choose the OK button or press Enter.

Word inserts the cross-reference field into your document. ☐

Table 11.1 describes some commonly used fields from Word's extensive collection of predefined fields. The Fields section of Word User's Reference manual lists all of Word's predefined fields and explains their functions in detail.

Table 11.1   ***Some Commonly Used Fields***

Field Type	Result
AUTHOR	Inserts the author's name, which is taken from the document's Summary Info dialog box.
DATE	Inserts the date that the field was last updated.
GLOSSARY	Inserts the specified glossary entry.
IMPORT	Inserts the specified .TIF graphic image file.
INCLUDE	Inserts the contents of another document or the contents of a bookmark from another document.
MACROBUTTON	Runs a specified macro when you double-click on the field.
PAGE	Places a page number on every page of your document. The page number is placed at the location where you inserted the field.
PAGEREF	Inserts the page number of a bookmark for cross-referencing.
TIME	Inserts the time that the field was last updated.

323

Updating and Navigating Fields

One of the powerful features of fields is the ability to update the field contents to reflect changes. Every time you print or repaginate a document, Word updates most of the fields in your document. Some special fields don't update in the same way as regular fields do (see the Word User's Reference manual to learn how these fields work). You can update a select field or group of fields at anytime by pressing F9.

You can lock a field result so that it can't be updated. To lock a field, select the field (or fields) and press Ctrl-F11 or Ctrl-Alt-F1. If you then press F9, print the document, or repaginate the document, Word does not update the field result. To unlock the field, select the field and then press Ctrl-Shift-F11 or Ctrl-Shift-Alt-F1. If a field inserts information in a document that you want to keep without ever updating again, you can unlink that information from the field by selecting the field result and pressing Ctrl-Shift-F9. Word then turns the information into regular document text and deletes the field that inserted the information.

You can move from field to field in your document by pressing F11 or Alt-F1. Either command moves the insertion point forward to the next field. Pressing Shift-F11 or Shift-Alt-F1 moves the insertion point back to the previous field.

Editing and Formatting Fields

There are two types of editing you can perform on fields in your documents: editing of the field code or editing of the field result. You can edit the field code directly in the document. Your editing then affects the document's actions or changes its source of information when it's updated. For example, using the INCLUDE field, suppose you inserted the wrong bookmark from another document. To correct the mistake, you can change the field instructions, such as the path, document, or bookmark name. To make the changes, place the insertion point within the field characters and make your changes as you would make any text changes. Remember, deleting field characters deletes the field.

To edit a field result, simply change the result as if it were part of the document text. In most cases, rather than changing the field result, we recommend that you make the changes in the field's source of information because, when you edit or format a field result, you're not changing the field itself, only its result. The next time the field is updated, your changes disappear, unless you lock the field by pressing Ctrl-F11.

You can apply formatting to a field result. The procedure is similar to applying formatting to text. However, like editing of a field result, any formatting applied to a field result is removed when the field is updated. You can format a field result by applying formatting commands to the selected field, including character, paragraph, and section formats to the field code. For example, suppose you want the text in your field result to be italic. First select the entire field code, and then choose the Italic button on the Ruler or choose the Italic check box in the Format Character dialog box. All the text in the field result is italicized. Any formatting you apply to the field affects the entire field result. In many cases you may want to format the source of the

324

field's information. This will allow you more flexibility in formatting the field result, such as including both italic and boldface type in the field result text.

Deleting, Copying, and Moving Fields

If you no longer want a field in your document, you can delete it just as you would text. With the field code displayed, simply select the first field character (｛). The entire field code will be selected. Then press the Del key. Word removes the field from the document. The entire contents of a field can be copied or moved to another location. The process is exactly like copying, cutting, and pasting regular document text.

To copy or move a field, select the field. Next, choose the Edit/Copy command (Alt,E,C) or press Ctrl-Ins to copy the field, or choose the Edit/Cut command (Alt,E,T) or press Shift-Del to move the field. Move the insertion point to the new location where you want to place the field and choose the Edit/Paste command (Alt,E,P) or press Shift-Ins. Word copies the field or moves it to the new location.

325

> ▶ **Tip:** If you find yourself frequently inserting a particular field, you can save time by saving the field as a glossary entry. To save a field as a glossary entry, select the entire field and then choose the Edit/Glossary command (Alt,E,O). Type a glossary entry name; then choose the OK button or press Enter.

Printing Field Codes in Your Document

By default, Word prints field results when you print your document. However, you can print your document with the field codes instead of the field results. Printing field codes can be useful for locating problems when your fields aren't working correctly. To print a document with field codes, first choose the File/Print command (Alt,F,P) or press Ctrl-Shift-F12. In the File Print dialog box, choose the Options >> button or press Alt-O; Word displays the expanded File Print dialog box. Choose the Field Codes check box or press Alt-L. Choose any additional settings you want, and then choose the OK button or press Enter to print your document with field codes.

> ▶ **Note:** The Update Fields check box in the File Print dialog box is turned on only for updating special fields that are not updated in the regular printing process. It doesn't need to be activated for most fields. See the Word User Reference manual for specific fields that need to have the Update Fields check box activated.

Adding Annotations to a Document

Annotation marks are the on-screen equivalent of the popular Post-it Notes. Like Post-it Notes, annotations can easily be added or removed from documents. Annotations aren't displayed with the body of the document, but instead appear in panes like footnotes. When you insert an annotation, an annotation mark appears as hidden text, showing the annotator's initials and an annotation number.

To insert an annotation into a document, move the insertion point to the spot where you want to insert the annotation, and then choose the Insert/Annotation command or press Alt,I,A. When you insert an annotation, Word displays an annotation mark, as shown in Figure 11.6. The annotation mark is made up of the initials entered in the Your Initials text box in the Utilities Customize dialog box, followed by an annotation number.

The insertion point then moves inside the Annotation pane, as shown in Figure 11.6. You can now enter your comments in the Annotation pane. A page field code is placed directly above the annotation mark in the Annotation pane. By using the page field code, you can easily reference annotations when they're printed. To switch between the Annotation pane and the main document window, simply move the mouse pointer to the location you want to move to and click. From the keyboard, press F6. To close the Annotation pane, choose the View/Annotations command or press Alt,V,A.

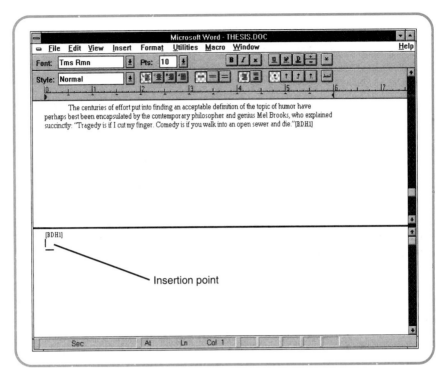

Figure 11.6   The insertion point in the Annotations pane.

 Adding Annotations

1. Move the insertion point to the spot where you want to add an annotation.	To change the annotation mark to indicate annotations made by someone other than the author, change the initials by choosing the Utilities/Customize command and entering the new initials in the Your Initials text box.
2. Choose the Insert/Annotation command or press Alt,I,A.	Word adds an annotation mark to your text (as hidden text) and moves the insertion point to the Annotations pane, as shown in Figure 11.6.
3. Type the annotation text.	The text appears in the Annotations pane.

4. To insert another annotation, press F6 and then repeat steps 1 through 3.

5. Choose the <u>V</u>iew/<u>A</u>nnotations command or press Alt,V,A.

Word closes the Annotations pane. You can also close the Annotations pane by dragging the window split box located on the scroll bar to the far right of the window split bar. □

To read annotations contained in a document, open the document and then open the Annotation pane by choosing the <u>V</u>iew/<u>A</u>nnotations command or pressing Alt,V,A. As you scroll through the document, the annotations in the Annotation pane scroll to match the current annotation mark. You can insert annotations by cutting and pasting text from the Annotation pane into your document. When you're finished viewing and working with annotations, choose the <u>V</u>iew/<u>A</u>nnotations command (Alt,V,A) again to close the Annotation pane. To delete an annotation, simply select the annotation mark and press the Del key. Word deletes both the reference mark and the annotation text, whether the Annotation pane is opened or not.

To print annotations with your document, choose the <u>F</u>ile/<u>P</u>rint command or press Alt,F,P, and then choose the <u>O</u>ptions >> button or press Alt-O to expand the Print dialog box. Choose the A<u>n</u>notations check box or press Alt-N, and then choose the OK button or press Enter. Word then prints your document, including the annotation marks and annotations. To print only the annotations and the page number that each annotation appears on, choose the <u>F</u>ile/<u>P</u>rint command or press Alt,F,P, and select the Annotations option from the <u>P</u>rint list box, as shown in Figure 11.7.

Adding Revision Marks to a Document

When more than one person is working on a document, you can turn on the revision marks feature to mark any changes made to a document. With Word's default settings, any text that is added to a document appears underlined, and any text that is deleted from a document appears with strike-through marks, rather than being cut or deleted from your document. Later you can review the document and accept or reject the changes.

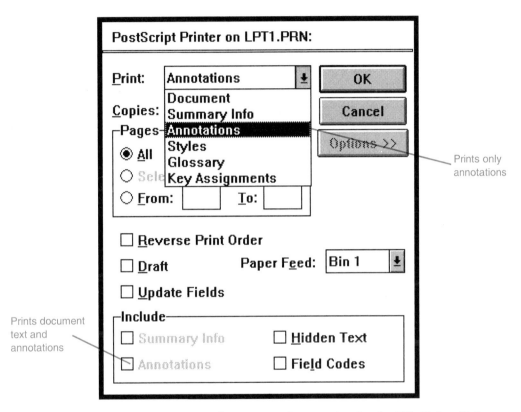

Figure 11.7   *The Annotations option in the File Print dialog box.*

329

To turn on the revision marks feature, first choose the Utilities/ Revision Marks command or press Alt,U,M. The Mark Revisions dialog box appears, as shown in Figure 11.8. Turn on the Mark Revisions check box or press Alt-M, and then choose the OK button or press Enter. To simplify the locating of revision marks, Word adds a vertical revision bar in the margin beside any changed text. Turn off the revision marks by choosing the Utilities/Revision Marks command (Alt,U,M) and then choosing the Mark Revisions check box or pressing Alt-M.

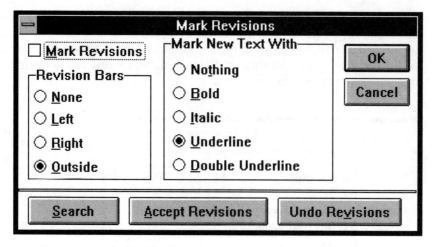

Figure 11.8   The Mark Revisions dialog box.

330   *Changing Word's Standard Revision Marks*

Word's standard revision marks can sometimes be confusing when you're viewing a document that contains text formatted with the same revision marks that Word uses. For example, a contract may have several sections containing strike-through text. The strike-through text could easily be confused with Word's revision mark deletions. You can change the way that Word marks your revisions by selecting a different method in the Mark New Text With box. For example, you can format altered text by using the Bold (Alt-B), Italic (Alt-I), Underline (Alt-U), Double-underline (Alt-D), or Nothing (Alt-T) option buttons.

You can also change where the revision bar is displayed, or you can choose the None option button so that it isn't displayed. Choosing the Left or Right option buttons displays the revision bar in the corresponding margin. If the document is formatted with mirror margins, you can choose the Outside option button or press Alt-O so that the revision bar appears on the outside margins of odd and even pages.

Accepting or Rejecting Revisions

To accept or reject a revision, first choose the Utilities/Revision Marks command (Alt,U,M), and then choose the Search button or press

Alt-S. Word moves to the first revision mark from the insertion point and selects the entire revision as a text block. If you want to accept the revision, choose the Accept Revisions button or press Alt-A. Word makes the changes to the selected text and removes the revision bar. To reject a revision, choose the Undo Revision button or press Alt-V. Word removes all added text and removes strike-throughs from text deleted with revision marks turned on. If you don't use the Search button or if you don't select text before choosing the Accept Revisions (Alt-A) or Undo Revisions (Alt-V) button, Word changes the entire document.

Comparing Two Versions of a Document

331

When you share or frequently revise a document, you may end up with several versions. The Utilities/Compare Versions command compares two versions of a document and adds underlines and revision bars (vertical lines in the margin) to the lines that don't match.

To compare two versions of a document, open the file to which you want to add the underlines and revision bars, and choose the Utilities/Compare Versions command or press Alt,U,V. Word displays the Compare Version dialog box. You can then enter a filename in the Compare File Name text box or select a file by using the Directories (Alt-D) and Files (Alt-F) list boxes. Choose the OK button or press Enter, and Word compares the two document files, under-lining differing text and adding revision bars beside the differing lines in the open document.

What You Have Learned

▶ *Bookmarks* let you reference portions of a document by using a unique name. They are useful in navigating large documents or in conjunction with fields to create cross-references. To create a bookmark, use the Insert/Bookmark command (Alt,I,M).

▶ To jump to a bookmark, use the Edit/Go To command (Alt,E,G) and choose the bookmark name from the Go To list box. If you know the name of the bookmark you want to move to, simply press F5 to display the Go To: prompt in the status bar and then enter the bookmark name.

▶ *Fields* are instructions that tell Word to retrieve and insert information or perform some kind of action. By using fields to insert information such as a spreadsheet or graphic into your document, you link that information to its original source.

▶ To insert one of Word's predefined fields into your document, choose the Insert/Field command (Alt,I,D).

▶ *Annotation marks* are the on-screen equivalent of the popular Post-it Notes. To insert annotations, use the Insert/Annotations command (Alt,I,A). To view and edit existing annotations, use the View/Annotations command (Alt,V,A).

332

▶ With Word's *revision marks* feature, others can make changes to your document without eliminating the original text. Any changes made are formatted differently than the original text, which by default is underlined. To activate the revision marks feature, choose the Utilities/Revision Marks command (Alt,U,M).

Creating Form Letters, Labels, Tables of Contents, and Indexes

About This Chapter 333

▶ *Creating form letters and mailing labels*
▶ *Adding a tables of contents to one or more documents*
▶ *Indexing a document*

Form letters are an efficient way of communicating standardized information. Word provides features that allow you to easily create and print form letters and mailing labels. Word also makes it easy to create a table of contents and index for a document. In this chapter, you'll learn the basics of merging and printing form letters and labels, as well as how to create tables of contents and indexes.

Creating and Printing Form Letters

The process of creating a form letter involves three steps. The first step is to create a *main document* containing the standard text for your form letter. The main document also contains field codes, which in turn contain bookmarks instructing Word where to insert the merged information. The second step is to create a *data document* in which you store any data you want to insert into your form letters, such as names, addresses, etc. The third step involves merging the data from the data document into the main document when you print your form letters. The result is the *merged document*. Figure 12.1 shows the relationship of the main, data, and merged documents.

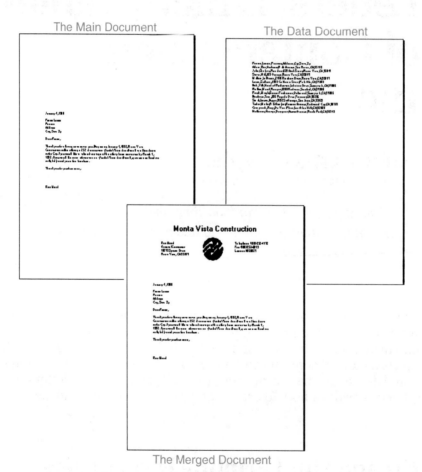

Figure 12.1   The relationship of the main, data, and merged documents.

Creating a Main Document

A main document incorporates three unique elements. The first element is the standard text for your form letter; this text remains the same in each form letter. The second element is the DATA field that identifies which data document to merge with the main document. You insert the DATA field at the beginning of the main document. The third element is the fields that contain bookmark names. These fields indicate the text in the data document that you want to merge into your documents, such as a name or address.

To insert the DATA field, choose the Insert/Field command (Alt,I,D) and select the DATA field option from the Insert Field Type list box (Alt-F) and add the name of the data document, or press Ctrl-F9 and enter the field code. The field code starts with the field DATA after the opening field character ({). Following DATA is the data document filename and then the closing field character (}). For example, pressing Ctrl-F9 and entering

```
{DATA C:\\DOCS\\ADDRESS1.DOC}
```

335

tells Word that the data to be merged into the main document will be found in a data document named ADDRESS1.DOC in the DOCS directory on the C: drive. Be sure to enter the extra backslashes in the path name (they distinguish the backslashes from field switches), or Word will display a message telling you it is unable to open the data document.

As you type the rest of your document, insert a field whenever you want Word to insert merged text. To insert a field, move the insertion point to the location where you want to insert merged text and press Ctrl-F9. Then, between the field characters, enter a bookmark name as a field code, such as {First_Name}, {Last_Name}, {Address}, etc. These fields are matched with the bookmarks that you will later create in your data document. When you use a bookmark name, be careful that you don't use a name that already exists for a field code, such as DATE, TITLE, etc. To verify that a bookmark name is not a Word field name, choose the Insert/Field command and scroll through the Insert Field Type list box to view Word's field names.

You can use bookmark names that match a field type by prefacing the bookmark with the REF field code. The REF field code informs Word that the bookmark name is a bookmark *not* a field type. For example, `{REF Headers}` indicates a bookmark named `Header`, not the Word field HEADER.

You can insert a bookmark name in several locations. For example, to insert a name in the greeting of a letter and then in the body of the letter, simply use the same field. In Figure 12.2, the `{Fname}` (First name) and the `{City}` fields are each used in two places. You can also add Word's predefined fields, such as the DATE field, anywhere in a document. Figure 12.2 shows a sample main document for creating form letters.

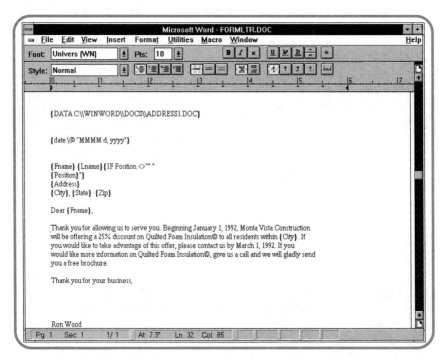

Figure 12.2   A sample main document for form letters.

Creating a Data Document

A data document stores a database of information that can be merged into your form letter. A *database* can be any collection of data, including such information as a person's first name, last name, street address, city, state, and zip code. All the information associated with each person is called a *record*. Each unit of information in a record, such as the first name, last name, job position, address, city, state, and zip code is called a *data item*.

Use your main document to determine the information you want to include in your database and the bookmark names you want to use. For example, to create a mailing list, you might use the following bookmark names: First_Name, Last_Name, Position, Address, City, State, and Zip.

Once you've determined the bookmark names you want, you can create your data document. A data document is a normal Word document file that is organized in the following way. The first paragraph is called a *header record*; it lists all the bookmark names for your records. Each record after the header record is a separate paragraph with data items entered in the same order as the bookmark names listed in the header record. Each data item within a record is separated by either a comma or a tab. You must choose only one data separator; you can't mix commas and tabs. To enter a comma as part of a data item separated by commas, enter a backslash before the comma (i.e., `Chief Engineer\, Manufacturing`). To enter a backslash, enter two backslashes together (`\\`).

If you don't have information for a particular field, leave it blank. However, be sure to add a comma to indicate the blank field, unless it is the last field in the paragraph. Figure 12.3 shows a sample data document containing blank fields.

> ▶ **Tip:** To use Word's premade templates to quickly print labels (as explained later), use the following bookmark names: Name, Street, City, State, and Zip.

Q Creating a Data Document

1. In the first paragraph of a new document, create a header record by typing the names of the bookmarks used in the main document, separating each bookmark with commas.

   The bookmarks in the header record must match the bookmarks (enclosed between the field characters) in your document. Remember, bookmarks can be only one word and there can be no spaces.

2. Press Enter to complete your header record.

3. Type the information for your first record in the same topical order as your header record.

Remember to separate each field with a comma or a tab. If there is no information for a data item, insert a comma by itself to indicate the blank data item (unless it is the last data item), as shown in the second record in Figure 12.3.

4. Press Enter when you've completed a record entry.

Word moves to the next line for your next record entry.

5. Repeat steps 3 and 4 for each record you want to enter in your data document.

6. When you've entered all your data, choose the File/Save command (Alt,F,S) or press Shift-F12 and enter the filename for your data document.

Word displays the File Save dialog box. Make sure that you save the file under the name you used in the DATA field in the main document. ☐

If you're creating a data document from scratch, you can also use a table as a data document. To create a table, choose the Insert/Table command or press Alt,I,T. In the Number of Columns text box (Alt-C), enter the number of bookmarks used in the document. Then choose OK or press Enter. In the first row, type the names of the bookmarks used in the main document.

If you already have a database file in another application that contains a mailing list, most likely the application will allow you to export it. *Exporting* means converting a file having one file format to another format. To convert the database file from another application to Word, choose your application's export command to save the file as a comma delimited ASCII file. You can then open the converted (ASCII) file in Word and save it as a Word data document. Once you've converted the file, you can easily check that each data item is entered correctly by selecting the text, choosing the Insert/Table command (Alt,I,T) and then choosing the Comma Delimited option button or pressing Alt-O to convert the data document to a table.

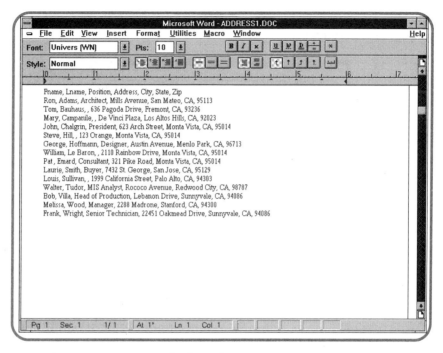

Figure 12.3   A sample data document.

Merging and Printing Form Letters

After creating a main document and a data document, you are ready to merge them. First, open the main document; then choose the File/ Print Merge command or press Alt,F,M. The Print Merge dialog box appears, as shown in Figure 12.4.

By default, the All option button is selected, which instructs Word to merge every record in the data document. You can limit the merge to a specific set of records by using the From (Alt-F) and To (Alt-T) text boxes. Word doesn't display record numbers in your data document but rather counts each record in the sequence it's listed in your data document. The first record after the header record is record 1, the next record number is 2, and so on.

To set a range of records, in the From box (Alt-F) enter the record number where you want to begin the merge, and in the To text box (Alt-T) enter the record number where you want to end. When Word merges the two documents, it first locates the data document file you've identified in the DATA command. Word then reads and merges the data document's records, beginning with and ending at the numbers you've indicated.

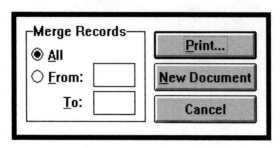

Figure 12.4   The Print Merge dialog box.

To begin printing the form letters, choose the Print button or press Alt-P. The Print Merge dialog box closes and the Print dialog box opens. You can then set the print options and choose the Print button or press Alt-P to begin printing. As the first letter is printed, the appropriate information from the data document fields is inserted where indicated by the merge field codes in your main document. Word continues merging information from the data document into the main document until it reaches the end of the data document. The status bar displays the number of records as they are merged.

When Word finishes printing, you will see the main document fields updated with the last set of records merged into the document. If Word cannot merge a field, a message is added to the main document as a field result for the fields that didn't work. Figure 12.5 shows the results of merging the main document shown in Figure 12.2 and the data document shown in Figure 12.3.

 Merging and Printing Form Letters

1. Open your main document.
2. Choose the File/Print Merge command or press Alt,F,M. | Word displays the Print Merge dialog box.
3. Choose the Print button or press Alt-P. | Word displays the Print dialog box.

340

4. Fill in any print options you want and choose the OK button or press Enter.

Word merges and prints your form letter. Word starts the merging and printing process and alternately displays two messages indicating it's either merging or formatting. Word continues printing form letters for all records in the data document. ☐

Monta Vista Construction

Ron Wood
General Contractor
10245 Spruce Drive
Monta Vista, CA 95014

Telephone (408) 252-1172
Fax (408) 252-6013
License #450024

341

November 15, 1991

Frank Wright
Senior Technician
22451 Oakmead Drive
Sunnyvale, CA 94086

Dear Frank,

Thank you for allowing us to serve you. Beginning January 1, 1992, Monta Vista Construction will be offering a 25% discount on *Quilted Foam Insulation*© to all residents within Sunnyvale. If you would like to take advantage of this offer, please contact us by March 1, 1992. If you would like more information on *Quilted Foam Insulation*©, give us a call and we will gladly send you a free brochure.

Thank you for your business,

Ron Wood

Figure 12.5   The results of merging a main and a data document.

Saving Merged Form Letters to a File

To store the results of your print merge without actually printing the form letters, choose the New Document button or press Alt-N while in the Print Merge dialog box. Word sends the results to a document named FORM LETTERS1. All the form letters are added to the FORM LETTERS1 document and are separated by section breaks. You can then edit the file or print the merged letters by printing the FORM LETTERS1 document. Each time you choose the New Document button or press Alt-N, Word increments the number in the filename by one so that the filename matches the number of print-merged documents.

When you exit or close the FORM LETTERS1 file, Word displays a message box asking if you want to save the changes to FORM LETTERS1. If you choose Yes or press Y, Word displays the File Save dialog box where you are to enter the filename for FORM LETTERS1. If you have performed multiple merges to document files, Word prompts you to save the changes for each merge.

Prompting for Information to Use in a Form Letter

Adding the ASK field to a main document causes Word to ask the user for information that will be put into the field before the form letter is printed. Use the Insert/Field command (Alt,I,D) or press Ctrl-F9 and then enter the ASK field and its instructions. The ASK field uses the following format:

```
ASK bookmark "text to prompt user"
```

where bookmark is the name of the field that is filled in with the information you type, and the text within quotes is the prompt message you want Word to display in a dialog box.

If you want Word to use your answer to fill in the specified field in all form letters, type \o after the text in the ASK field. For example, pressing Ctrl-F9 and adding the following text between the field characters prompts the user to enter the name of a product:

```
{ASK Product "Enter the product to reference" \o}
```

The \o instructs Word to fill in the bookmark named Product for all the form letters.

By default, the entry last entered in an ASK dialog box appears as the new default entry. You can specify a different default by adding the \d switch to the ASK instruction followed by the default text. The following instruction shows a sample ASK field with a \o and \d switch, and Figure 12.6 shows the results of this field's instructions in a form letter.

```
{ASK Payment "Enter method of payment" \d "Check" \o}
```

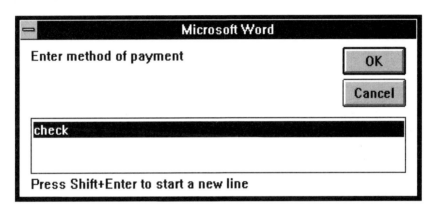

343

Figure 12.6   The ASK field inserted in a form letter.

Skipping Records in a Form Letter

Using the SKIPIF field causes Word to print a form letter only if the records in your data document meet certain conditions. Insert the SKIPIF field in your main document by using the following format:

```
SKIPIF Conditional Test
```

You can use any of the following operators to exclude records from being printed:

Operator	Description
>	Greater than
<	Less than
>=	Greater than or equal to
<=	Less than or equal to
< >	Not equal to

Choose the Insert/Field command or press Alt,I,D, and select the Skip if option from the Insert Field Type list box. You can then add a condition to instruct Word when to skip a record. You can insert the SKIPIF field directly in your document by pressing Ctrl-F9 and adding the SKIPIF field and the conditional test for the records you want to skip. The following example uses the SKIPIF field to skip every record in which the state is not equal to CA:

```
{SKIPIF State <> "CA"}
```

The result of the SKIPIF field depends on the result of the conditional test that follows it. In the previous example, any state other than CA causes Word to skip to the next record without printing the letter. The SKIPIF instruction might also be used to create invoices by testing for an amount due. For example, suppose you have a data document containing the data item `Due`. You could use the SKIPIF field to print invoices for customers owing money by entering the following:

```
{SKIPIF Due < .01}
```

Suppressing Blank Lines from Printing

Suppressing blank lines in a mailing label can be a little tricky, but the results are worth the effort. To suppress the printing of a blank line when Word encounters an empty data item, you must understand how to use the IF field to test whether a data item in the data document is empty or contains text. To use the IF field, you insert it into your main document by choosing the Insert/Field command (Alt,I,D) and then selecting the IF field from the Insert Field Type list box (Alt-F). You can also insert it by pressing Ctrl-F9 and entering the field and its conditions within the field characters. The IF field uses the following format:

```
IF Conditional Test If-TrueResult If-FalseResult
```

The first argument of the IF instruction is a *conditional test,* an expression that is either true or false. If the conditional test is true, then the instruction returns the true result. If the conditional test is false, the instruction returns the false result.

344

The following example shows the first three lines of an address in which the IF field tests for an empty data item. The purpose of testing for the empty data item is to prevent the printing of a blank line in the address. Word is instructed to omit the blank line whenever the `Position` bookmark is empty.

```
{First_Name} {{Last_Name}{IF Position <>"" "¶
{Position}"}
{Address}
```

Notice that the test for the blank data item is placed on the same line as the line containing the bookmarks `First_Name` and `Last_Name`. Notice, too, that the paragraph mark (¶) is inside the true result to ensure that no blank line occurs when the `Position` bookmark is empty. To enter the paragraph mark, press Enter. When you press Enter to insert the paragraph mark into the true result, the insertion point moves to the next line. Continue typing the merge instruction on the next line as though you were entering the merge instruction on a single line.

345

When Word performs the merge, the IF field tests to make sure that the `Position` data item does not equal (<>) a blank field (""). The true result causes Word to begin a new line and enter the Position bookmark's current data item. If the Position bookmark's data item is false (no data item), Word moves to the `Address` field without inserting a blank line.

Filling in a Field for Different Conditions

Another use for the IF field is to cause Word to print a bookmark's contents in a form letter only when certain conditions are met. For example, you might instruct Word to print one result if a condition is true and another result if the condition is false. To insert the IF field, choose the Insert/Field command (Alt,I,D) and select the IF field from the Insert Field Type list box (Alt-F), or press Ctrl-F9 to enter the field directly in your document.

In the following example, Word is instructed to change the closing of a form letter depending on whether the customer owes a balance or is paid up:

```
{IF {Due} < .01 "Thank you for your business" "Please
note the amount due is" "{Due}"}
```

The first message within quotations is printed if the condition is true, that is, if no amount is due. The second message within quotations (and the amount due) prints if the condition is false, that is, if an amount is due. To test a field to see if it meets several conditions, you can enter multiple IF statements—a technique commonly referred to as *nesting*. The next example has two IF statements:

```
{IF {Orders} > 20 {IF {Due} < .01 "Congratulations,
You are entitled to a 10% discount on your next order."}}
```

In the preceding example, the first IF field checks to see whether the form letter recipient has placed more than 20 orders and nests a second IF statement to ensure that the recipient doesn't have an outstanding balance. If these conditions are met, a congratulatory line is included, informing the recipient that he or she is entitled to a 10% discount on the next order. Because there is only a true result in the nested IF statement, nothing is done if the Due data item is greater than one cent.

In the previous example, two IF statements were combined and tested to see whether both IF conditions were met. This type of statement is known as a logical AND statement. You can combine two IF statements and test to see whether only one condition is met. This is a logical OR statement, as shown in the following example:

```
{IF {Orders} > 50 "Congratulations, You are entitled to a 15%
discount on your next order."}{IF {Purchased} > 1000
"Congratulations, You are entitled to a 20% discount on your
next order."}}
```

Remember, only one IF instruction can be true in order to print the conditional text. In the previous example, the text telling the customer that he or she is entitled to a 20% discount is printed only if the first conditional statement is false and the second conditional statement ({Purchased} > 1000) is true.

Supplying Information for a Field Not in the Data Document

To supply information for a field in your main document rather than merging it in from the data document, use the SET field. In some cases, you might want to keep only the records for a mailing list in the data document and use the SET instruction for information that varies. The SET field uses the following format:

```
{SET bookmark "text"}
```

For example, pressing Ctrl-F9 and entering

```
{SET Trip "Caribbean Cruise"}
```

inserts the words `Caribbean Cruise` in the field containing the bookmark `Trip` without having to add the field to the data document.

Creating and Printing Mailing Labels

Once you have created a data document, you can easily edit it to create another data document containing only the addresses needed for mailing labels. To do this, use the File/Save As command. Then create a main document formatted to match the size and type of labels you're using. To simplify the printing of labels, Word provides a number of label templates:

Label Template Name	Result
LBL15COT.DOT	1.5-inch labels in a single column, continuous label
LBL1COLT.DOT	1-inch labels in a single column, continuous feed
LBL2COL.DOT	1-inch labels in two columns, sheet feed
LBL2COLT.DOT	1-inch labels in two columns, continuous feed
LBL3COL.DOT	1-inch labels in three columns, sheet feed
LBL3COLT.DOT	1-inch labels in three columns, continuous feed

To use one of these templates, choose the File/New command or press Alt,F,N, and select a label template name in the Use Template list box (Alt-U). Be sure to select the template that matches the type of printer and the number of labels you want to create.

Figure 12.7 shows the results of selecting the LBL3COL.DOT template. To use this predefined template, you must make a few minor adjustments. First make sure that the DATA field indicates the correct path and name for your data document. By default, Word includes the filename ADDRESS. Next you need to make sure that the table cells will fit the size of your labels so that text will not spill over from one label to the label below it.

348

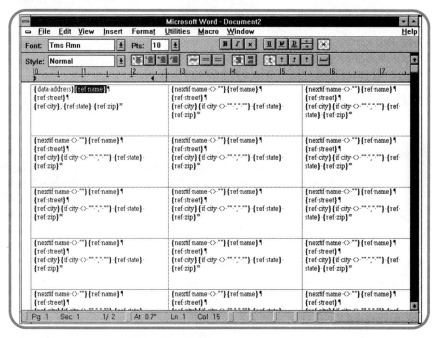

Figure 12.7   The LBL3COL.DOT template.

By default, Word inserts a section break at the end of each record's merged text and prints one document for each data record in the data file. For address labels, you need to print as many addresses per page as you have address labels. Thus, you need to insert a field that instructs Word to print more than one data record per page and omit the section breaks. Notice that the NEXTIF field is added to the beginning of each NAME field after the first label in Word's LBLCOL3.DOT template, as shown in Figure 12.7.

The NEXTIF field is a predefined field that is a combination of the NEXT and IF fields. The NEXTIF field tests for a condition and, if the condition is true, instructs Word to move to the next data record and use its data items for the fields that follow without adding a section break. If the conditional test is true (data exists), Word issues a NEXT instruction, moving to the next record of the data document. Using the NEXTIF field enables Word to merge and print multiple records (labels) on a single page.

 Creating and Printing Mailing Labels with a Predefined Label Template

1. Modify your data document to contain the following fields: NAME, STREET, CITY, STATE, and ZIP. Save the data document with the name ADDRESS.

    You can use a different name for your data document, but be sure to change the DATA field in the template to match the new name. Figure 12.8 shows a sample data document for use with the LBL3COL.DOT template.

2. Choose the File/New command or press Alt,F,N.

    Word displays the File New dialog box.

3. Select the template in the Use Template list box (Alt-U), and then choose the OK button or press Enter.

    Word's predefined label templates begin with LBL. The number in the template name matches the number of columns of labels that will print. If you are using a printer with a tractor feed, make sure that the template ends with the letter *T*. After choosing the OK button or pressing Enter, Word displays the new document using the selected template.

4. Change the DATA field to include the entire path name for your data document file. Remember to include the extra backslash before each backslash used in the path name.

    By default, Word uses the filename ADDRESS without a path name. A sample DATA field might be entered as {data c:\\winword\\address.doc. If you didn't save the data document with the name ADDRESS, replace ADDRESS with the filename under which you saved the data document.

349

5. Choose the File/Print Merge command or press Alt,F,M.

Word begins merging and printing labels. If your data document is large, it will take a while to perform the merge before printing. Press Esc to stop printing. □

Figure 12.8   A data document (in table form) set up for mailing labels.

Sorting Records in a Data Document

Word prints form letters in the same order as the records appear in your data document. However, you can change the order of your records in a data document to affect the order in which your form letters print. For example, you can sort your data document's records by zip code and then print your form letters and mailing labels in that order.

You can sort a data document on individual columns. First, select the column records you want to include in the sort, but *do not* include the header record. Choose the Utilities/Sort command or press Alt,U,O. In the Key Type list box (Alt-K), make sure that the Alphanumeric option is selected. This option allows you to sort data that contains letters and/or numbers. Choose OK or press Enter, and Word sorts your selected records.

Creating a Table of Contents

The easiest way to create a table of contents, and the method explained in this chapter, is based on outline headings. The outline headings are formatted by using Word's outlining features or by applying heading styles. Chapter 7, "Creating Tables and Outlines" explains how to use these features. Using the Insert/Table of Contents command compiles all the paragraph headings in your document and formats them into a standard table of contents, as shown in Figure 12.9. The Insert/Table of Contents command utilizes the TOC (Table of Content) field. Word allows you to create a table of contents from one or more document files.

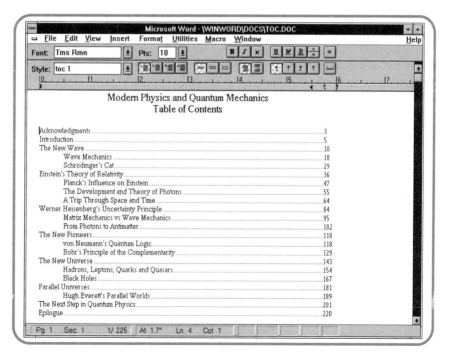

Figure 12.9   A sample table of contents.

Creating a Table of Contents

1. Place the insertion point where you want the table of contents to appear, usually at the beginning of your document.

2. Choose the Insert/Table of Contents command or press Alt,I,C.

   Word displays the Insert Table of Contents dialog box, as shown in Figure 12.10. The default option button settings are Use Heading Paragraphs and All. If you want to use only certain heading levels in your table of contents, type the beginning level number in the From text box and the ending level number in the To text box. For example, if you want the table of contents to contain only heading levels 1 and 2, type 1 in the From text box and type 2 in the To text box.

3. Use the default option button settings and choose the OK button or press Enter.

   Word compiles the headings from the document and displays either the TOC field code or its results, depending on the viewing option settings you've activated. To view the results of the TOC field, make sure that the Show All feature and the View/ Field Codes command are turned off.

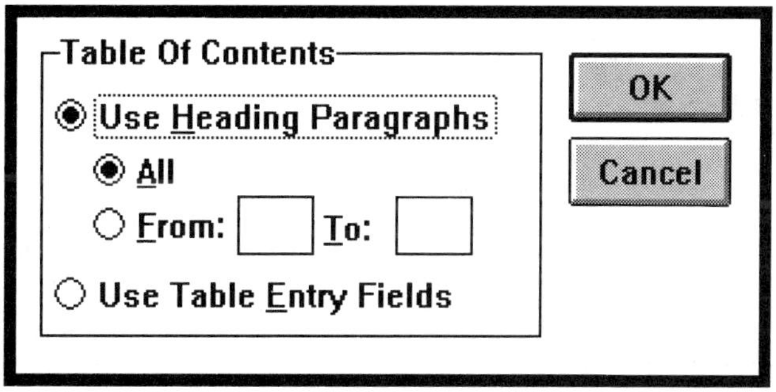

```
┌─────────────────────────────────────────────────────┐
│  ┌─Table Of Contents──────────┐    ┌──────────────┐  │
│  │ ⦿ :Use Heading Paragraphs:  │    │     OK       │  │
│  │                             │    └──────────────┘  │
│  │ ⦿ All                       │    ┌──────────────┐  │
│  │ ○ From: [    ] To: [    ]   │    │   Cancel     │  │
│  │                             │    └──────────────┘  │
│  │ ○ Use Table Entry Fields    │                      │
│  └─────────────────────────────┘                      │
└─────────────────────────────────────────────────────┘
```

Figure 12.10   The Insert Table of Contents dialog box.

Creating a Table of Contents from Multiple Document Files

At times you may want your table of contents to integrate headings from several document files, such as chapters of a book. Word can create a table of contents for any group of document files you specify. Remember, to use the technique explained here, every paragraph heading you want in the table must have a heading style applied to it.

When you create a table of contents from multiple document files, keep in mind that Word inserts page numbers based on the page numbering for each document file. By default, the page numbering starts at page 1. To display page numbers sequentially for multiple document files, you must change the page numbering settings in each document file.

In the first document file that you want to include in the table of contents, note the last page number. In the second document file you want to include in the table, set the first page number to start after the last page number of the first document file. For example, if the first document file ends on page 10, you would start the page numbering of the second document on page 11. To change a document's page numbering, use the Start at text box in the expanded Edit Header/Footer dialog box, as shown in Figure 12.11. Replace Word's default Auto option with the appropriate starting page number for each chapter.

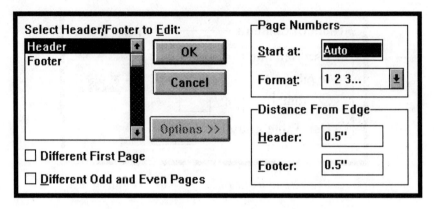

Figure 12.11   The expanded Edit Header/Footer dialog box.

 Creating a Table of Contents from Multiple Document Files

1. Choose the File/New command or press Alt,F,N to open a new document window. Choose the OK button or press Enter.

2. Choose the Insert/Field command or press Alt,I,D.

    Word displays the Insert Field dialog box.

3. Choose the `Referenced doc.` field from the Insert Field Type list box.

    Word displays the field type code, RD, in the Field Code text box.

4. Choose the Field Code text box or press Alt-C and press the Right Arrow key.

    The insertion point is displayed in the text box after the field type name.

5. Type the path and the document filename that you want to include in the table of contents, for example, `c:\\winword\\book\\chap1.doc.`

    When entering the path for a document file, you must use a double backslash (\ \) to separate the drive, directory, and document names.

6. Choose the OK button or press Enter.

    Word inserts the field in your document.

7. Repeat steps 2 through 6 for each additional document you want to include in the table of contents.

    Each RD field needs to be on a separate line in the order you want it listed in the table of contents.

8. Place the insertion point on a new line after all the RD fields and choose the Insert/Table of Contents command or press Alt,I,C.

Word displays the Insert Table of Contents dialog box. The default option button settings are Use Heading Paragraphs and All.

9. Use the default option button settings and choose the OK button or press Enter.

Word compiles the headings from the documents you've specified and displays either the TOC field code or its results, depending on the viewing option settings you've activated. To view the results of the TOC field, make sure that the Show All feature and the View/Field Codes command are turned off. □

355

Updating, Editing, and Formatting the Table of Contents

Working with the table of contents field is the same as working with any other field. The table of contents is updated whenever you print or repaginate your document or select the TOC field and press F9. Each update reflects any changes you've made to your document's headings. You can edit and format the text in the table of contents as you would edit and format any other text; however, remember that your changes are lost when the field is updated, unless you lock the field by pressing Ctrl-F11.

You can apply character, paragraph, and section formats directly to the field code, and these formats affect the entire TOC field's results. The TOC field can be copied, moved, and deleted as for any other field by using the Edit/Copy, Edit/Cut, and Edit/Paste commands. To view the results of the TOC field, make sure that the Show All feature and the View/Field Codes command (Alt,V,C) are turned off.

> ▶ **Note:** For more information on working with fields, see
> Chapter 11, "Using Bookmarks, Fields, and Document
> Revision Features."

Creating an Index

An *index* is a list of important terms and topics contained in a
document, with page numbers indicating where the terms and
topics can be found. Word allows you to create an index for a single
document file or from several document files. Like creating a table
of contents, creating an index uses fields.

Creating an index is a two-step process. The first step involves
inserting an index entry field marker next to each term you want to
reference in your document's index. To do this, you use the Insert/
Index Entry command. After inserting the index entry fields
throughout your document, you instruct Word to compile the index
entries to create an index by using the Insert/Index command. Figure
12.12 shows an index created by Word based on compiled index
entries from a document.

Inserting Index Entries

You can designate existing text on a page as an index entry, or you
can type new text for an index entry. The new text is then referenced
to the page where the insertion point is located. Either way, you
insert an index entry field that is formatted as *hidden text*, meaning
that these fields don't appear in your document when printed,
unless you activate the Field Codes check box (Alt-L) in the expanded File Print dialog box. If you want to view these fields on your
screen, make sure that the Hidden Text check box (Alt-I) is turned
on in the View Preferences dialog box.

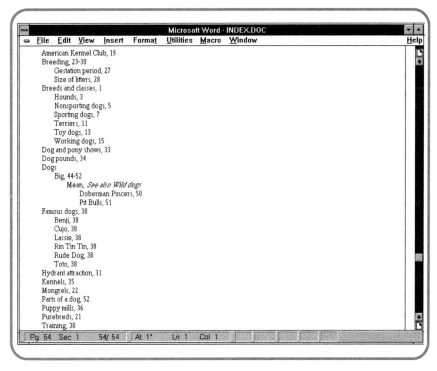

Figure 12.12   An index created using the Insert/Index command.

Inserting Index Entries in Your Document

1. Select the text you want as an index entry. Or, if you're typing the index entry, place the insertion point next to the text you want to reference in the index entry.

2. Choose the Insert/Index Entry command or press Alt,I,E.

Word displays the Insert Index Entry dialog box. If you selected text as an index entry, it's displayed in the Index Entry text box. If you didn't select text in your document as an index entry, the Index Entry text box is empty. To format an index entry's page number format, simply choose the Bold (Alt-B) or Italic (Alt-I) check box option.

3. Edit the existing text or type the text you want for the index entry in the Index <u>E</u>ntry text box.

4. Choose the OK button or press Enter.

Word closes the Insert Index Entry dialog box and inserts the index entry field in your document.

5. Repeat steps 1 through 4 for each index entry you want to insert in your document.

□

Additional Index Entry Features

Word provides several additional features to create more sophisticated indexes. These include creating subentries for the document index, marking an index entry that spans several pages, and marking cross-references in index entries.

Indexes usually have two levels of entries: the *main entry* and *subentries*. To indicate a main index entry and its subentry, you insert a colon (:) between the main entry and the subentry in the Index <u>E</u>ntry text box found in the Insert Index Entry dialog box. For example, to create an index subentry `Big` under the main index entry `Dogs`, type `Dogs:Big` in the Index <u>E</u>ntry text box. You can use colons to mark the entry and multiple levels of subentries, such as `Dogs:Big:Mean`. The main entry is always the first entry, with each subsequent level separated by colons.

Word automatically inserts backslashes before colons in selected text. To ensure that an index subentry is created, and not treated as a colon, be sure to eliminate the backslash or edit the contents of the index entry field. To edit the index entry field, choose the <u>V</u>iew/Pr<u>e</u>ferences command (Alt,V,E). Then choose the H<u>i</u>dden text check box (Alt-I) or choose the Show All button on the Ruler. The index entries are displayed so that you can edit them.

When the subject of your index entry spans several pages, you will want to indicate a range of pages in the printed index, such as, `Dogs, 75-79`. To create this type of index entry, you first need to create a bookmark that contains all the pages of text you want to reference in the index entry. In the Index Entry text box in the Insert Index Entry dialog box, type the text for the index entry as you want it to appear in the index. Next, choose the Range list box or press Alt-R. Select the bookmark name from the list, and then choose the OK button or press Enter. Word keeps track of the page range that the bookmark spans.

In addition, Word allows you to add cross-reference text after an index entry instead of a page number; for example, under the *Dogs, Big, Mean* entry, you could type See also Wild dogs, as shown in Figure 12.13. To create this type of cross-reference, first create an index entry. In the Draft mode, choose the Show All button. In the index entry, type a \t switch (the t stands for text) followed by the cross-reference text enclosed in quotation marks. For example, to create the cross-reference shown in Figure 12.13, the index entry would be {XE "Dogs:Big:Mean" \t "See also Wild dogs"}. The quotation marks tell Word that the quoted text is cross-reference text to insert after the index entry. The quotation marks do not appear in your index. You can format your cross-reference text by selecting the text within the quotation marks and choosing the character format you want to use from the Format Character dialog box or the Ribbon. The words *See also Wild dogs* are formatted for italic in the example.

359

Compiling Index Entries to Create the Index

When you've inserted the index entries for your document, you're ready to create the index. You can choose to create a "normal" index, where the subentries are indented. This is the most commonly used style. Or you can choose a "run-in" index, where subentries continue on the same line after main entries, separated by semicolons.

You can also choose a heading separator to separate sections alphabetically, with each section separated by the appropriate letter heading, as shown in Figure 12.13. Alternatively, you can decide to have no separation in your index or only a single blank line to separate the sections of your index. The Quick Steps explain how to create a normal index for a single document, using letter separators between sections in the index.

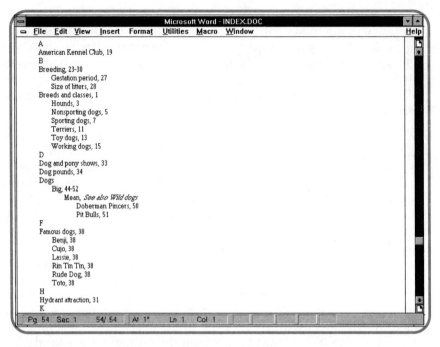

Figure 12.13   A normal index using letter separators.

🅠 Creating an Index

1. Place the insertion point where you want the index, usually at the end of a document.

2. Choose the Insert/Index command or press Alt,I,I.

   Word displays the Insert Index dialog box shown in Figure 12.14. The default settings are the Normal Index option button and the None option button in the Heading Separator box.

3. Choose the Letter option button or press Alt-L.

   Word activates the letter separator option to display a letter heading before each letter group of index entries.

4. Choose the OK button or press Enter.

Word closes the Insert Index dialog box and inserts the Index field in your document at the insertion point location. To view the results of the Index field, make sure that the Show All feature and the View/ Field Codes command are turned off. □

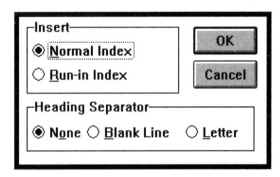

Figure 12.14   The Insert Index dialog box.

361

Creating an Index from Several Document Files

Creating an index from several document files is similar to creating a table of contents from several documents. To display page numbers sequentially for multiple document files, you must change the page numbering settings in each document file. In the first document file you want to include in the index, note the last page number. In the second document file you want to include in the index, set the first page number to start after the last page number of the first document file. For example, if the first document field ends on page 10, start the page numbering of the second document on page 11.

To change a document's page numbering, use the Start at text box in the expanded Edit Header/Footer dialog box. Replace Word's default Auto option with the appropriate starting page number for each chapter.

Creating an Index from Multiple Document Files

1. Choose the File/New command or press Alt,F,N to open a new document window. Choose the OK button or press Enter.

2. Choose the Insert/Field command or press Alt,I,D.

    Word displays the Insert Field dialog box.

3. Choose the field type, `Referenced doc.`, from the Insert Field Type list box.

    Word displays the field type code, `RD`, in the Field Code text box.

4. Choose the Field Code text box or press Alt-C and press the Right Arrow key.

    The insertion point is displayed in the text box after the field type name.

5. Type the path and the document filename that you want to include in the index, for example, `c:\\winword\\book\\chap1.doc.`

    When entering the path for a document file, you must use a double backslash (\ \) to separate the drive, directory, and document names.

6. Choose the OK button or press Enter.

    Word inserts the field in your document.

7. Repeat steps 2 through 6 for each additional document that you want to include in the index.

    Each RD field needs to be on a separate line in the order in which you want it listed in the index.

8. Place the insertion point on a new line after all the RD fields, and choose the Insert/Index command or press Alt,I,I.

    Word displays the Insert Index dialog box. The default option button settings are Normal Index and None in the Heading Separator box.

9. Use the default Normal Index option button setting and choose the Letter option button (Alt-L).

10. Choose the OK button or press Enter.

    Word compiles the index entries from the documents you've specified and displays either the INDEX field code or its results, depending on the viewing option settings you've activated. To view the results of the Index

362

field, make sure that the Show All feature and the View/Field Codes command are turned off. □

Editing, Formatting, and Deleting Index Entries and the Index

The Insert/Index command is based on the INDEX field. Working with this field is the same as working with any other field. The INDEX field is updated whenever you print or repaginate your document or select the INDEX field and press F9. Each update reflects any changes you've made to your document's index entries. You can edit and format the text in the index as you would edit and format any other text. However, remember that your changes are lost when the field is updated, unless you lock the field by pressing Ctrl-F11.

363

You can apply character, paragraph, and section formats directly to the field code. These formats then affect the entire INDEX field's results. The INDEX field can be copied, moved and deleted as for any other field by using the Edit/Copy, Edit/Cut, and Edit/Paste commands. To view the results of the INDEX field, make sure that the Show All feature and the View/Field Codes (Alt,V,C) command are turned off.

 Formatting an Index Field Code to Start on a New Page and as Double-Column Text

1. With the INDEX field highlighted, choose the Insert/Break command or press Alt,I,B.	Word displays the Insert Break dialog box.
2. Choose the Next Page option button (Alt-N), and then choose the OK button or press Enter.	Word inserts a new page break line marker above the INDEX field.
3. Choose the Format/Section command or press Alt,T,S.	Word displays the Format Section dialog box.
4. In the Number text box, type 2.	By default, the New Page option is chosen in the Section Start list box.

5. Choose the OK button or press Enter.

Word closes the Format Section dialog box. To change the font style or size of the text, choose the Font and/or Pts list box on the Ribbon, as needed. To view the results of the formatted INDEX field, make sure that the Show All feature and the View/Field Codes command are turned off. □

What You Have Learned

▶ Creating a *form letter* involves three steps: (1) creating a *main document* (your form letter text containing field codes), (2) creating a *data document* (a database of records, such as names and addresses), and (3) merging the data from the data document into the main document when you print your form letters. To merge and print form letters, use the File/Print Merge command (Alt,F,M).

▶ Word provides several predefined label templates for merging and printing mailing labels using the File/Print Merge command (Alt,F,M).

▶ The Insert/Table of Contents command (Alt,I,C) creates a table of contents based on a document's outline headings.

▶ You can create a table of contents that includes headings from multiple document files by using the `Referenced doc.` field in the Insert Field dialog box (Alt,I,D) and then choosing the Insert/Table of Contents command (Alt,I,C).

▶ To create index entries to be compiled into an index, select the index entry text and use the Insert/Index Entry command (Alt,I,E).

▶ Choosing the Insert/Index command or pressing Alt,I,I compiles your predefined index entries into an index.

▶ You can create an index that includes index entries from multiple document files by using the `Referenced doc.` field in the Insert Field dialog box (Alt,I,D) and then choosing the Insert/Index command (Alt,I,I).

Appendix A

Installing Word for Windows

The first part of this appendix explains the computer system requirements needed to install the Word for Windows program. The second part provides step-by-step instructions for actually installing Word for Windows.

Computer System Requirements of Word for Windows

Word for Windows is designed to be used in the Microsoft Windows environment. Because Microsoft Windows is an extension of the Disk Operating System (DOS) software, it provides an easy-to-use graphical environment that overlays the operating system. The graphical environment consists of windows, menus, and icons. The Windows foundation on which Word for Windows is based allows you to produce documents easier and faster than text-based word processors.

Because Word for Windows is a graphical-based program, its hardware and software requirements are more demanding than traditional text-based word processing programs. You will need the following hardware and software to install and use Word for Windows:

▶ The latest versions, if possible, of Windows and Word for Windows. In the first version of Word for Windows (version 1.0), the user could install and use the program without actually installing Windows by including a run-time (stripped-down) version of Windows. However, Word for Windows version 1.1 requires that Windows 2.11 or higher be installed on your computer system. Because of the significant improvements in both the new versions of Windows and Word for Windows, we strongly recommend that you upgrade from Windows 2.11 and Word for Windows 1.0.

> ▶ **Note:** Microsoft provides an upgrade program at a nominal fee to users of Word for Windows version 1.0. As part of the upgrade promotion, you can purchase Microsoft Windows at a substantially discounted price. For more information, contact Microsoft at (800)426-9400.

366

▶ An IBM or compatible computer, with an 80286 or later microprocessor, such as an 80386SX or 80386.

▶ From 2MB to 4MB of extended (or expanded) memory. While you can get by with 640K to 1MB of memory, we strongly recommend the additional memory if you're using Windows with other Windows-based applications.

▶ At least one hard disk drive and one floppy disk drive, preferably a 1.44MB (3.5-inch disk) or a 1.2MB (5.25-inch disk). The Word for Windows package includes both 1.44MB and 1.2MB disks. If you have only a 360K or 720K drive, Microsoft provides a form with which you can order free 360K or 720K disks in the Word for Windows package.

▶ A Hercules, EGA, or higher resolution (VGA) graphics adapter and monitor.

▶ A Microsoft or compatible mouse. While a mouse is optional, you will find that it becomes an indispensable tool for working in Word for Windows.

> ▶ **Tip:** If you don't have a mouse, purchase the Microsoft mouse. Its state-of-the-art mouse technology offers superior sensitivity that translates into less mouse movement required to move the mouse pointer.

Before Installing Word for Windows

Before installing Word for Windows, you must have Windows 2.11 or higher already installed on your hard disk. For Windows installation instructions, see the *Microsoft Windows User's Guide*. Also, make sure there is enough space on your hard disk to install the Word for Windows program. Installing the entire Word for Windows requires approximately 4.2MB. To economize on disk space, you can skip the tutorial program installation and save 1.2MB.

Installing Word for Windows

To install Word for Windows, you must use its Setup program. This program leads you through the installation process, detecting your computer system's configuration, asking you questions, providing options to select from, and copying the appropriate files onto your hard disk. The files on the Word for Windows' disks are compressed to reduce the number of disks you need to work with. Because these files are compressed, you must use the Setup program to install Word for Windows. The Setup program uncompresses the files and copies the files to your hard disk.

367

The instructions given here explain how to install Word for Windows (version 1.1) by using the 1.44MB or 1.2MB disks included in the Word for Windows package. Regardless of which disk set you use (1.44MB or 1.2MB), the disks are labeled the same: Setup, Conversions, Learning/Writing Aids, and Utilities.

Normally, you use drive A to install Word for Windows onto your hard disk. However, the Setup program also allows you to use drive B if you need to. The Setup program automatically prompts you to insert disks in the drive you specify when starting the Setup program. The following instructions are based on using drive A, but you can substitute drive B if needed. To exit the Setup program, press Ctrl-X.

1. Insert the Word disk labeled Setup into drive A, type `a:setup` at the DOS prompt, and then press Enter. Word displays a screen informing you that you need to know the configuration of your computer system, such as what kind of graphics adapter you have, or which port your printer is connected to. In most

cases, you don't have to worry about answering these questions because the Setup program automatically identifies them for you. Remember that these system configuration options have already been identified when you installed Windows. Press Enter to continue with the Setup program.

2. The Setup program then displays a screen asking if you want to install the Word for Windows program. The `Skip copying, Continue` option is used when you've already installed Word for Windows but want to add some additional features that you didn't specify in the original installation. Press Enter to choose the `Install Word for Windows and utilities` option. The next screen informs you that you need to have Windows 2.11 or higher installed on your system. Press Enter to continue. The Setup program detects the hard disk(s) on your computer system and highlights the hard disk on which it recommends you install Word for Windows. To confirm the recommended hard disk as the destination of the Word for Windows program files, press Enter. If you want to use another hard disk, use the Up or Down Arrow key to highlight the drive you want and then press Enter.

3. After you have selected the hard disk you want, the Setup program proposes the specific directory name WINWORD. Press Enter to accept Word's recommended directory name. To use a different name for your Word for Windows directory, use the Backspace key to erase the current selection, type the new directory name, and then press Enter. The Setup program copies the Word for Windows program files to the drive and directory you've specified.

4. When the Word for Windows program files have been copied, the Setup program prompts you to insert the disk labeled Conversions into drive A. Insert the disk in the drive and press Enter; the Setup program copies additional files. The Setup program then asks if you want to install file conversion programs. These programs allow you to convert files created in other programs, such as WordPerfect or Word for DOS. If you don't want to add any conversion program files, choose the `Do not install conversions` option and press Enter. To install a conversion program, press Enter to choose the `Install conversions` option. The Setup program displays a list of available file conversion programs for selected software packages. Keep in mind that each conversion program file requires 100K of disk space. To select a file conversion program option from the list, use the Up or Down Arrow key to highlight the option you want and then press Enter. An asterisk is dis-

played next to the option you've chosen and the list is redisplayed for choosing another conversion program. After you've selected all the file conversion programs you want, highlight the `Continue With Selected Conversions` option at the top of the list and then press Enter.

5. After the conversion program file screen, the Setup program displays a new screen asking if you want to install graphics filters. Graphics filters work similarly to conversion programs, except that they allow you to use graphics files in Word for Windows that were created using popular graphics and drawing programs. If you don't want to install any graphics filter options, choose the `Do not install graphics filters` option and press Enter. To install graphics filters, choose the `Install graphics filters` option and press Enter. As it did when you were choosing a conversion program, the Setup program displays a list of available graphics filter options to choose from. To select a graphics filter file from the list, use the Up or Down Arrow key to highlight the option you want and then press Enter. An asterisk is displayed next to the graphics filter you've chosen, and the list is redisplayed for choosing additional graphics filters. After you've selected all the graphics filters you want, choose the `Continue With Selected Filters` option at the top of the list and then press Enter. The Setup program copies the files for the graphics filters you've specified. For an explanation of the available graphics filter options, see Chapter 8, "Enhancing Documents with Pictures and Spreadsheets."

369

> ▶ **Tip:** By default, Word for Windows can open TIFF files. In addition, we recommend that you select the CGM, PCX, and Windows Metafile graphics filters because these are popular file formats for many graphics programs.

6. The Setup program next displays a screen asking if you want to install the tutorial lessons program. These tutorial lessons require about 1.2MB of disk space and are installed within a subdirectory named WINWORD.CBT. If you have the space on your hard disk, these lessons can provide a useful overview of how to work with Word for Windows. You can always remove the tutorial lessons subdirectory later to make more room on your hard disk. If you don't want to install the tutorial lessons, choose the `Do not install tutorial lessons` option

and press Enter. To install the tutorial lessons, choose the `Install tutorial lessons` and press Enter. The Setup program copies additional files from the Conversions disk (already in your drive) and then prompts you to insert the disk labeled Utilities into drive A. Insert the disk in the drive and press Enter; the Setup program copies additional files.

7. Following the tutorial lessons screen, the Setup program prompts you to insert the disk labeled Learning/Writing Aids in drive A. Insert the disk into the drive and press Enter; the Setup program copies additional files. After copying these files, the Setup program displays a screen asking if you want to install printer drivers that enable you to use printers supported by DOS for Word (version 4.0), but not by Windows. Most likely, you won't need to install these printer drivers, so choose the `Do not install Word for DOS printer drivers` option and press Enter to continue the Setup program.

8. If the Setup program detects that an HP-PCL printer has been installed in your Windows environment, it displays a screen asking if you want to install soft fonts. The soft fonts allow you to print Greek letters and equation symbols on your HP LaserJet or compatible printer. Soft fonts are downloaded to your printer from the Word for Windows program. If you don't want to install these special symbol fonts, choose the `Do not install symbol soft fonts` option and press Enter. To install the symbol fonts, choose the `Do install symbol soft fonts` option and press enter. The Setup program prompts you to insert the disk labeled Setup in drive A. Insert the disk in the drive and press Enter. The Setup program creates a directory named PCLFONTS on your hard disk's root directory and then copies the soft font files into the new directory.

9. After the Setup program has finished installing Word for Windows on your hard disk, Word displays a final message screen instructing you to press Ctrl-Alt-Del to reboot your computer system. Make sure you remove the Setup disk from your floppy disk drive before rebooting. After rebooting your computer, you can then start Word for Windows by typing `winword` at the DOS prompt. (If you have Windows /386, type `win386 winword`.) If at a later time you decide you want to add additional conversion or graphics filter files, you can use the Setup program again.

Index

B

background pagination, 105-106
background printing, 150
backup files, 69-70
BASIC template, 280
basing new styles on existing styles, 269-270
basing new templates on existing templates, 281
bit-mapped fonts, 155
blocks, 42
bold character formats, 122-123
Bookmark (Insert menu) command, 314-316
bookmarks
  cross-referencing with fields, 322
  deleting, 316
  inserting, 314-315
  jumping to, 316-317
  redefining, 316
borders
  graphics, 241
  paragraphs, 116-119
  tables, 206-207
Break (Insert menu) command, 182-185, 188
BRIEF template, 280
BROCHURE template, 280
bulleted lists, 169-171
buttons, 2
  Minimize, 6
  Restore, 6

C

Calculate (Utilities menu) command, 212
calculations, 212
captioning graphics, 242-243
case-sensitive
  searches, 77
  sorting, 210-211
centered tabs, 127-129
CGM graphics file format, 230
Character (Format menu) command, 120-123
Character dialog box, 120-123
characters
  ANSI character set, 168-169
  counting, 95-96
  deleting, 35

formatting, 120-122
  emphasis, 122-123
  fonts, 124-126
  hidden text, 123
  kerning, 123
  Ribbon, 120-122
charts, importing from Excel, 234-236
check boxes, 18
Check Spelling dialog box, 85-88
checking spelling, 84
  main dictionary, 84
  single words, 88-89
  user dictionaries, 84, 89-90
    adding words, 90-92
    deleting words, 92
choosing commands from menus, 15-17
clipboard, 56
  copying text, 60
  deleting text, 60-61
  moving text, 58-59
  replacing text from, 83-84
  viewing contents, 57
closing windows, 304
columns
  adjusting width, 186-187
    in tables, 202
  deleting from tables, 199-200
  inserting breaks, 188
  inserting in tables, 199-200
  selecting, 55-56
  snaking, 184-187
  space between in tables, 202
commands
  Edit/Copy, 59-60
  Edit/Cut, 56, 58-59
  Edit/Glossary, 254-257
  Edit/Go To, 48-49, 316-317
  Edit/Header/Footer, 130-134
  Edit/Paste, 57-59
  Edit/Paste Link, 251
  Edit/Repeat, 62
  Edit/Replace, 76, 79-84, 119-120
  Edit/Search, 76-79, 119-120, 125-126
  Edit/Summary Info, 65
  Edit/Table, 199-200, 208-209
  Edit/Undo, 62
  File/Exit, 28-30
  File/Find, 285-290

373

375

377

379

381

383

385

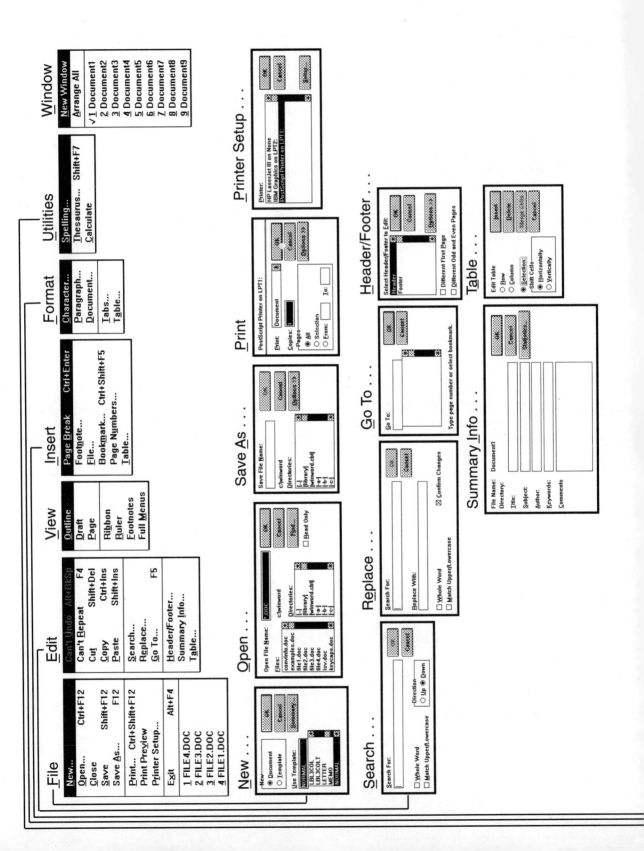